"This book profoundly faces the tension between social science/evaluation and the world of lies, distortions, and un-truths. Whether addressing Brexit or Trump, this book does not shy away from the confrontation of these two forces playing out in countries across the globe. As the editors see it, we are now in the midst of "the death of expertise" as emotions lure people and politicians more than facts and evidence do. One of the brilliantly addressed tensions in the book is that between knowledge and power. The tensions are manageable, especially if there are safeguards erected by democratic institutions. But when these safeguards are challenged or eroded, as in the times we are presently experiencing, democracy becomes more fragile and frail. The ten chapters in this volume focus on democratic countries and their public policy decision-making for two reasons: First, the democratic environment is the most common arena for the evaluative function; and second, the post-truth phenomenon is most visible in the democratic space."

Ray C. Rist, *Former Senior Advisor*
(Retired), The World Bank

"Like many others, I have been puzzled by the increasing tension between the discrediting of science and expertise on the one hand, and the pressure for evidence-based policymaking, on the other hand. This tension is the focus of this book, which has been initiated and written during the last turbulent years with Trump, COVID, and the Ukraine war. The aim of the book is to raise awareness and provoke reflections on the factors that influence evaluations and policy-related work in such challenging environments. The first part deals with the relationship between policy problems and evaluation, the second with the relationship between politics and expertise, and the third with the complexity of evaluation in the institutional and political systems. The underlying conviction is that for an evaluating society to flourish, citizens and professionals have to develop a capacity to be inquisitive, systematic in their inquiry, judicious in their claims, truth seeking, analytical, intellectually humble, sympathetic to opposing points of view, self-critical, and open-minded—not simply open-minded in the sense of being tolerant of other points of view, but open-minded in the sense of recognizing the challenges to one's own way of seeing things that arise from others' ways of making distinctions of worth."

Per Oyvind Bastøe, *International Evaluation*
Adviser, Formerly Evaluation Director and
Chair of OECD/DAC Evaluation Network

Evaluation in the Post-Truth World

Evaluation in the Post-Truth World explores the relationship between the nature of evaluative knowledge, the increasing demand in decision-making for evaluation and other forms of research evidence, and the post-truth phenomena of anti-science sentiments combined with illiberal tendencies of the present day. Rather than offer a checklist on how to deal with post-truth, the experts found herein wish to raise awareness and reflection throughout policy circles on the factors that influence our assessment and policy-related work in such a challenging environment. Journeying alongside the editor and contributors, readers benefit from three guiding questions to help identify specific challenges but tools to deal with such challenges: How are policy problems conceptualized in the current political climate? What is the relationship between expertise and decision-making in today's political circumstances? How complex has evaluation become as a social practice? *Evaluation in the Post-Truth World* will benefit evaluation practitioners at the program and project levels, as well as policy analysts and scholars interested in applications of evaluation in the public policy domain.

Mita Marra is Associate Professor of Political Economy at the University of Naples in Italy. She also taught at the Trachtenberg School of Public Policy and Public Administration at the George Washington University (2016–2021), at Maastricht University (2006) and within the International Program of Development Evaluation (IPDET, 2016–2018). Mita Marra has a PhD in Public Policy from the George Washington University, an MA in International Relations at the School of Advanced International Studies of the Johns Hopkins University and a BA in Economics at the University of Naples Federico II, in Italy. Her current research interests revolve around public sector governance and policy evaluation in the field of regional development, innovation, and gender equality. Dr Marra has published extensively in peer-reviewed journals such as American Journal of Evaluation, Systems Research and Behavioral Science, and European Urban and Regional Studies. Dr Marra is Editor-in-Chief for the international peer-reviewed journal Evaluation and Program Planning (2015–present), past president of the Italian Evaluation Association (AIV, 2013–2017), and a current member of the Board of the European Evaluation Society, and the Council of the International Evaluation Academy.

Karol Olejniczak is Associate Professor of Public Policy at SWPS University, Warsaw, Poland, and co-founder of the Polish policy research company, Evaluation for Government Organizations (EGO s.c.). He was an Ostrom Policy Analysis Workshop fellow (2006), Kosciuszko Foundation fellow (2012), and Fulbright fellow (2021). Dr. Olejniczak's work focuses on the intersection of policy design and evaluation, and the use of evidence in decision-making. In his research and teaching, he utilizes games, experiments, and behavioral design. He has published the six-volume series *Ministerstwa Uczace Sie* (Learning Ministries), and articles in scientific journals such as the *American Journal of Evaluation, Policy Design and Practice*, and *Policy & Politics*.

Arne Paulson pursued a career in international development, working as an economist in a number of international organizations, including the World Bank, UNCTAD (Geneva), the International Energy Agency (Paris), and the Inter-American Development Bank (IDB), from which he retired in 2007. At the IDB, he worked in all aspects of evaluation, including ex-ante economic evaluation, ongoing monitoring of projects in execution, and ex-post evaluation of completed projects financed by the IDB. At the corporate level, he reported on the overall development effectiveness of IDB operations to the bank's board of directors and at international conferences.

Comparative Policy Evaluation

Edited by Ray C. Rist

The Comparative Policy Evaluation series is an interdisciplinary and internationally focused set of books that embodies within it a strong emphasis on comparative analyses of governance issues—drawing from all continents and many different nation states. The lens through which these policy initiatives are viewed and reviewed is that of evaluation. These evaluation assessments are done mainly from the perspectives of sociology, anthropology, economics, policy science, auditing, law, and human rights. The books also provide a strong longitudinal perspective on the evolution of the policy issues being analyzed.

Evaluation and Turbulent Times
Edited by Jan-Eric Furubo, Ray C. Rist, Sandra Speer

Speaking Justice to Power
Edited by Kim Forss, Mita Marra

Success in Evaluation
Edited by Steffen Bohni Nielsen, Rudi Turksema, Peter van der Knapp

Doing Public Good?
Edited by R. Pablo Guerrero O., Peter Wilkins

Cyber Society, Big Data, and Evaluation
Edited by Gustav Jakob Petersson, Jonathan D. Breul

The Evaluation Enterprise
Edited by Jan-Eric Furubo, Nicoletta Stame

Crossover of Audit and Evaluation Practices
Edited by Maria Barrados, Jeremy Lonsdale

Long Term Perspectives in Evaluation
Edited by Kim Forss, Ida Lindkvist, Mark McGillivray

The Realpolitik of Evaluation
Edited by Markus Palenberg, Arne Paulson

Changing Bureaucracies
Edited by Burt Perrin, Tony Tyrrell

Ethics for Evaluation
Edited by Rob D. van den Berg, Penny Hawkins, Nicoletta Stame

Towards Sustainable Futures
The Role of Evaluation
Edited by Per Øyvind Bastøe, Kim Forss, Ida Lindkvist

Evaluation in the Post-Truth World
Edited by Mita Marra, Karol Olejniczak, Arne Paulson

Evaluation in the Post-Truth World

Edited by Mita Marra, Karol Olejniczak, and Arne Paulson

NEW YORK AND LONDON

First published 2024
by Routledge
605 Third Avenue, New York, NY 10158

and by Routledge
4 Park Square, Milton Park, Abingdon, Oxon, OX14 4RN

Routledge is an imprint of the Taylor & Francis Group, an informa business

© 2024 selection and editorial matter, Mita Marra, Karol Olejniczak, and Arne Paulson; individual chapters, the contributors

The right of Mita Marra, Karol Olejniczak, and Arne Paulson to be identified as the authors of the editorial material, and of the authors for their individual chapters, has been asserted in accordance with sections 77 and 78 of the Copyright, Designs and Patents Act 1988.

With the exception of Chapter 6 and Conclusion, no part of this book may be reprinted or reproduced or utilised in any form or by any electronic, mechanical, or other means, now known or hereafter invented, including photocopying and recording, or in any information storage or retrieval system, without permission in writing from the publishers.

Chapter 6 and Conclusion of this book are available for free in PDF format as Open Access at www.taylorfrancis.com. It has been made available under a Creative Commons Attribution-Non Commercial-No Derivatives (CC-BY-NC-ND) 4.0 license.

Trademark notice: Product or corporate names may be trademarks or registered trademarks, and are used only for identification and explanation without intent to infringe.

Library of Congress Cataloging-in-Publication Data
Names: Marra, Mita, editor. | Olejniczak, Karol, editor. | Paulson, Arne, editor.
Title: Evaluation in the post-truth world / edited by Mita Marra, Karol Olejniczak, and Arne Paulson.
Description: New York, NY: Routledge, 2024. | Series: Comparative policy evaluation | Includes bibliographical references. |
Identifiers: LCCN 2023047244 (print) | LCCN 2023047245 (ebook) | ISBN 9781032719313 (hardback) | ISBN 9781032719931 (paperback) | ISBN 9781032719979 (ebook)
Subjects: LCSH: Political planning–Evaluation. | Political planning–Decision making. | Truthfulness and falsehood–Political aspects. | Disinformation–Political aspects.
Classification: LCC JF1525.P6 E83 2024 (print) | LCC JF1525.P6 (ebook) | DDC 320.6–dc23/eng/20240130
LC record available at https://lccn.loc.gov/2023047244
LC ebook record available at https://lccn.loc.gov/2023047245

ISBN: 978-1-032-71931-3 (hbk)
ISBN: 978-1-032-71993-1 (pbk)
ISBN: 978-1-032-71997-9 (ebk)

DOI: 10.4324/9781032719979

Typeset in Times New Roman
by Deanta Global Publishing Services, Chennai, India

The Open Access version of Chapter 6 and Conclusion was funded by SWPS University.

Contents

Foreword	*xi*
List of Contributors	*xiii*

Introduction: Questions rather than alternative facts   1
MITA MARRA, KAROL OLEJNICZAK, AND ARNE PAULSON

1   Co-creating evaluation for policy relevance: The challenges of the post-truth world   10
MITA MARRA

2   Free trade, populism, and post-truth: An evaluation perspective   29
R. PABLO GUERRERO O

3   Evidence as enlightenment versus evidence as certainty: Appropriate uses of evaluative information to inform policy in a post-truth world   37
RICHARD BOYLE AND SEAN REDMOND

4   Lies and politics: Until death do us part …   57
STEVE JACOB AND JEANNE MILOT-POULIN

5   Heuristics and biases in the post-truth era—a piece of advice for policy-makers   76
JAKUB KRAWIEC AND PAWEŁ ŚLIWOWSKI

6   In search of effective communication with decision-makers for the post-truth era: Discourse strategies from pre-imperial China   97
KAROL OLEJNICZAK AND MARCIN JACOBY

7   Do citizens even want to hear the truth?: Public attitudes toward evidence-informed policymaking   116
PIRMIN BUNDI AND VALÉRIE PATTYN

x *Contents*

8   Sustaining momentum for evidence-informed policymaking:
    The case of the US government   134
    NICHOLAS HART AND KATHRYN NEWCOMER

9   Participatory budgeting, evaluation, and the post-truth
    world: Where are we, and where do we go from here?   150
    YAERIN PARK

10 Evidence use in a post-truth world: A unique opportunity for
    evaluators?   176
    STEFFEN BOHNI NIELSEN AND SEBASTIAN LEMIRE

    Conclusions: Some suggestions for evaluators'
    daily work in a post-truth world   192
    KAROL OLEJNICZAK, MITA MARRA, AND ARNE PAULSON

    Index   *201*

Foreword

A common assumption among its theorists and practitioners is that evaluation is a rational enterprise that takes place in a political context. The independent, objective, external evaluator generates data and transforms it into evidence of the success (or failure) of program and policy implementation and intended outcomes. This practice takes place in a highly complex, often chaotic, political environment where decision-makers exert pressure on evaluation researchers for decisive answers to pressing social and environmental problems. This view of the evaluation-politics relation dates at least to 1973 when Carol Weiss explained that politics and evaluation entwine because (a) programs and policies are the creatures of political processes and decisions, (b) the reports produced by evaluators feed into the political process where evaluative evidence competes with other influences on decision-making, and (c) that evaluation itself makes political statements about the problematic nature of some programs and others as unchallengeable, and even the appropriate role of the evaluation researcher in policy and program formation.

Fifty years on, the field has grown wiser about the evaluation-politics connection, realizing that evaluators are not simply one of many participants in politically charged arenas dealing with social problems but that the practice itself is political and value-laden. Many evaluators now recognize that evaluation can be used as a means of political legitimation; that evaluation might be of greater value and use by democratizing the production of evaluation knowledge and returning control of the process and product to program users (i.e., doing participatory and action-oriented evaluation); that evaluation practices are not disengaged, eternal judgments of effectiveness and efficiency but active agents in the power politics of evidence and results-based management and thus must inevitably confront the question of what evidence matters and to whom; that political decision-making cannot be usefully informed by so-called neutral facts—neutral in the sense that they do not serve any particular set of interests or promote any value judgment; and that a sociological perspective on the practice requires evaluators to consider the structural bases of inequality in societies. In short, evaluation does not simply operate in a world of political constraints as first imagined years ago but is itself socially constructed and politically expressed. Evaluation is given meaning by multifaceted social and political relations, and at the same time it contributes to the creation of those relations.

xii *Foreword*

Sorting out the aims and means of professional evaluation practice as well as its claims to be of use in view of this realization of the politics-evaluation nexus is not for the faint hearted. The task has taken on new urgency in the current climate of post-truth politics, the increasing disregard for evidence in decision-making at levels of both policy and practice, and the distrust and often outright rejection of the independence and objectivity of scientists and scholars. Ironically, the evidence from cognitive psychology reveals that renewed appeals to confront misinformation and the manufacture of alternative facts with the "real" facts of the matter and to double down on the assumption that most people respond rationally to data and evidence that contradict their long-held positions simply will not work. Evaluators must now learn to navigate an interlocking set of considerations that include the following: Revisiting the fact-value relationship to critique the faulty assumption that facts and values are somehow added together in decision-making; learning to confront, manage, and counteract asymmetries of power long ignored in simplistic models of stakeholder participation in evaluation; looking to fields such as public management and public policy creation to understand how evaluation practices can be part of the co-production and co-creation of policies and programs; finding ways to restore emotion to reason, refusing to treat the former as an enemy of the latter; learning to incorporate indigenous knowledges, global south epistemologies, and culturally responsive inquiries into methods for judging the value of social and environmental interventions; and returning the critical examination of values to the center of what it means to evaluate. The current volume aims to help with this very challenging and complicated task. My hope is that the advice found here is tempered with yet another observation on the added value of evaluation by Carol Weiss and colleagues made in 2005:

Evaluation is fallible.
Evaluation is but one source of evidence.
Evidence is but one input into policy.
Policy is but one influence on practice.
Practice is but one influence on outcomes.

[Carol Hirschon Weiss, Erin Murphy-Graham, Sarah Birkeland, "An Alternate Route to Policy Influence: How Evaluations Affect D.A.R.E." *American Journal of Evaluation*, Vol. 26 No. 1, March 2005, 12–30]

Thomas A. Schwandt
Bloomington, Indiana USA
April 15, 2023

Contributors

Richard Boyle is an independent researcher and former head of research at the Institute of Public Administration in Ireland. He has carried out a wide range of research and consultancy studies on aspects of public service management with an emphasis on public sector reform, performance measurement, and evaluation. He has published extensively on the Irish public service. Internationally, he has conducted research on behalf of the European Commission, the OECD, and the World Bank. He is a former member of the board of the European Evaluation Network and was a founding member of the Irish Evaluation Network.

Pirmin Bundi is Associate Professor of Public Policy and Evaluation at the Swiss Graduate School of Public Administration (IDHEAP), University of Lausanne. His research, publications, and expertise focus on policy evaluation, public policy, and political elites. He has published extensively in academic journals, such as the *American Journal of Evaluation, Journal of European Public Policy, Policy Studies Journal,* and *Policy Sciences.* He recently co-edited the *Handbook of Public Policy Evaluation* published by Edward Elgar Publishing. Previously, he was Visiting Professor at Venice International University and Visiting Scholar at the University of California, Los Angeles.

R. Pablo Guerrero is an Economist and former Advisor at the World Bank. He has graduate degrees in Economics and Business and did his postgraduate executive education at Harvard University. He is a former Chief of Evaluation at the Inter-American Development Bank and Advisor to the Director-General of Evaluation at the World Bank. Among his contributions are the launching of the Evaluation Capacity Development Program at the World Bank, managing the World Bank's Secretariat for the Comprehensive Development Framework, and developing the World Bank's Strategy for Middle-Income Countries. He has done consulting work on country strategies and finance for the World Bank and, since the 1990s, has contributed to several books in the Comparative Policy Evaluation Series: *Evaluation Capacity Development, Success in Evaluation,* and *Doing Public Good?*

xiv   *Contributos*

Nick Hart is President and CEO of the Data Foundation, a Washington, DC-based non-profit organization that champions the use of open data and evidence-informed policymaking to improve society. He is an adjunct professor of program evaluation at George Washington University and a fellow of the National Academy of Public Administration. He has written extensively about the need to collect, manage, govern, and use data to generate useful evidence for policymakers, including co-authoring two books: *Evidence-Building and Evaluation in Government (2022, with Kathy Newcomer)* and *Evidence Works: Cases Where Evidence Meaningfully Informed Decision-Making (2019)*. He earned a Ph.D. from George Washington University's Trachtenberg School of Public Policy and Public Administration, specializing in program evaluation.

Steve Jacob is a Full Professor in the Department of Political Science at Université Laval (Québec City, Canada). He is the Director of the Research laboratory on the performance and evaluation of public action (PerfEval) and also the Scientific Director of the International Observatory on the Societal impacts of AI and digital technology (OBVIA). Trained as a political analyst and historian, Steve Jacob conducts research dealing with the mechanisms of performance management and evaluation: professionalization, institutionalization, and capacity building in Europe and Canada, ethics in public administration, and the digital transformation of the public sector. His research has been published in numerous journals. He is also the author and editor of 12 books focusing on evaluation and experts' involvement during the policy process. Steve Jacob has been an invited professor at several universities in Europe, Africa, and North America. In 2013, he was awarded the Prix reconnaissance from the Société québécoise d'évaluation de programme (SQÉP) for his outstanding contributions to program evaluation in Quebec.

Marcin Jacoby is Associate Professor (Ph.D. in Chinese literature from the University of Warsaw), Dean of the Faculty of Humanities, and Head of the Department of Asian Studies at the SWPS University, Poland. Sinologist, translator, and interpreter, Jacoby specializes in Chinese pre-imperial literature and political thought. Jacoby also translates Chinese classical literature into Polish (Zhuangzi, Liezi, and Zhanguoce) and is Co-editor-in-chief of the "Asia-Pacific" biannual academic journal.

Jakub Krawiec is Psychologist, Ph.D. candidate, lecturer, and staff member at the Department of Economic Psychology and Business, Faculty of Psychology, SWPS University in Warsaw. He has interned at the Policy Research Group, University of Cambridge (2018), and Oslo Metropolitan University (2022). Before joining SWPS University, he worked at the Sotrender Research Agency and the Polish Economic Institute as a project manager, focusing on behavioral and digital data analysis. His research interests include behavioral economics and the psychology of decision-making and public policy.

Contributors xv

Sebastian Lemire, PhD, is Senior Scientist at Abt Associates with decades of experience designing and managing evaluations of education and workforce development programs. He has extensive experience with a broad range of evaluation approaches, quasi- and non-experimental designs, qualitative and quantitative data collection and analysis methods, as well as systematic evidence reviews. Sebastian has published over 40 peer-reviewed articles and book chapters on a broad range of methodological topics, including alternative approaches for impact evaluation, theory-based evaluation, and development and use of theories of change for program design, implementation, and evaluation. He is a current board member of the American Evaluation Association and a former board member of the European Evaluation Society and the Danish Evaluation Society.

Kathryn Newcomer is Professor at the Trachtenberg School of Public Policy and Public Administration at George Washington University. She was the founding director of the Trachtenberg School in 2003 and served as its director for 14 years. She is a Fellow of the National Academy of Public Administration. She served as president of the American Evaluation Association (AEA) in 2017 and also as president of the National Association of Schools of Public Affairs and Administration (NASPAA) for the period 2006–2007. Kathryn has published ten books, including, *Evidence-building and Evaluation in Government* (2022), *Engagement for Equitable Outcomes: A Practitioner's Playbook* (2022), *Federal Inspectors General: Truth Seekers in Turbulent Times* (2020), and *The Handbook of Practical Program Evaluation*,4th edition (2015), and dozens of articles. She earned her B.S. in Education and an M.A. in Political Science from the University of Kansas, and her Ph.D. in Political Science from the University of Iowa.

Steffen Bohni Nielsen (PhD) is Director General at the Danish National Research Centre for the Working Environment, NFA and a member of the Danish National Research and Innovation Council. He is a member of INTEVAL and has published extensively in the field of evaluation on topics such as theory-based evaluation, evaluation capacity building, results-management, public leadership, Big Data, and Artificial Intelligence. He is the editor of several journal special issues and books. He is a member of the editorial advisory board of the *American Journal of Evaluation.*

Yaerin Park is Assistant Professor in Public Service and Public Policy at Hainan University (HNU)–Arizona State University (ASU) Joint International Tourism College (HAITC), Hainan University. Her multidisciplinary research interests include Participatory Budgeting (PB), open government, social justice and equity (particularly in the public budgeting process), and public management innovation. She has expertise in quantitative, qualitative, and mixed methods research methodology, and possesses experience incorporating behavioral insights by using experimental methods in public

xvi *Contributos*

administration research. Yaerin received her Ph.D. degree in Public Policy and Administration from George Washington University in Washington DC, USA.

Valérie Pattyn is Associate Professor at the Institute of Public Administration at Leiden University and Visiting Professor at KU Leuven Public Governance Institute. Her work focuses broadly on comparative public policy, evidence-informed policy-making, and policy evaluation. In addition to fundamental research in these areas, she engages in applied evaluation research and policy consulting. She is a co-chair of the Permanent Study Group on Policy Design and Evaluation of the European Group for Public Administration and is an active member of both the Flemish and Dutch Evaluation Associations. She has published in a wide range of public administration, public policy, and evaluation journals.

Dr Sean Redmond is seconded by the Department of Justice to the School of Law, University of Limerick (UL) in Ireland. Seán is leading a national project to develop the evidence base to improve youth crime policy decision-making. From 2012 to 2016 Sean worked in the Research and Evaluation Unit of the Department of Children and Youth Affairs with the lead responsibility for evaluation. Over the last 25 years Sean has held positions as Head of Young Offender Programmes Irish Youth Justice Service; Assistant Director of Children's Services, for a national NGO, Barnardos and Director of PACE, a prisoners' resettlement service. Sean is a registered social worker and holds a doctorate in Governance.

Pawel Śliwowski is Deputy Director of the Polish Economic Institute – governmental socio-economic think tank based in Warsaw. Śliwowski previously worked as researcher at the University of Warsaw and also as a policy consultant, delivering advisory and training services for public organizations in the European Union and Poland, such as the European Commission, the European Investment Bank, the Chancellery of the Prime Minister of Poland, the Polish Ministry of Development, and various local governments across Poland.

Introduction

Questions rather than alternative facts

Mita Marra, Karol Olejniczak, and Arne Paulson

Does the growing practice of appealing to emotions and opinions, rather than evidence, affect evaluation in democratic political and institutional settings? This collection of essays addresses this question with the intensity that only writing a book permits. The book has evolved in keeping with the turmoil of our times: over the past three years, we have observed how destructive post-truth can be for the decision-making of democratic countries. We began in 2019 with the realization that populism—with Brexit and the election of Donald Trump in the West as examples—has contributed to a post-truth world with a looming crisis of trust in science and a diminished role of expertise in political arenas. In 2020, as the Covid pandemic spread out, that realization has reinforced our conviction that a post-truth world exposes evaluators' work to additional resistance and antagonism when designing and implementing policies. Finally, the Russian aggression in Ukraine in 2022 has further exacerbated the national and global public policy landscape. In current geopolitics, the mechanisms of post-truth, especially through disinformation, can be weaponized into propaganda and lies, and used by malicious dictatorships in an open war against democratic global order (Rid, 2020).

The point of departure of our reasoning is that expertise at any level in a democratic society has been challenged and seriously questioned. This phenomenon has been labeled as "post-truth" and broadly defined as circumstances in which facts are eroded and less influential in shaping decision-making than appeals to emotions, personal beliefs, or even fiction (McIntyre, 2018: 5). A 2018 report by the Rand Corporation (Kavanagh & Rich, 2018), entitled *Truth Decay: An Initial Exploration of the Diminishing Role of Facts and Analysis in American Public Life* has investigated the diminishing role of facts and analysis that, over the past two decades, has compromised civil discourse, caused political paralysis, and led to public uncertainty and disengagement. Authors point out that this context becomes extremely challenging for developing effective public policy solutions.

By the same token, Schmieg et al. (2018) assert that polarization and politicization of national and international techno-scientific and economic innovation policy programs have influenced the way information is developed and used. The authors observe politicization pervading international and national

DOI: 10.4324/9781032719979-1

regulatory policies for implementing sustainability-centred policies—including Sustainable Development Goals (SDGs) (Schmieg et al., 2018; Marra, 2021a). Regulatory solutions at the macro level get influenced by vested interests that often win over social sustainability goals and aims, whereas, at the local level, welfare politics rests on particularistic needs and interests (Schmieg et al., 2018).

Along the same lines, the influential report by Mair et al. (2019) of the Joint Research Council of the European Commission focuses on the complexity of political behavior, highlighting policymakers' and citizens' vulnerability to disinformation, but also on the partisan leadership that undermines the capacity of governments to use evidence effectively. The report points out that polarized politics is likely associated with the unwillingness to use evaluation to assess policy choices and may lead to governments seeking to weaken independent scientific authorities and to reduce the visibility of evidence critical of partisan leadership. Nichols (2017), in his insightful and popular book, simply labels this situation as "the death of expertise" as emotions lure people and politicians more than facts and evidence.

And yet, a casual observer may be impressed by the lofty achievements in the domains of genetics, modern electronics, and any other topic in human knowledge. In social policies and welfare programs, remarkable progress has emerged in exploring societal change against such difficult or "wicked" problems as inequality, racism, and poverty. As the British physicist, Czercky (2016) points out, on the surface, science is more democratic than ever—a rapidly increasing proportion of all scientific contributions are freely available online; university websites overflow with information about current research, and scientists and experts across different policy domains are increasingly visible to the rest of society. In the age of Google and ChatGPT, the frontiers of knowledge are not inaccessible but misleadingly comprehensible. Modern science remains full of complexities because our reality is complex. The accessibility of science means that we may not see the complex context before arriving at each nugget of information—and often, we don't want to (Czercky, 2016). Thus, explaining the state-of-the-art of our knowledge and even using it to support policy choices becomes a daunting undertaking that draws on the foundations that connect science to society, politics, and the policies they underpin—and that's where the problem lurks.

In postmodern philosophies, the relationship among science, society, politics, and policies sees knowledge and power as either competing or complementary goods (Voß & Freedman, 2017). When they are in competition, knowledge and power are safeguarded by democratic institutions that act within their respective functional systems—that is, the sphere of science, on the one hand, and the sphere of politics, on the other. Along these lines, Wildavsky's seminal work—*Speaking Truth to Power*—as well as Habermas' dialogic discourses, delve into the dialectic between knowledge and power as separate fields of interaction (Wildavsky, 1979; Habermas, 2003). When no longer in competition, knowledge and power merge as in Foucault's thinking of governmentality (Gordon,

Introduction 3

1980), whereby governance structures and relations stem from different forms of knowledge. Accordingly, the German thinker Mannheim (1940), discussing Seinsge-bundenheit, that is, being-bounded, sheds light on the epistemic processes that underlie politics.

Following the latter interpretation, recent studies on the policy process have emphasized the situated nature of decision-making, rejecting a universally rational foundation for decision-making (Cairney, 2020). Policymakers do not inhabit a lofty perspective that yields an objective vision of the problem and its solutions. More pragmatically, decision-makers bring their own situated perspective to the issue at hand and do the best they can, under all circumstances, to reach a fair, effective, and efficient choice. In this context, decision-making draws on scientific evidence and the tacit and contextual knowledge that stakeholders share in democratic regimes (Voß & Freedman, 2017). And evaluation, incorporating technical and contextual insights, causal analyses, and policy recommendations, contributes to the diversified knowledge sets that potentially support decision-making.

The focus and audience of the book

This book reflexively reconstructs the socio-political climate that contradictorily characterizes our epoch: we witness the underlying tensions between the open discrediting of science and expertise on the one hand and the pressure for evidence-based policymaking (EBPM) on the other. Polarization of politics, old and new media dynamics, lack of trust in science, and the ever-rising complexity of policy issues are some features and trends that influence the environment where evaluators work (across different levels and jurisdictions) to design and improve specific policies and public interventions. Even when constructive consensus does exist between commissioners or managers and evaluators, the latter may face uncertain and unfavorable circumstances. As opinionated individuals or vocal collective stakeholders ignite protest and contestation, a cloak of silence may hamper dialogue and information sharing. Within an unfriendly climate of suspicion, distrust, skepticism, and conflict, performance and impact assessments risk stressing their punitive effect rather than their potential for organizational learning and results-based management (Considine & Afzal, 2011).

In such circumstances, evaluators may face the denial of the evidence they collected and the emotional reaction that challenging performance information may generate, realizing their own implicit biases within organizations (Sah, 2017; Marra, 2021b). Evaluators may also have to cope with the increasing demands for information associated with the movement of evidence-based policymaking (EBPM). For the past two decades, national and subnational governments—and even several big cities—have experienced what Haskins (2018) calls an evidence-based uprising that is helping them to select or develop effective social and educational programs, and then improve them. The 2018 special issue entitled *The Role of Evaluation in Building Evidence-Based Policy* by the *Annals of the American Academy of Political and Social Science*, provides a survey of the field of evidence-based practices and policymaking, while a growing consensus has emerged around the phrasing of *Evidence-Informed Policymaking* to acknowledge, from a critical stance, the multiple sources, and ways of knowing that can support policy decisions besides scientific evidence.

Thus, this book explores the relationship between the nature of evaluative knowledge with its increasing demand in decision-making for evaluation and other forms of research evidence and the post-truth phenomena of anti-science sentiments combined with the illiberal tendencies of our times. There are two reasons why we focus on democratic countries and their public policy decision-making. First—as earlier volumes of this Comparative Policy Evaluation series show—the democratic, deliberative environment is the natural and most common habitat for the evaluation practice (see: Eliadis et al., 2011; Furubo et al., 2002). Second, the implications of the post-truth phenomenon are most visible in democratic settings. Here, post-truth defies the fundamental mechanism of improving decision-making with a critical reflection based on facts and research.

Our primary audience is evaluation practitioners at the program and project levels, as well as policy analysts and scholars interested in applying evaluation in the public policy domain. We do not intend to offer a practical checklist on how evaluators should deal with post-truth although, in our conclusions, we do provide some suggestions—after all, evaluators always expect some recommendations. Instead, the primary goal of this volume is to raise policy analysts' and evaluators' awareness and provoke a reflection throughout policy circles on the factors that influence our assessment and policy-related work in such a challenging environment. The essays included in the volume, in various degrees, address the following three guiding questions:

(1) How are policy problems conceptualized in the current political climate?
(2) What is the relationship between expertise and decision-making in today's political circumstances?
(3) How complex has evaluation become as a social practice?

The first question concerns how today's democratic systems interpret such policy problems as climate change, social inequality, and vulnerability. Here, a greater awareness of public opinion toward these social problems and their related policies, a greater attention by decision-makers and experts to policy evaluation, and a significant increase in the data made available to researchers and analysts have improved the ability to observe and analyze both goals and outcomes. This heightened policy evaluation capacity is perhaps the most important advance of our times, thanks to efforts by national and international statistical institutions to provide increasingly complete and updated data. Notwithstanding persistent limitations in measurement, aspects and problems that until a few years ago were studied through qualitative observations and very limited sampling surveys are now subject to systematic monitoring because of the supply of information provided by robust statistical systems of data collection. However, since problems get perceived and addressed if metrics detect their size and intensity, policies may risk being considered only for their measurement dimensions. While potentially enhancing reflexivity, this noise—paraphrasing Kahneman et al. (2021)—contributes to losing sight of the problems, the subjects, and the dynamics that, for various reasons, remain outside the radar screen of measurement and evaluation and are confined to silence and invisibility because of their immeasurable or residual nature. An additional risk is that a technocratic vision of public policies that overlooks consideration of dimensions, subjects, and problems that are not visible or measurable enough to be treated, fuels populism and data misrepresentation.

Our second question deals with the relationship between expertise and decision-making. Many politicians use easily refutable statements to promote their political agenda or oversimplify to make their point in public. Modern media public discourse favors clear-cut, brief assertions. As Czercky (2016) notes, people often perceive an overwhelming complexity they cannot bear, whereas researchers know that theories often require revision or radical rethinking as a normal part of the scientific process; their rethinking follows systematic questioning methods and distinguishes facts from interpretations. Yet, the public and policymakers—encouraged to think of science as a matter of certainty—may consider these changes to reflect either a lack of authority or expertise or that everything is debatable. That context creates a substantial challenge for establishing a constructive relationship between science and decision-making in developing effective public policies.

Finally, our third question focuses on the complexity of the evaluation enterprise as a social practice (see also Furubo & Stame, 2019 in our Policy Evaluation Collection). Modern states have built surveillance systems to face wicked problems considering the bounded rationality of individual and organizational endeavors (Simon, 1976; Scott, 1999). The institutionalization of evaluation in the legislative and executive branches of democratic systems has contributed to systematically supporting policymaking and institutional operations. And yet, how and to what extent do evaluators, citizens, and policymakers innovate their ways of thinking and doing things by learning from their collaboration experiences? Here, the third question examines how complex evaluation has become as a social practice and what type of ambiguity arises regarding its design and concrete functioning (Marra, 2018).

Over the past three decades, most governments have institutionalized evaluation through investments in policy and organizational capacity building (Furubo et al., 2002; Stockmann & Meyer, 2016). To assess the Sustainable Development Goals (SDGs), for instance, Schmieg et al. (2018) point to the architecture

6 *Marra, Olejniczak, and Paulson*

of informational surveillance systems at the global level that has created an infrastructure of international technical and financial facilities operating at the national level. While the commonly-shared goal is to assure transparency, the operating systems may fail to follow up on data gathering and dissemination. The weakness is often related to the capacity of collecting the information on the ground, which requires invested time and resources to siphon off for other, more urgent purposes, especially in critical circumstances. As a result, the exercise of accountability may get downgraded to mere numerical accounting practices and indicators for oversight with no involvement of stakeholder groups in the co-production of policy measures based on research insights (Ostrom, 1996). Here, the need exists for broadening and intensifying citizen participation while cultivating traits or dispositions that evaluators aim to promote in others and among themselves, including procedures and institutions that facilitate reflexivity.

The structure of the book

As this volume is not a compendium of all issues related to our post-truth world, the book structure unfolds along the relevance of chapters as grouped around the three basic questions outlined in second section in this introduction. While we draw readers' attention to the fact that some of our authors touch upon more than one of these questions, we have oriented our discussion to what we regard as the most salient aspects of each chapter. Each author describes not only specific challenges but also practical ideas for the community of evaluators to deal with those challenges.

The first part of the volume groups the chapters that address the relationship between policy problems and evaluation. Marra's chapter sets the stage for a reflexive endeavor by highlighting the challenges that evaluators face in the current political economy. The author explores the epistemological, behavioral, and political-economic pathways evaluators can follow to interact with policymakers and citizens and cope with anti-science sentiments, illiberal tendencies, and post-truth phenomena, pointing out the need for co-creation and co-evaluation to address those challenges.

In the same vein, the chapters by Guerrero and Boyle and Redmond explore what normative and theoretical underpinnings permeate wicked problems or policy issues through multiple policy circles and epistemic communities. In particular, Guerrero points out value-laden and cognitive insights that influence how policymakers interpret free trade policies and their economic and social consequences—and search for alternative interpretations that evaluators ought to assess against observable effects on the ground. The author discusses how framing free trade in the sole dimension of distributional effects has created a blind spot and discrepancy in economic evaluations, creating a fertile environment for rising social discontent and political opportunism. The main takeaway is the need for critically revisiting theories and their simplified assumptions that drive mainstream economic policies.

Introduction 7

Boyle and Redmond examine youth crime and water quality and their respective policy measures as assessed across different policy networks. Although these problems are inherently diverse, similar interpretations emerge within the Irish policy community. Looking at in-depth monitoring and evaluations of youth justice and water quality programs in Ireland, the authors detect commonly shared patterns in the plural nature of evaluative information, drawing both on scientific evidence and craft knowledge based on contextual, organizational, and tacit knowhow. This diversified knowledge body can help us understand complex policy issues beyond stereotypical categories associated with beneficiaries and outcomes.

The second part groups chapters that address the relationship between politics and expertise. Jacob and Milot-Poulin's chapter proposes an erudite reconstruction of how politicians are often prone to lying, providing readers with a spectrum of decision situations and tactics applied in politics to use, but often also abuse, information, evidence, and facts. Building upon behavioral science and cognitive psychology, Krawiec and Sliwowski, in their chapter, illustrate the mechanisms that explain the generalized preference for simplification among policymakers and citizens. Olejniczak and Jacoby draw on the pre-imperial China political discourse to identify specific strategies of persuasion that might inspire more effective communication between evaluators and decision-makers in the post-truth era. By contrast, exploring the citizenry reaction, Bundi and Pattyn discuss findings of a survey on evidence-informed policymaking across six countries. They show how political polarization influences public attitudes toward using evidence for planning and conclude that knowing which citizens and social communities are more open or skeptical about evidence can help evaluators design targeted strategies to overcome potential resistance.

The third part groups chapters that deal with the complexity of evaluation in our political-institutional systems that increasingly ask for evidence-based information to make collective decisions. Newcomer and Hart retrace the steps the US has taken to build an administrative machinery enabling policymakers to assume evidence-based policy choices. The authors examine how the Commission for Evidence-based Policymaking has emerged with the set of reforms aimed to improve objective information available to politicians and the public alike. Park delves into participatory budgeting. Building upon the experience initiated in Porto Alegre, Brazil, in the late 1980s that has recently spread to other parts of the world, the author gleans relevant lessons for program evaluation, especially concerning knowledge co-production and participatory approaches to decisionmaking. Finally, Bohni and Lemire describe how some of the characteristics and complexities of evaluation provide unique opportunities for evaluators to promote professionalization, and the trans-disciplinary nature of the evaluative knowledge, while mastering the evaluation marketplace and the commissioning processes. The authors propose some tools evaluators have used to anticipate and manage different stakeholder needs, tools that could be relevant and valuable for researchers navigating the post-truth landscape.

8 Marra, Olejniczak, and Paulson

The answers this volume seeks are far from delineating an exhaustive and definitive overview of the challenges that evaluation faces and the solutions to alternative facts and fake news within the current socio-political climate. However, some advances can be acknowledged and valued. First, this volume links post-truth changes in the public domain with evaluation craft that is often perceived as a technical exercise conducted in neutral organizational environments, screened off the dynamics occurring at the national, international, and transnational levels. Second, this volume raises the implications of political trends, translating them into specific evaluation practices that seek to counteract the post-truth drift. Third, this volume brings together different perspectives and critical views—not only populist politics and rationally bounded policymaking but also the complexity of evaluation and science more broadly considered.

We argue that these are a means of assuring that evaluation continues to have a constructive role in the public debate considering the new challenging circumstances of post-truth policy-making. In agreement with Schwandt (2008), we posit that for an evaluating society to flourish, citizens and professionals have to develop a capacity to be inquisitive, systematic in their inquiry, judicious in their claims, truth-seeking, analytical, intellectually humble, sympathetic to opposing points of view, self-critical, and open-minded—not simply open-minded in the sense of being tolerant of other points of view, but open-minded to recognize the challenges to one's way of seeing things that arise from others' ways of making distinctions of worth.

References

Cairney, P. (2020). *Understanding public policy: Theories and issues* (2nd ed.). New York: Red Globe Press.

Clarke, J., & Newman, J. (2017). 'People in this country have had enough of experts': Brexit and the paradoxes of populism. *Critical Policy Studies*, 11(1), 101–116. https://doi.org/10.1080/19460171.2017.1282376

Considine, M., & Afzal, K. (2011). Legitimacy. In *The SAGE handbook of governance* (pp. 369–385). SAGE Publications Ltd. https://doi.org/10.4135/9781446200964

Czercky, H. (2016). *Storm in a teacup: The physics of everyday life*. New York, W.W. Norton and Company.

Eliadis, P., Furubo, J. E., & Jacob, S. (2011). *Evaluation: Seeking truth or power?* London: Routeldge.

Furubo, J.-E., Rist, R. C., & Sandahl, R. (2002). *International atlas of evaluation*. New Brunswick: Transaction Publishers.

Furubo, J. E., & Stame, N. (2019). *The evaluation enterprise. A critical view*. New York: Routledge.

Gordon, C. (Ed.). (1980). *Michel Foucault. Power/knowledge: Selected interviews and other writings, 1972–79*. New York: Pantheon Books.

Habermas, J. (2003). *Truth and justification*. Cambridge, MA: The MIT Press.

Haskins, R. (2018). Evidence-based policy: The movement, the goals, the issues, the promise. *The ANNALS of the American Academy of Political and Social Science*, 678(1), 8–37. https://doi.org/10.1177/0002716218770642

Kahneman, D., Sibony, O., & Sustain, C. R. (2021). *Noise. A flaw in human judgment.* New York: William Collins.

Kavanagh, J., & Rich, M. D. (2018). *Truth decay. an initial exploration of the diminishing role of facts and analysis in American public life, rand corporation America.* https://www.rand.org/pubs/research_reports/RR2314.html

Mair, D., Smillie, L., La Placa, G., Schwendinger, F., Raykovska, M., Pasztor, Z., & Van Bavel, R. (2019). *Understanding our political nature: How to put knowledge and reason at the heart of political decision- making.* Publications Office of the European Union. https://op.europa.eu/en/publication-detail/-/publication/6574c875-a90a-11e9-9d01-01aa75ed71a1/language-en

Mannheim, K. (1940). *The concept of social control: Planning as the rational mastery of the irrational, in Karl Mannheim, man and society in an age of reconstruction* (pp. 265–273). London: Routledge.

Marra, M. (2018). The ambiguities of performance-based governance reforms in Italy: Reviving the fortunes of evaluation and performance measurement. *Evaluation and Program Planning, 69,* 173–182. https://doi.org/10.1016/j.evalprogplan.2017.02.006

Marra, M. (2021a). Meso evaluation for SDGs' complexity and ethics. *Ethics, Policy & Environment.* https://doi.org/10.1080/21550085.2021.1940450

Marra, M. (2021b). A behavioral design to reform Italy's evaluation policy. *American Journal of Evaluation, 42*(4), 483–504. https://doi.org/10.1177/1098214020972791

Marra, M. (2023). Editorial. *Evaluation and Program Planning, 100,* 102352. https://doi.org/10.1016/j.evalprogplan.2023.102352

McIntyre, L. C. (2018). *Post-truth.* Cambridge, MA: MIT Press.

Nichols, T. M. (2017). *The death of expertise: The campaign against established knowledge and why it matters.* New York, NY: Oxford University Press.

Ostrom, E. (1996). Crossing the great divide: Coproduction, synergy, and development. *World Development, 24*(6), 1073–1087.

Rid, T. (2020). *Active measures: The secret history of disinformation and political warfare.* London: Profile Books.

Sah, S. (2017). Policy solutions to conflicts of interest: The value of professional norms. *Behavioural Public Policy, 1*(2), 177–189. DOI:10.1017/bpp.2016.9

Schmieg, G., Meyer, E., Schrickel, I., Herberg, J., Caniglia, G., Vilsmaier, U., Laubichler, M., Hörl, E., & Lang, D. (2018). Modeling normativity in sustainability: A comparison of the sustainable development goals, the Paris agreement, and the papal encyclical. *Sustainability Science, 13*(3), 785. https://doi.org/10.1007/s11625-017-0504-7

Schwandt, T. (2008, June). Educating for intelligent belief in evaluation. *American Journal of Evaluation, 29*(2), 139–150.

Scott, J. (1999). *Seeing like a state: How certain schemes to improve the human condition have failed (the institution for social and policy St).* Yale University Press.

Simon, H. A. (1976). *Administrative behavior: A study of decision-making processes in administrative organization.* New York: Free Press.

Stockmann, R., & Meyer, M. (2016). *The future of evaluation global trends, new challenges, shared perspectives.* London: Palgrave.

Voß, J. B., & Freeman, R. (2017). *Knowing governance.* London: Palgrave.

Wildavsky, A. (1979). *Speaking truth to power: The art and craft of policy analysis.* Boston: Little, Brown.

1 Co-creating evaluation for policy relevance

The challenges of the post-truth world

Mita Marra

Introduction

Current social and political realities have recently transformed the way politicians, media, citizenry, and experts—including the evaluators—address social problems and their solutions. What is at stake is the notion of facts and scientific evidence, and the role of expertise in the capacity and legitimacy to bring to bear viable improvements to social welfare. The book by Tom Nichols, *The Death of Expertise,*—and other influential contributions[1] along the same lines—explores the declining trust in science and rationality in today's society. "Not only do increasing numbers of laypeople lack basic knowledge,—Nichols writes—they reject fundamental rules of evidence and refuse to learn how to make a logical argument. In doing so, they risk throwing away centuries of accumulated knowledge and undermining the practices and habits that allow us to develop new knowledge" (Nichols, 2017: 3).

Has the age of Enlightenment come to the end?[2] Political economist William Davies argues that: "Contemporary notions of truth, scientific expertise, public administration, experimental evidence, and progress are all legacies of the seventeenth century [...] But this project—the author asserts—has run aground. The media is less trusted than ever; traditional politicians are ignored or doubted; institutions of all stripes are seen as uninterested in trying to achieve anything other than the preservation of their own privilege; populist demagogues have risen around the world. The results are widespread social strife and seemingly unresolvable conflicts about the nature of reality" (Davies, 2019).[3]

The current distrust in science is associated with post-truth and fake news that have pervaded public discourse throughout North America, Europe, and other non-Western countries. Oxford English Dictionary defines "post-truth politics" as "relating to or denoting circumstances in which objective facts are less influential in shaping public opinion than appeals to emotion and personal belief." This political dynamic centers on emotionally charged discourse and seeks the passions of the audience in an increasingly fractioned media landscape (Suiter, 2016). Since the media no longer filters reliable information, providing a balanced perspective, the current information system presents a significant challenge to citizens' political thinking (Chadwick, 2019). Politicians can communicate directly with the electorate. But, skepticism of the establishment is such that many believe

DOI: 10.4324/9781032719979-2

little the media says as lies and rumors spread almost instantaneously across networks and borders (Chadwick, 2019). And we know from the work of Nobel Prize–winning psychologists Daniel Kahneman and Amos Tversky that when faced with a truth that contradicts a bias we hold, we are likely to ditch the truth.[4] This is the "backfire effect," Nichols writes, "in which people redouble their efforts to keep their own internal narrative consistent, no matter how clear the indications that they are wrong" (Nichols, 2017: 43). As a result, extreme views are amplified online, just as fake news and propaganda easily go viral.

Post-truth thrives on polarization, exaggerated difference, and divisions among citizens, which have lately grown sharper regarding geography, formal education levels, and value systems (Suiter, 2016). Supporters of dynamism and diversity increasingly clash with proponents of stability and homogeneity, beneficiaries of technological change with those harmed by the resulting economic shifts (Gallston, 2018: 8). For instance, post-election analyses in the United States, United Kingdom, and the European Union showed that concerns about immigration largely drove the Brexit referendum, the 2016 US presidential election, and the gains of far-right parties across Europe (Gallston, 2018: 9). Failures to deal with waves of immigration in ways that commanded largely shared support within society were associated with perceptions of immigrants as not only competing for jobs and social services but also threatening established cultural norms and public safety. In these circumstances, factual claims come to be judged according to their emotional and ideological consistency and we cannot expect that lobbing more factual claims into the public domain necessarily challenge anyone's beliefs. The presentation of contrary evidence may reinforce people's view that experts will almost inevitably present different unreliable advice (Lockie, 2017; Chadwick, 2019).

What role can evaluation play in these political circumstances? Does evaluation provide constructive critique and informed judgment to improve public policies? Does it help bring to bear factual knowledge to counter misinformation and propaganda? Can evaluation confront ignorance and uncertainty, and open policymakers and citizens to learning to solve seemingly intractable problems? Do current political dynamics require new designs, analytical techniques, methodological choices, or communication tools to overcome skepticism and resistance? And finally, what normative stances and ethical standards can inform the evaluation practice to preserve pluralism and participation across different jurisdictions?

This chapter addresses these questions through the lenses of evaluators who have navigated the complexities of political and administrative arenas throughout a variety of institutional settings and organizational cultures. The analysis is a reflexive endeavor that intends to share the point of view of those "experts" who have always been in the trenches, engaged in the front lines to bring about organizational advancement and social betterment. It is also an attempt to understand the limits of the evaluation enterprise and the potential that can be exploited in current political and societal transformations.[5]

12   Mita Marra

The reader may wonder why they should be interested in evaluation and not in other, perhaps more compelling themes, such as democracy, state reform, accountability, or citizen participation. By reconstructing the phenomenology of evaluation in the present political climate I can face post-truth challenges through a public policy frame. This perspective encourages to ask unconventional questions about the implementation, the impact, and use of evidence in current policymaking and institution working. The public policy lens examines both the formal hierarchy and the informal relationships that characterize representative democracies in their current problematic manifestations. Drawing upon the experiences and knowledge of the actors in the field, the evaluators' account offers critical insights about the challenges these experts face, the roots of these challenges, and solutions across scales and contexts.

The role of evaluation in the current political situation is a thorny issue. Societal and economic mega-trends that underlie the post-truth world are deep-seated (Lewandowsky et al., 2017). The increasing availability of digital data on economic and human development does not explicitly underpin a public policy, and a social justice agenda by national and international authorities involved (Taylor, 2017). While long-established neoliberal pressures tend to minimize the role of deliberative institutions to harness globalized markets, growing populist pressures favor the over-simplification of social interests, reducing the public debate to mere propaganda. Reflecting on the worths and merits of political choices—so that they can be less partisan and more competent—has increasingly been contested and resisted. Populist appeal to "the people" and the denunciation of the "elite" involve a thorough critique of the establishment and liberal institutions. According to many commentators, populism is not merely an emotion-laden expression of disappointment over frustrated economic expectations, resentment against rigged rules and special interests, and fear of threats to physical and cultural security situations (Gallston, 2018: 10). Populism threatens to shrink democratic pluralism, as it supports illiberal tendencies that reduce the space for reasoned debate in public policy and political deliberation (Hugh, 2017).

Exploring the way evaluation can address these political challenges is what this chapter is all about. Of course, the stance is not that evaluation can rescue our societies from obscurantism and authoritarianism. With a more modest and constructive purpose, this chapter aims to highlight political, epistemological, and behavioral dimensions of evaluation that may help policymakers, citizens, and evaluators themselves cope with anti-science sentiments, illiberal tendencies, and post-truth phenomena related to the rising trend of "datafication." The analysis will unfold along three axes—a political, epistemological, and behavioral line of analysis—which do not unfold separately but overlap and intertwine systematically.

From a political-economy standpoint, evaluation can inform policymaking considering the evolutions of the broader political environment. This lens helps reconstruct the big picture where evaluators can identify the tangled roots of post-truth phenomena, provide illustrations from around the world, and examine their practical implications for the modern public sphere. In such circumstances, evaluative knowledge can generate powerful arguments, decisive evidence, and compelling reason through institutional processes that evaluation research can criticize and question (see on this Collier, 1992). In the relationship between institutional and expert authority (Collier, 1992), evaluation can work as a democratic governance mechanism promoting collective intelligence[6] (Mair et al., 2019), and co-produce knowledge relevant to policy problems and critical of (and for) policy solutions.

From an epistemological perspective, evaluation can provide concrete cases of evidence-informed policy assessments, which combine expert, practitioner, and users/citizen observations to feed reasoned planning and management of public programs. What evaluation presents is a creative mix between technical and tacit or situational knowledge that strengthens competence and expertise. Building upon Patton's (2005) notion of "situational responsiveness," evaluation experts make decisions about "evaluation design and use that include program variables (e.g., size, complexity, history), evaluation purposes (formative, summative), evaluator experience and credibility, intended users, politics, and resource constraints" (Patton, 2005: 390). The interplay of technical and tacit knowledge enables evaluators alongside other stakeholders involved in the political arena to recognize diversity, enhance pluralism, attenuate distrust, and counter the manipulation of information.

From a cognitive/behavioral perspective, evaluation can go deeper into the analysis of the heuristics that policymakers, citizens, and experts show in their exposure to evidence. Evaluative research can explore the ways effective actors frame questions to address ambiguity in the interpretation of the world and specific issues as policy problems (Cairney et al., 2016; Wellstead et al., 2018). Actors compete to draw attention to one "image" of a problem at the expense of all others and, if successful, they limit attention to a small number of feasible solutions (Majone, 1989; Baumgartner and Jones, 1993: 7; Kingdon, 1984). The competition to resolve ambiguity drives the demand for evaluation through an eminently political, not a scientific process—aimed to objectively research open-ended issues without reflecting on how we define them. Furthermore, the behavioral perspective helps reject the commonly-expressed idea that policymakers suffer from a "knowledge deficit" to be solved by more evaluation, in the pursuit of comprehensive rationality (Crow and Jones, 2018). In its place should be the image of policymakers seeking efficient ways to select that evidence that allows them to make choices decisively. Those evaluators' approaches, methods, techniques, instruments that can overcome cognitive shortcuts and help decision-makers apply evaluative knowledge, need to be acknowledged and valued. This is also a space to show what innovative solutions evaluators can take on board from other practices to tackle cognitive biases (psychology, design, public management, problem solving, etc.) (Barzelay, 2019; Marra, 2021).

The three perspectives highlighted can underpin more concrete approaches to face the challenges of the post-truth world: namely, (i) co-production of evaluation in the current political environment; (ii) the hybrid forms of evaluative

14   *Mita Marra*

knowledge that combines expert, user, practitioner, and citizen science; and (iii) behavioral heuristics of evaluation designs and use in policymaking and organizational management. Across the three axes, there is a need to assure high policy relevance, which does not map directly onto a narrow scientific view of quality (Topp et al., 2018) but relates more to the demand for evidence stemming from a competition to define policy problems. The rest of this chapter illustrates these three axes. Next section deals with co-production, while the two following sections respectively explore the epistemological and the behavioral dimensions associated with evaluation. The last section presents a few concluding remarks.

Co-producing evaluation against politically devoid rhetorics

"Resistance to intellectual authority" is not new in our history. At the end of the past century, Foucault's view of "the sciences of discipline and normalization, of surveillance and control of bodies and souls, of marginalization and exclusion of the deviant, the abnormal, the insane interrogated the limits and powers of '[…] reason as despotic enlightenment'" (Foucault, 1972 in Gordon, 1980: 54). Much earlier Alexis de Tocqueville theorized that the distrust in intellectual authority is ingrained in the nature of American democracy. When "[…] citizens, placed on an equal footing, are all closely seen by one another—he wrote—they were constantly brought back to their own reason as the most obvious and proximate source of truth. It is not only confidence in this or that man which is destroyed, but the disposition to trust the authority of any man whatsoever" (Tocqueville in Nichols, 2017: 17).

Max Weber emphasized that, contrary to any other form of power, authority is exercised legitimately not only from the point of view of those who exercise it and of society, but also from the point of view of those who are subject to it. Thus, the emphasis placed on the dimension of legitimation explains the "force of persuasion" of authority within a relationship that is not between "equal" (Collier, 1992: 151). Those who are subject to authority do not passively suffer it, while those who exercise it can have the right to do so because of some principle and belief, which are commonly recognized and valued.

Today, Gallston (2018) notes that the tacit compact between people, on the one hand, and elected representatives together with unelected experts, on the other, has waned. This compact had held as long as elites delivered sustained prosperity that steadily improved living standards for the people. But when elites stopped managing the economy effectively, the growing competition from developing nations put pressure on policies designed to protect the citizens of advanced democracies against labor-market risks. Further economic pressures added uncertainty to an already weakened manufacturing sector, while the urbanization of opportunity—the shift of economic dynamism away from smaller communities and rural areas toward a handful of metropolitan centers—destabilized geographic regions and political structures, rising significant inequality (Gallston, 2018: 5).

Co-creating evaluation for policy relevance 15

Populist politics was the answer to the growing perception that the globalized economy served the interests of most people in developing countries and elites in rich countries at the expense of the interests of the working and middle classes in the advanced economies (Lewandowsky et al., 2017; Mudde, 2017; Gallston, 2018: 5). In this respect, as Davies (2019: xvi) puts it:

> If people don't feel safe, it doesn't matter whether they are objectively safe or not; they will eventually start to take matters into their own hands. Telling people that they are secure is of limited value if they feel that they are in situations of danger. For this reason, we have to take people's feelings seriously as political issues, and not simply dismiss them as irrational.
>
> (Davies, 2019: xvi)

Both liberals and conservatives failed to respond to the feelings and claims of insecurity that populists rode on. As liberals refused to engage with populists, their approach ended up confirming the very narrative whereby the elites do not respect "ordinary people" (because they don't respect their representatives). Furthermore, the strategy of all non-populist parties uniting also validated populists' position that the ideological differences among "establishment" parties do not really matter since they all combine to protect gained privileges (Rose, 2018).[7]

A conservative approach to populism drew on the very populist rhetoric shifting from a position of total disrespect—whatever populists say we can discount as false—to a stance that accorded them credit in knowing what was truly happening at the core of our societies (Rose, 2018). Conservatives did share with populists the diagnosis of the problem, but not the solutions that continued to adhere to neoliberal economic policy. Such an "opportunistic" posture was, therefore, unable to win the votes and the consensus populists have gained in North America, Europe and Brazil, Russia, and India, just to name advanced and emerging economies.

Finally, a technocratic approach to populism rested on considering populists as the purveyors of irresponsible policies and misleading promises as opposed to the rational solutions technocrats could provide for every major policy challenge. Any dissent revealed as essentially irrational (and therefore undeserving of standing in policy debates), paving the way for populists to claim (not without good reasons) that democracy without choices is a contradiction in terms (Rose, 2018).

There is a paradox here. While citizens want to exercise greater power over their own lives—hence, any forms of institutional and intellectual authority is questioned (Collier, 1992)—none of the traditional political approaches have provided persuasive answers to the growing anxieties associated with future economic and social prospects. Since the size and complexity of government have enormously increased, it became more difficult for voters with limited knowledge to monitor, and evaluate the policies, and programs (Somin, 2015). By the same token, experts themselves could not always keep up with the uncertainty and the ambiguity of the policy process. If uncertainty hampers any accurate forecast of how critical phenomena will play out, ambiguity is a key characteristic of democratic systems. The latter can be defined as changing definitions of the policy problem, variation of the venues where the search for alternatives is carried out, and actors that come and go in the different venues—hence ambiguity implies instability of the network of actors (Radaelli, 2018).

In such circumstances, can evaluation help debunk populist discourse and adequately account for "feelings" and "claims" of insecurity? A possible political answer to this question resonates with Hirschman's (1991) conception of rhetoric as associated with discourse devoid of meaning—often employed to deceive listeners regarding an agent's true intentions (McCloskey, 1998). Against all political rhetorics, evaluation can become a weapon to avoid a "dialogue among deaf," breaking the wall of incommunicability between opposing political forces. Revealing the roots and background of reactionary, progressive, and technocratic discourse, arguments based on evaluative information can be brought to bear to raise the quality of democratic dialogue beyond slogans or skirmishes, tactically oriented to gain consensus (Hirschman, 1991). For public policy reform debates, we can then resort to evaluation to add to the knowledge of the means of persuasion, becoming "a delectably powerful tool for rhetors and the citizens who, in the end, are the ones who must make all judgements" (Finlayson, 2006: 556).

Some may argue that what it takes to use evaluation as an effective argument to counter other rhetorics is to better communicate findings and recommendations. Thus, more powerful channels can contribute to constructing and spreading persuasive arguments, drawing on facts and values. Yet, communication per se does not prevent different political forces at play from a manipulative use of evaluative information. Many studies have demonstrated that evaluation can degenerate into control-focused activity, misinformation, or mere bureaucratic compliance (MacDonald, 1976; Pollitt, 2013; Dalher-Larsen, 2014; Marra, 2017, 2019, 2021; Boswell, 2018). To forge factual knowledge and constructive criticism, only collaborative governance structures, and networks can foster and coordinate priority-setting and mainstream and experiment with innovative practices (Hölscher et al., 2019). In other terms, co-creating evaluation may encourage dialogue among multiple actors, providing diverse sources of information and perspectives (Miller and Wyborn, 2020).

Co-production is often described as more effective than simply seeking advice from experts (Frantzeskaki et al., 2016). Particularly when scientific uncertainty is high, there is no simple recourse to expert authority, and there is a predisposition to listen to what others have to say and to reconsider one's preferences (Dunlop and Radaelli, 2018: 260). In such cases, open dialogue, for people to use deliberative techniques to piece together their disparate knowledge and communicate the social norms crucial to cooperation, may curb high politicization and the elite capture of the political arena (Aeberhard and Rist, 2009).

Collaborative governance may attenuate emotionally charged dynamics. The very notion of collaborative governance suggests a significant change as policy-takers, no longer passive consumers of public services, participate in defining and generating what relevant policies and programs and related outcomes are and how programs should be organized, and assessed. Actors learn how to use each other's competencies and develop new ways to address public-sector challenges. User experience becomes a key standard against which policies are planned and evaluated (Zeitlin, 2016) and recipients hold tacit knowledge which is highly valuable to frame goals, needs and expected outcomes, including the perception of what measures work and what side effects are likely to emerge (see Hood et al., 2001). Knowledge co-production can also spur social dialogue and public debate, drawing on different sources of information, expertise, and citizens' science to attenuate science trust crisis and polarized politics, as explained in the next section.

Techné and mētis for democratic evaluation

In the book *Seeing Like a State* (1999), Scott recalls the classical distinction between *episteme* (certain, acquired and codified knowledge), *techné* (technical-methodological knowledge), and *mētis* (practical-experiential knowledge) to underline how among these forms of knowing, *techné* is the knowledge commonly used in institutional processes (see also Polanyi, 1966). To reduce risk and uncertainty, administrative and legislative activity requires to register, file, classify, list, order, reorder, and arrange. These are techniques designed to isolate and domesticate those aspects of politics that can be quantified and subjected to systematic and impersonal rules. Knowledge thus produced can be easily assembled, documented, and formally transferred —although these techniques alone cannot explain how that very knowledge was created, that is, whether it arose from deductive thinking or from practical inference (Scott, 1999).

Being *techné*, evaluation comprises multiple conceptual and methodological approaches, which are underpinned not only by disciplinary systems of knowledge (i.e., economics, sociology, psychology, political science, management, etc.) but also trans-disciplinary constructs (see Patton, 2018). In government institutions, evaluative information was associated with the economic performance of public investments based on cost-benefit and multi-criteria analysis. The tradition of program evaluation emerging out the North American strand of applied social sciences has, over time, contributed to generating a variety of policy-oriented research approaches, drawing on statistical and qualitative methods as well as experimental and theory-based designs (see on this Vedung, 1996; Weiss, 1998).

Although evaluation is not a unified field of studies and practices (Stockmann and Meyer, 2016), it is broadly understood as an applied research activity aimed to examine the outcomes of multi-objective, multi-site, and multi-actor interventions at various jurisdictions and in different time spans. In this respect, both experimental (and counter-factual) and non-experimental approaches have set

18 Mita Marra

out to reconstruct the theory of change underlying policy interventions and investigate non-linear causal links (Weiss, 1998). Over the past two decades, evaluation has also encompassed the assessment of organizational performance by measuring the work effort made by individuals and teams to improve the division of labor and the organization of production.

Yet, as Davies (2019) convincingly argues, for all its impressive data collection and sophisticated modeling and analysis, the facts produced by experts, including evaluators, do not necessarily capture lived reality for many people. Besides technical expertise (the Greek notion of *techné*), the need exists for a more inclusive type of knowledge relying on the Greek notion of *mētis*, that is user and citizen experience and the direct participation and collaboration of beneficiaries in defining, deciding, and assessing success, more within states (at the level of regions and municipalities) rather than among states. As Scott (1999: 315) writes:

> Mētis is most applicable to broadly similar but never precisely identical situations requiring a quick and practiced adaptation that becomes almost second nature to the practitioner. The skills of mētis may well involve rules of thumb, but such rules are largely acquired through practice (often in formal apprenticeship) and a developed feel or knack for strategy. Mētis resists simplification into deductive principles which can successfully be transmitted through book learning, because the environments in which it is exercised are so complex and non-repeatable that formal procedures of rational decision making are impossible to apply. In a sense, mētis lies in that large space between the realm of genius, to which no formula can apply, and the realm of codified knowledge, which can be learned by rote.
>
> (Scott, 1999: 315–316)

This kind of evaluative knowledge gets shared within organizations, where evaluators collaborate with managers and executive leaders on a daily basis. In such contexts, evaluation contributes to organizational learning and management and it is not reducible to an attempt to rationalize administrative work. Nor does it provide a technological solution, characterized by techniques, metrics, and standards or algorithms (Barry, 2006). Politics and administration rely on evaluative information to focus on problems and solutions, to formulate assumptions, or arguing positions. This is a cognitive and political process that requires in-depth analysis to understand its credibility and impact on organizational and public life. For instance, in dealing with drug addiction, psychological support and pharmacological methods require coordination among managers, social workers, and physicians. If performance is measured as saving time and money, medicalization may be preferred, but at what price? The choice is then between valuing more responsibility in using public resources or internal organizational learning practices.

Multiple and at times competing evaluation criteria underpin political goals and administrative routines, which generate real effects on users, citizens, and political leaders. As a system of technical and practical knowledge, firmly anchored to the context, evaluation can help unearth the change embedded within dense social, organizational, and institutional networks and interactions. Politicians, managers, and administrators draw on evaluation constructs and evidence in addition to the rest of available codified and tacit knowledge that can inform decision-making and management. Political decisions will, therefore, build on context-specific information, the consultation of key stakeholders, the experiential learning of previous successes and failures in planning and management. This "experimentalist governance"—in Sabel's and Zeitlin's (2012) words—relies on metrics and indicators but also on interpersonal modes of coordination, management, and evaluation. The practical form of knowledge that is involved within these processes is crucial to understand the unique and not replicable nature and dynamics of decision-making in the time and space where it takes place. As Scott (1999) argues, although we can always think about forestry, urban planning, agriculture, and rural settlements in broad terms, that kind of abstract knowledge will never allow us to understand how a specific forest, city, or farm will grow in reality (Scott, 1999: 289). In other terms, aggregate data and modeled social phenomena can never be able to solve the uncertainty and account for the heterogeneity of contexts, providing usable knowledge for policymaking (Lindblom and Cohen, 1979). Scott writes:

> The power of practical knowledge depends on an exceptionally close and astute observation of the environment. [...] Mētis, with the premium it places on practical knowledge, experience, and stochastic reasoning, is of course not merely the now-superseded precursor of scientific knowledge. It is the mode of reasoning most appropriate to complex material and social tasks where the uncertainties are so daunting that we must trust our (experienced) intuition and feel our way.
>
> (Scott, 1999: 324–327)

Indeed, the focus on the tacit and situational knowledge feeding into evaluation processes suggests at least three applications. First, situational, reflective, and interpersonal practice helps form effective evaluation skills (Kuji-Shikatani, 2015). Credentials for practitioners emphasize that the evaluator needs to recognize dynamics of power, multicultural diversity, and social conflicts, and reflect on their own practices to systematically question premises and results. As a political actor, the evaluator must be able to listen, negotiate, mediate, facilitate teamwork and respect the differences of all those partaking in the evaluation process. The capacity to master situational dimensions of evaluation practice has, therefore, clear ethical foundations.

Second, from a political point of view, the capacity to observe the specificities of any social environment is congenial with pluralism and inclusive participation. Only by recognizing the heterogeneity of contextual realities can diverse interests and

20 *Mita Marra*

policy dynamics be acknowledged and democratically addressed. As Dewey (1916) pointed out, democracy, here, is more than a form of government. It is an experience of collective intelligence where everyone reports his/her own action to that of the others to overcome barriers of class, race, and ethnicity that have prevented from grasping the full meaning of human activity (Dewey, 1916). Recognizing the importance of situational knowledge suggests promoting a democratic evaluation that nurtures experiential and pluralist approaches to debunk dogmas, fake news, and any other intransigent rhetoric. Finally, there is an economic advantage associated with tacit knowledge in innovation processes both within and between companies, universities, and other government institutions according to well-known triple or multiple helix models (Etzkowitz and Leydesdorff, 2000). In such configurations, all actors involved exchange ideas and practices and thus create value. In unique conditions, evaluative knowledge can enhance a situational awareness that no other form of artificial intelligence (even generative) can provide (Marra et al., 2022).

Behavioral heuristics in evaluation and the policy process

As previously mentioned, populist politics builds upon the assumption that policymakers pay insufficient respect to expertise or attention to good evidence. Evaluation theory and research, and the tradition of policy studies tell a less alarmist story. First, policymakers have always combined "rational" and "irrational" cognitive shortcuts to evidence. No person or organization can process extant information. Cognitive efficiency is necessary for policy choice. Thus, it would be a mistake to assess evidence quality narrowly with a hierarchy of evaluation methods, or exaggerate the extent to which evaluators adhere to this hierarchy. Second, policymakers identify problems and place certain demands on evaluation: to help solve problems, and maintain their image of governing competence, credibility, or political support. Policy relevance and availability are necessary gauges of quality, and an evidence-informed solution must be technically and politically workable. Third, too many commentators declare policymaking failure compared to an ideal-type, such as the policy cycle, in which (a) a core group of policymakers can make choices, and process them in a straightforward evidence-informed way, through a series of orderly stages, and (b) evaluators know how, and when to present evidence. Policymaking is, instead, better understood as a complex environment or system over which the "center" has limited control. Policymakers must delegate most responsibilities in favor of many other organizations and networks, and respond to socio-economic conditions and events out of their control. Thus, the "action" takes place in numerous parts of the system, there are multiple "rules of the game," and policy often seems to emerge locally without central direction. If we think of these dynamics as inevitable features of political systems—and not as dysfunctions to be solved—we can produce more pragmatic ways to encourage evidence-informed policymaking (Cairney, 2018: 2).

Co-creating evaluation for policy relevance   21

Policy studies seek to capture the effect of "bounded rationality," which describes the cognitive limitations of individual actors and the equivalent resource constraints of organizations. Classic postwar accounts—produced before the rise of psychology-informed behavioral economics—contrast bounded rationality with the ideal-type "comprehensive rationality" (Simon, 1976; Lindblom, 1959; Marra, 2021). The ideal-type describes the ability of (i) individual policymakers to separate their values from facts, and rank their preferences consistently, and of (ii) policymaking organizations to process policy in linear "stages" and analyze policy and the policymaking context comprehensively. Bounded rationality describes the limitations to each action, and the ways in which policymakers address them, such as by using cognitive shortcuts and organizational standard operating procedures.

Modern advances in scientific method and information technology appear to help solve these limitations, which most remain as follows:

- the ambiguity of problems—or the many ways in which we could interpret them—makes them difficult to define well enough to gather evidence comprehensively;
- the "radical uncertainty" of policy problems, and the large number of potential actions to solve them, makes them difficult to predict (Tuckett and Nicolic, 2017);
- the experts hold unconscious conflict between personal and professional interests (Sah, 2017);
- more evidence does not help us adjudicate between the unclear preferences of individual actors or the preferences contested by many actors;
- the policy process remains complex, and the language of policy cycles and stages does not epitomize its unpredictability;
- policy-relevant science is infused with value choices, from the decision to ask a specific research question on a problem to how evidence is used to evaluate the success of a policy solution;
- policymakers "learn" but acquiring new knowledge and skills is a political process with clear limits (Botterill and Hindmoor, 2012; Dunlop and Radaelli, 2018).

Cairney and Kwiatkowski (2017) describe cognitive shortcuts provocatively as: "rational," to use simple rules—including trust in expertise, or in the rules that experts use to define and synthesize good evidence—to identify good enough sources of information; and, "irrational," to use their beliefs, emotions, habits, and familiarity with issues to identify policy problems and solutions (see Kahneman, 2012; Lewis, 2013; Sloman and Fernbach, 2017; Dunlop and Radaelli, 2015). However, the latter can be described more positively as "computationally cheap" and "fast and frugal heuristics" (Gigerenzer, 2001).

Recently, there has been an explosion of academic and practitioner interest in the heuristics or "cognitive biases" that people use to limit their exposure to evidence. In policy studies, examples include:

22 *Mita Marra*

- The "framing effects," that is, the competition to draw attention to, and define, policy problems based on emotional and moral judgments.
- The "representativeness heuristic," whereby people overestimate the probability of events because of their vivid nature, and the "availability heuristic" (or "processing fluency"), when people relate the size, frequency, or probability of a problem to how easy it is to remember or imagine (Alter and Oppenheimer, 2009).
- The "Prospect theory" describes people valuing the losses they fear more than the equivalent gains they might receive. It helps explain why "advocacy coalitions" think that their competitors are more powerful than they are, contributing to their tendency to romanticize their cause and demonize their opponents (Sabatier et al., 1987).
- "Cognitive dissonance" describes the discomfort associated with holding conflicting beliefs, such as when fresh evidence challenges an extant belief (Festinger, 1957). Actors may address this discomfort by ignoring more recent evidence.
- Motivated reasoning shows that the more people reflect analytically about a certain issue, the more likely they are to engage in ideologically motivated reasoning (JRC, 2019: 12).
- Illusion of control in distinguishing between events determined by chance and skill (Langer, 1975). This hinders policymakers from understanding their limited impact on outcomes, such as when they make emotional connections between their action and perceived success and seek to boost their ego by repeating their success (Dunlop and Radaelli, 2015).
- The "need for coherence," identifying patterns and causal relationships, helps explain the power of narratives with a simple hero and moral (Jones et al., 2013).
- Policymakers use of exemplars of social groups to represent overall experience and describe why they reward and punish populations (Schneider et al., 2014).
- The "status quo bias," the "sunk costs fallacy," and "optimism bias" (unrealistic expectations about our plans working out well when we commit to them) help explain inertia and the "path dependance" of institutions.
- "Groupthink" and other aspects of organizational psychology place crucial limits on comprehensive searches for policy relevant information (Kam, 2005).

As previously pointed out, our general focus on cognitive shortcuts has two immediate applications. The framing of evaluation within current political realities makes us aware to the uncertainty and ambiguity that contribute to soliciting the demand for evaluation. Second, the behavioral perspective helps us discuss the high and low policy relevance of evaluation as well as to understand their audience, that is, their beliefs and evidence demands, to tailor engagement accordingly.

Conclusions

This chapter has meant to highlight the political economy of evaluation in times of science trust crisis. Schematically, current challenges have to do both with the demand and supply side of evaluation. From the supply side of evaluation, there is a need to dig out elements, practices, and dynamics that can make this form

Co-creating evaluation for policy relevance 23

of knowledge and expertise relevant to policy problems. From a demand side of evaluation, the need is to understand the broader and fast changing political environment that asks for evaluative information for a variety of reasons, and uses. The contention here is not only the manipulative uses of evaluation—that is a very well-known issue in the evaluation literature (Alkin and King, 2017; King and Alkin, 2018)—but a more generalized attitude of resistance and opposition to evidence based on scientific knowledge and empirical analysis. Polarized politics is likely associated with the unwillingness to use evaluation to assess previous government choices, politicized appointments, and limited recruitment and retention of high-quality civil servants. Polarized politics also leads to some governments seeking to weaken independent scientific authorities and to reduce the visibility of evidence critical to partisan leadership (Mair et al., 2019; see also Marra, 2021).

Science trust crisis signals a deeper skeptical turn against evaluation (Dahler-Larsen, 2019) that questions it in the first place. This is a democratic threat to the extent it may influence policy agendas, and specifically the issues that can dominate evaluation concerns, including the role assigned to evaluative information and evaluators in policy processes. However, this political environment can also endorse co-production and evaluation can then play a role in concrete collaborative governance experimentation.

This chapter highlighted three ways of thinking about evaluation in response to the current challenges. My analysis unfolded along a political-economy, an epistemological, and a behavioral perspective to understand constitutive features of evaluation that might act not only as an antidote against populism and post-truth tendencies but also rationalist determinism of evidence-based policymaking. The political-economy perspective asks evaluators to be aware of their public role in the institutional and administrative settings where they operate. Evaluators are not just methods experts, but actors that embrace values, including human rights and democracy.

The epistemological perspective helps evaluators better grasp what types of knowledge they generate and feed into the evaluative information. Evaluators need both technical and transversal skills to face and contrast skepticism, manipulations, and "alternative realities." As the digital transformation asks for new analytical techniques to navigate big data and social networks, so does experiential learning become crucial to operate within organizations and political arenas (Kolb, 1984). As previously noted, the situational dimensions of evaluation processes add to the credibility of the technical information that is offered to policymakers and citizens. Furthermore, the practical knowledge that is infused in evaluation findings and recommendations reveals the shared values that underlie any attempt to make sense of reality. This epistemological reflection can also provide the space for innovations in designs and methods as they emerge in policy practice, not yet discussed in the literature. For instance, co-production of services (evaluation is often used there as a part of the testing stage), and co-decision approaches (e.g., deliberative panels) may provide compelling narratives showing new ways of sharing knowledge to make policy choices.

24　*Mita Marra*

Finally, the behavioral perspective helps evaluators develop an understanding of the cognitive features of human-bounded rationality. As both users and producers of evaluation are subject to cognitive bias in decision-making, ethical and political implications arise. While experts may unconsciously hold conflicts between personal and professional interests, policymakers and all different stakeholders in the political arena may embark on "irrational" and emotionally charged policies that lack objective justification. Building upon behavioral sciences, evaluators have to come to terms with their tendency to conformism and complacency (Marra, 2021) and deal with the emotional reaction that challenging performance information may generate. Peer-review practices could strengthen methodological expertise, ethical standards, and communities of practices to enhance professionalization and leadership.

New pathways for knowledge co-production and collaborative governance ask for higher participation of stakeholders and the active promotion of different social groups' and users' experience alongside expert knowledge to frame goals, needs, expected outcomes, and potential positive and negative side effects. For this purpose, concrete ways to counter post-truths may include:

- Involving political leaders in defining epistemic/techno-scientific norms;
- Developing open debates to set goals for action;
- Encouraging and speed up innovation and bottom-up initiative;
- Mobilizing collaborations across sectors;
- Acknowledging virtuous change at micro-level;
- Disseminating success stories to build trust;
- Revising goals following upon small-scale evaluations;
- Being always alert of the macro trends; and, last but not least,
- Enforcing democratic accountability for results.

Notes

1 Al Gore's *The Assault on Reason*, Susan Jacoby's *The Age of American Unreason*, Robert Hughes's *Culture of Complaint,* and the 1963 classic *Anti-Intellectualism in American Life* by Richard Hofstadter (1963); see Michiko Kakutni (2017) "The Death of Expertise Explores How Ignorance Became a Virtue" in *New York Times*.
2 To understand this dynamic a 2019 report of the European Commission's Joint Research Council—drawing on the project "Enlightenment 2.0"—has identified the key drivers of political behavior and the strategies that allow political decisions to be informed by evidence and how can they be implemented ethically.
3 Despite the growing and gloomy outlook of current situation, there is also a collection of pundits, academics, and think tank operatives who endorse an optimist account. They have been labelled "the New Optimists," a name intended to evoke the rebellious skepticism of the New Atheists led by Richard Dawkins, Daniel Dennett, and Sam Harris. Psychologist Steven Pinker (2012) would argue this claim is just wrong— health, prosperity, peace, knowledge, and happiness are all on the rise today. In his book *Enlightenment Now* (2018), he argues, the Enlightenment is still gradually spreading the problem-solving mentality that finds its fullest expression in science. Also the Swedish historian Johan Norberg has recently published the book entitled *Progress:*

Ten Reasons to Look Forward to the Future (2016) where he traces the progress made over the past two hundred years considering the ten most important indicators of quality of life, such as food, sanitation, life expectancy, poverty, violence, the state of the environment, literacy, freedom, equality, and conditions of childhood. Just to give an example, in 1882, only 2% of New York's houses had running water; in 1900, life expectancy worldwide was 31 years, due to the extremely high infant mortality rate.

4 Cognitive dissonance describes the discomfort associated with holding conflicting beliefs, such as when new evidence challenges an existing belief (Festinger, 1957). Actors may address this discomfort by ignoring new evidence.

5 See on this Furubo and Stame (2019).

6 The theory of argumentative reasoning explains that the function of reasoning and people's ability to argue convincingly are a social competence that benefit the community. See Mercier, H., Sperber, D. (2011), "Why do humans reason? Arguments for an argumentative theory" *Behavioral and Brain Sciences*, 34(2): 57–74. See also Sloman and Fernbach (2018).

7 For instance, it seemed clear confirmation of all the accusations put forward by Beppe Grillo against "la casta" of professional (and corrupt) politicians, when, in the end, Matteo Renzi and Silvio Berlusconi could work together on a set of proposed changes to the Italian political system (see Gallston, 2018).

References

Aeberhard, A. and Rist, S. (2009) Transdisciplinary co-production of knowledge in the development of organic agriculture in Switzerland, *Ecological Economics*, 68, 1171–1181.

Alkin, M. C. and King, J. A. (2017) Definitions and factors associated with evaluation use and misuse, *American Journal of Evaluation*, 38(3): 434–450.

Alter, A. and Oppenheimer, D. (2009) Uniting the tribes of fluency to form a metacognitive nation, *Personality and Social Psychology Review*, 13(3): 219–235.

Barry, A. (2006) Technological zones, *European Journal of Social Theory*, 9(2): 239–253.

Barzelay, M. (2019) *Public Management as a Design-Oriented Professional Discipline*, Cheltenham, UK: Edward Elgar Publishing.

Baumgartner, F. (2017) Endogenous disjoint change, *Cognitive Systems Research*, 44: 69–73.

Baumgartner, F. and Jones, B. (1993; 2009) *Agendas and Instability in American Politics* (1st and 2nd eds.), Chicago, IL: Chicago University Press.

Boswell, C. (2018) *Manufacturing Political Trust: Targets and Performance Measurement in Public Policy*, Cambridge University Press.

Botterill, L. C. and Hindmoor, A. (2012) Turtles all the way down: Bounded rationality in an evidence-based age, *Policy Studies*, 33(5): 367–379.

Cairney, P. (2016) *The Politics of Evidence-based Policymaking*, London: Palgrave Pivot. http://dx.doi.org/10.1016/j.cogsys.2017.04.001.

Cairney, P. and Kwiatkowski, R. (2017) How to communicate effectively with policymakers: Combine insights from psychology and policy studies, *Palgrave Communications*, 3: 37. https://www.nature.com/articles/s41599-017-0046-8

Chadwick, A. (2019) *The New Crisis of Public Communication: Challenges and Opportunities for Future Research on Digital Media and Politics. O3C 2*, Online Civic Culture Centre, London: Loughborough University.

Collier, C. W. (1992) Intellectual authority and institutional authority, *Journal of Legal Education*, 42(2): 151–185.

Crow, D. and Jones, M. (2018) Narratives as tools for influencing policy change, *Policy & Politics*, 46(2): 217–234.

26 Mita Marra

Dahler-Larsen, P. (2014) The constitutive effects of performance indicators: Getting beyond unintended consequences, *Journal of Public Management Review*, 16(7): 969–986.

Dahler-Larsen, P. (2019) The skeptical turn in evaluation, in E.-J. Furubo and N. Stame (eds.), *The Evaluation Enterprise*, London and New York: Francis and Taylor.

Davies, W. (2019) *Nervous States: Democracy and the Decline of Reason*, New York: W. W. Norton & Company.

Dewey, J. (1916) *Democracy and Education: An Introduction to the Philosophy of Education*, New York: Macmillan.

Dunlop, C. A. and Radaelli, C. (2015) Overcoming illusions of control: How to nudge and teach regulatory humility, in A. Alemanno and A.-L. Sibony (eds.), *Nudge and the Law: A European Perspective*, Oxford: Hart Publishing.

Dunlop, C. A. and Radaelli, C. (2018) The lessons of policy learning: Types, triggers, hindrances and pathologies, *Policy & Politics*, 46(2): 255–272.

Etzkowitz, H. and Leydesdorff, L. (2000) The dynamics of innovation: From national systems and "mode 2" to a triple helix of university-industry-government relations, *Research Policy*, 29(2): 109–123.

Festinger, L. (1957) *A Theory of Cognitive Dissonance*, Evanston, IL: Row & Peterson.

Finlayson, M. (2006) Assessing the Need for Services. In: Kielhofner, G., Ed., *Research in Occupational Therapy— Methods of Inquiry for Enhancing Practice*, F.A Davis, Philadelphia, 591–606.

Frantzeskaki, N., Kabisch, N. and McPhearson, T. (eds.). (2016) Advancing urban environmental governance: Understanding theories, practices and processes shaping urban sustainability and resilience. *Environmental Science & Policy*, 62: 1–144.

Furubo, J.-E. and Stame, N. (eds.). (2019) *The Evaluation Enterprise. A Critical View*, New York and London: Routledge.

Gallston, W. A. (2018) The populist challenge to liberal democracy, *Journal of Democracy*, 29(2): 5–19.

Gigerenzer, G. (2001) The adaptive toolbox, in G. Gigerenzer and R. Selton (eds.), *Bounded Rationality: The Adaptive Toolbox*, Cambridge, MA: MIT Press.

Gordon, C. (Ed.). (1980) *Michel Foucault. Power/Knowledge: Selected Interviews and Other Writings, 1972–79*, New York: Pantheon Books.

Hirschman, A. (1991) *The Rhetoric of Reaction: Perversity, Futility, Jeopardy*, Cambridge: Belknap Press of Harvard University Press.

Hofstadter, R. (1963) *Anti-Intellectualism in American Life*. New York: Vintage Books.

Hölscher, K., Frantzeskaki, N. and Loorbach, D. Steering transformations under climate change: Capacities for transformative climate governance and the case of Rotterdam, the Netherlands, *Regional Environmental Change*, 19: 791–805.

Hood, C., Rothstein, H. and Baldwin, R. (2001) *The Government of Risk Understanding Risk Regulation Regimes*, Oxford: Oxford University Press.

Hugh, G. (2017) From Brexit to Trump: Anthropology and the rise of nationalist populism, *American Ethnologist*, 44(2): 209–214.

Jones, R., Pykett, S. and Whitehead, M. (2013) Psychological governance and behavior change, *Policy & Politics*, 41(2): 159–182.

Kahneman, D. (2012) *Thinking Fast and Slow*, London: Penguin.

Kam, C. D. (2005) Who toes the party line? Cues, values, and individual differences, *Political Behavior*, 27(2): 163–182.

King, J. A. and Alkin, M. C. (2018) The centrality of use: Theories of evaluation use and influence and thoughts on the first 50 years of use research, *American Journal of Evaluation*, 40(3): 431–458.

Kingdon, J. (1984; 1995) *Agendas, Alternatives and Public Policies* (1st and 2nd eds.), New York, NY: Harper Collins.

Kolb, D. A. (1984) *Experience as the Source of Learning and Development*, Englewood Cliffs, N.J.: Prentice-Hall.

Kuji-Shikatani, K. (2015) Credentialed evaluator designation program, the Canadian experience, in J. W. Altschuld e M. Engle (a cura di), *Accreditation, Certification, and Credentialing: Relevant Concerns for U.S. Evaluators, in "New Directions for Evaluation"* (Vol. 145, pp. 71–85). Hoboken: Wiley Online.

Langer, E. J. (1975) The illusion of control. *Journal of Personality and Social Psychology*, 32(2): 311–328.

Lewandowsky, S., Eckerb, U. K. H. and Cook, J. (2017) Beyond misinformation: Understanding and coping with the "post-truth" Era, *Journal of Applied Research in Memory and Cognition*, 6(4): 353–369.

Lindblom, C. E. (1959) The science of "muddling through", *Public Administration Review*, 19(2): 79–88.

Lindblom, C. E. and Cohen, D. K. (1979) *Usable Knowledge: Social Science and Social Problem Solving*, New Haven: Yale University Press.

Lockie, S. (2017) Post-truth politics and the social sciences, *Environmental Sociology*, 3(1): 1–5.

MacDonald, B. (1976) Evaluation and the control of education, In Tanwey, D.A. (ed.) *Curriculum Evaluation Today: Trends and Implications*, London: MacMillan.

Mair, D., Smillie, L., La Placa, G., Schwendinger, F., Raykovska, M., Pasztor, Z. and Van Bavel, R. (2019) *Understanding Our Political Nature: How to Put Knowledge and Reason at the Heart of Political Decision-Making*, Publications Office of the European Union. https://op.europa.eu/en/publication-detail/-/publication/6574c875-a90a-11e9-9d01-01aa75ed71a1/language-en

Majone, G. (1989) *Evidence, Argument and Persuasion in the Policy Process*, New Haven, CT: Yale University Press.

Marra, M. (2007) How does evaluation foster accountability for performance? Tracing accountability lines and evaluation impact within the World Bank and the Italian local health-care providers, in M. L. Bemelmans-Videc, J. Lonsdale, and B. Perrin (eds.), *Making Accountability Work: Dilemmas for Evaluation and Audits* (pp. 193–216). New Brunswick: Transaction Publishers.

Marra, M. (2018) The ambiguities of performance-based governance reforms in Italy: Reviving the fortunes of evaluation and performance measurement, *Evaluation and Program Planning*, 69: 173–182.

Marra, M. (2019) Italian evaluation policy. Centralization and judicially-enforced accountability, in J. E. Furubo and N. Stame (eds.), *The Evaluation Enterprise. A Critical View* (pp. 147–165). New York: Routledge.

Marra, M. (2021) A behavioral design to reform Italy's evaluation policy, *American Journal of Evaluation*, 42(4): 483–504.

Marra, M., Alfano, V. and Celentano, R. M. (2022) Assessing university-business collaborations for moderate innovators: Implications for university-led innovation policy evaluation, *Evaluation and Program Planning*, 95. http://doi.org/10.1016/j.evalprogplan.2022.102170.

McCloskey, D. N. (1998) Bourgeois virtue and the history of P and S., *The Journal of Economic History*, 58(2): 297–317.

Miller, C. A. and Wyborn, C. (2020) Co-production in global sustainability: Histories and theories, *Environmental Science & Policy*, 113: 88–95.

28 Mita Marra

Mudde, C. (2017) *Populism: A Very Short Introduction*, Oxford: Oxford University Press.

Nichols, T. (2017) *The Death of the Expertise. The Campaign Against Established Knowledge and Why It Matters*, Oxford: Oxford University Press.

Norberg, J. (2016) *Progress: Ten Reasons to Look Forward to the Future*, London: Oneworld Publications.

Patton, M. Q. (2005) *Qualitative Research*, Thousand Oaks, CA: Sage.

Patton, M. Q. (2018) Evaluation science. *American Journal of Evaluation*, 39(2): 183–200.

Pinker, S. (2012) *The Better Angels of Our Nature: Why Violence Has Declined*, New York: Penguin Books.

Polanyi, A. (1966) *The Tacit Dimension*, Chicago: University of Chicago Press.

Pollitt, C. (2013) The logics of performance management, *Evaluation*, 19(4): 346–363.

Rose, D. C. (2018) Avoiding a post-truth world: Embracing post-normal conservation, *Conservation and Society*, 16(4): 518–524.

Sabatier, P., Hunter, S. and McLaughlin, S. (1987) The devil shift: Perceptions and misperceptions of opponents, *The Western Political Quarterly*, 40(3): 449–476.

Sah, S. (2017) Policy solutions to conflicts of interest: The value of professional norms, *Behavioral Public Policy*, 1(2): 177–189.

Scott, J. (1999) *Seeing Like a State: How Certain Schemes to Improve the Human Condition Have Failed (The Institution for Social and Policy St)*, New Haven: Yale University Press.

Schneider, A., Ingram, H. and deLeon, P. (2014) Democratic policy design: Social construction of target populations, in P. Sabatier and C. Weible (eds.), *Theories of the Policy Process* (3rd ed.), Boulder, Colorado: Westview Press.

Simon, H. (1976) *Administrative Behavior*, London: Macmillan.

Sloman, S. A. and Fernbach, P. (2017) *The Knowledge Illusion: Why We Never Think Alone*, New York: Riverhead Press.

Sloman, S. A. and Fernbach, P. (2018) *The Knowledge Illusion: Why We Never Think Alone*, London: Penguin.

Somin, I. (2015) *Democracy and Political Ignorance: Why Smaller Government Is Smarter*, Stanford, CA: Stanford University Press.

Stockmann, R. and Meyer, W. (eds.). (2016) *The Future of Evaluation Global Trends New Challenges, Shared Perspectives*, London: Palgrave.

Suiter, J. (2016) Post-truth politics, *Political Insight*, 7(3): 25–27.

Taylor, L. (2017) What is data justice? The case for connecting digital rights and freedoms globally, *Big Data & Society*, 1–14.

Topp, L., Mair, D., Smillie, L. and Cairney, P. (2018) Knowledge management for policy impact: The case of the European commission's joint research Centre, *Palgrave Communications*, 4: 87. https://doi.org/10.1057/s41599-018-0143-3.

Tuckett, D. and Nicolic, M. (2017) The role of conviction and narrative in decision-making under radical uncertainty, *Theory and Psychology*, 27(4): 501–523.

Vedung, E. (1997) *Public Policy and Program Evaluation*, New Brunswick: Transaction.

Wellstead, A., Biesbroek, R., Cairney, P., Davidson, D., Dupuis, J., Howlett, M., Rayner, J. and Stedman, R. (2018) Comment on "Barriers to enhanced and integrated climate change adaptation and mitigation in Canadian forest management", *Canadian Journal of Forest Research*, 48(10): 1241–1245.

Weiss, C. (1998) *Evaluation: Methods for studying programs and policies* (2nd ed.), Englewood Cliffs, NJ: Prentice Hall.

Zeitlin, J. (2016) EU experimentalist governance in times of crisis, *West European Politics*, 39(5): 1073–1094.

2 Free trade, populism, and post-truth

An evaluation perspective

R. Pablo Guerrero O.

About post-truth and populism

This has become a popular catchall expression that journalists and ideologues of all stripes have used to denigrate opposing views. Post-truth, chosen as word of the year in 2018 by the Oxford Dictionary, has become a synonym with obfuscation of facts real or imagined (McIntyre 2018). The label has become both a key wedge in coming to terms with policy disagreements and a barrier to reaching political consensus. The clamor has exacerbated divisiveness among socio-economic groups, and political candidates have used it sometimes to their own detriment. It is the elites in academic and news circles that gave US Presidential Candidate Clinton fodder to label opponents a basket of deplorable and afterward, when the dust settled, it was these same elites that launched a campaign to label all they disagreed with as based on alternative facts and therefore fake. It was a sad but educational episode in the evolution of politics and is much alive in 2021.

So what is post-truth? To find a cogent answer one must look a bit deeper into what truth is. Moran (2020) states that the concept of truth both pragmatically and philosophically follows conflicting theories. She says that "truth can be both concrete and abstract, linguistic and non-linguistic, directly perceived or indirectly validated though in many instances it can be non-verifiable." This is a tall order even for celebrated philosophers who spent their lives studying the matter. For example, the Cambridge philosophers in the late 1800 and early 1900 debated this question. Among them, Moore, Russell, Wittgenstein, and Ramsey had a serious debate about this notion of what is truth and they could not agree (Misak 2020). Simplifying the problem, they could not sort out whether truth must be fact based and validated independently, or that truth depends not on fact but on perceptions of what facts are, that is, truth lies in the eye of the beholder. Ramsey stated that "truth is not a relation between a proposition and a fact, but is primarily an attribute of thoughts and opinions" (Misak 2020). Ramsey (1926) concluded that truth is a property of our fallible human judgments and beliefs, such as the proposition that "free trade is preferable to protection." This discourse on truth should give pause to anyone who bandies about the concept of truth and post-truth.

So, in the earlier example, to admonish people who experience life differently as living in post-truth reality and to point fingers at them as exhibiting aberrant behaviors, seems to miss the mark and be wholly counterproductive. The tenet

DOI: 10.4324/9781032719979-3

30   *R. Pablo Guerrero O.*

of this discussion is to try to elucidate why what has been pejoratively labeled populism may indeed have a substantial base in reality and that so-called populists at the very least perceive reality as they see it and how it affects them and this has real political consequences.

About free trade

What are the realities of free trade? What does the theory tell us and what does the practice show? These are basic issues I address. Cohen et al. (1996) have laid out in detail the complexities and issues of trade and it is beyond the scope of this essay to lay them all out. Free trade, in simple form, is about the removal of tariff and not-tariff barriers to the exchange of commerce across nations (Heller 1973). The removal of such tariffs would over time lead to a specialization of production in the countries which have a comparative advantage in producing traded goods given their resource endowments, that is, the availability of the essential factors of production—capital, labor, and technology. In theory the flow of factors of production would be in the direction of where their productive use is better than the alternative. Over time, productivity would be reflected in the prices of goods and services being traded. In such a scenario, consumers in trading countries would be better off by paying lower prices than before and thereby deriving welfare gains from the trade. This is what the theory promises: increases in welfare gains by engaging in free trade. In reality nations do not allow for the free movement of factors of production across borders, or they allow it under constraints. Each of these constraints introduces a degree of inefficiency in the trading process that limits the welfare gains from trade. Free-Trade Agreements codify the conditions under which free trade will occur. There are familiar Agreements such as the North American Free Trade Agreement (NAFTA) and the European Union Agreements from which the controversial British Exit (BREXIT) is the most recent example. These Agreements contain a maze of regulations that eventually weigh heavy on the welfare gains they produce, and, more to the point in this essay, how these welfare gains are distributed among the socio-economic groups affected by the Agreements. The Agreements themselves are political in nature, and although there are economic reasons for their provisions, social reasons are seldom spelled out. Trade theory says that if Free Trade produces welfare gains at the national level by the process described above, then that is a sufficient test of whether it is justified. Welfare theory suggests that it is not enough to produce national-level welfare gains, and that those socio-economic groups who lose due to Free trade should be compensated so that they are not worse off than without free trade. Heller (1973) has addressed the changes in economic welfare that are experienced by a socio-economic group within a trading country. A country that has a comparative disadvantage in the production of a commodity will suffer when the country engages in free trade as it will have to reduce the production of that commodity. If there is a factor of production that is specialized in the production of that commodity, it will be impossible for this factor, say labor, to find employment in that industry and this will lead to a reduction in welfare gains accruing to it. Heller shows that the opposition of individual socio-economic groups to changes in trade policy may very well be justified, even if the country as a whole is better off. As we discussed, the gains realized by one socio-economic group consist of the gains that accrue to the country as a whole and are reaped by gainers; the losses are experienced by another socio-economic group, e.g., displaced labor. If the gainers can compensate the losses suffered, they must still reap additional gains for the trade to produce net welfare gains. The conclusion is that all persons can be made better off with trade if appropriate compensations are arranged for (Heller 1973). Since no one has been able to define a social welfare function that identifies society's social preferences, it is impossible to determine the optimal combination to be consumed by each member of a socio-economic group or the optimal combination of commodities to be produced, or the optimal amount of trade.

In reality such compensatory mechanisms fall short or fail. In a political environment, it is often impossible to directly compensate those who lose. Elected Governments create subsidy programs, but the resources tend to flow in a myriad of ways, often creating overlapping and inefficient public programs to favor those who support such governments. More commonly Governments find it easier to reintroduce protections for the affected groups via tariffs. The USA is case in point where amendments to NAFTA were made to clawback concessions, for example, to auto manufacturers by requiring limits on the import content that each vehicle produced abroad and sold in the USA should have. Significant distortions occur in such an environment, and the gains from trade are no longer so evident. But the losses are evident and they accrue to different socio-economic groups.

These agreements have led to the movements of manufacturing across borders leaving behind an unhappy lot of unemployed and displaced workers who have seen their incomes dwindle and their futures take an uncertain and bleak path. In some industries these effects are more pronounced, for example, in the rust belt. Or in border areas where migrants come in to challenge for the jobs at reduced costs. Past statistics on displacement effects show very large job losses. The real effects of trade is that it both creates and destroys jobs (Scott 2003). These trends have continued. Increases in US exports tend to increase jobs, but increases in imports tend to destroy them as they displace domestic production. Politicians in the past have tended to highlight the effects of exports while usually ignoring imports, although the last Republican administration took a strong stand by imposing tariffs on "strategic" imports. These tariffs were designed to restart domestic production in certain sectors and most surely have led to increases in prices of the goods affected. But the incidence of this loss of value has not affected all consumers equally. Those who lost jobs did not gain as the gains accrued to a different socio-economic group. For example, NAFTA created specific clauses that provide for compensation for lost investments and loss of future profits aiding the investor class.

32 *R. Pablo Guerrero O.*

A justification for NAFTA was that it would promote greater consumption in the trading partner, e.g., Mexico. It would lead to an expansion of the middle class in that country and an increase in imports of consumer goods from the US. But the reality is that most US exports to Mexico consist of parts and components shipped across the border for assembly into final products and re-export to the US overwhelmingly surpassing the value of US exports (Scott 2003). The increasing and seemingly uncontrollable deficits in the US balance of trade provide evidence. According to Scott, all states experienced a net job loss during NAFTA; and more jobs have been lost due to growing imports than gained by increasing exports.

Paul (2015) provides a concise summation and states "Free trade is not free. The gains from trade are marginal, and the sunk costs of creative destruction can outweigh the near-term gains. Although the global economy has generated millions of new jobs in developing economies, these countries do not have the regulatory infrastructure to maintain labor, safety, and environmental standards. Workers are exploited, and production methods are not sustainable. Regulatory competition among developing countries prevents them from raising standards, which leads to the problem of social dumping."

Rodrik 2018 concludes that economists as policy-makers can be counted on to parrot the wonders of comparative advantage and free trade whenever Free-trade agreements come up. And, they have consistently minimized distributional concerns even though it is clear that the distributional impact of, e.g., NAFTA was significant for the most directly affected socio-economic groups and communities. Rodrik further concludes that this reluctance to be honest about trade has not only cost economists their credibility with the public but it has fed the narrative of free-trade opponents.

For example, in BREXIT a large part of the discontent could be traced to unchecked migration, allowed under the EU Free Trade agreements, from Eastern Europe into the UK, flooding the market with cheaper labor and displacing opportunities for citizens.

So this creates a fertile environment for rising discontent. And this engenders what is now condescendingly labelled populism. Astute politicians and political opportunists recognize that this is a force that cannot be ignored. And this has had political consequences. Populists are electing governments and are trying to redress what they perceive as an injustice. Having sat on the sidelines and not participated in the political process they come out of the woodwork to support politicians who promise to do their bidding.

About welfare gains

The theory says that for public policies, such as free-trade, to be justified on economic welfare grounds, these must be "Pareto optimal," that is, no one must be worse off because of the policy (see E.J Mishan 1973). Furthermore,

Free trade, populism, and post-truth 33

if there are losers the policy must produce gains sufficient to compensate for the losses. In effect, the nation's gains accrue to certain socio-economic groups and the nation's losers must wait for the host governments to tap the gains, usually through taxation, to distribute via transfers to them, or a subsidy mechanism, to redress the losses incurred. This rarely happens. The gains get captured and losses get internalized by those who bear them. And, this is not all, in addition these are usually quantifiable economic losses and not the difficult-to-quantify social costs, including job displacement and the loss of economic opportunities. The counterargument is that free-trade gains materialize from the migration of factors of production to more effective uses. But where such migration, say of labor, would be called for, in most cases this doesn't happen. Nations engaged in free trade retain constraints to the free movement of the factors across borders. In the NAFTA case, capital flows from the USA to Mexico where labor wages are comparatively low, that is, the opportunity cost of labor is low because labor is abundant and of low productivity. In the BREXIT case, the situation is similar as labor flows into the UK where wages are higher and employment can be obtained by displacing local labor. But in both cases there is labor displacement. The country that shifts employment to less costly locations leaves a vacuum for those who lose their jobs. And in many cases, depending on the age structure of the unemployed, older workers cannot simply find new opportunities, or be re-trained, and they become discontented with the policies that led them there and with the governments that enacted them. Sometimes labor moves across borders surreptitiously and presents an additional challenge to the existing legal order. As mentioned earlier, the political orientation of those who enact the policies becomes intertwined with the interests of those who gain and lose.

Timiraos (1999) discusses the Trade Adjustment Assistance (TAA) program that failed to be approved by Congress. This program proposed to compensate those who lost their jobs because of production shifts overseas or due to import competition. The program was to provide relocation assistance, subsided health care insurance, and extended unemployment benefits, but the displaced workers had to enroll in job retraining to receive the unemployment benefits. The problem was, the older displaced workers who could not or would not be retrained. Another more significant problem was that the funding for this TAA had to come from cuts in Medicare and imposition of customs duties. One could venture to generalize and say that conservative politicians tend to place a bigger weight on gains accruing to the nation as a whole, and to keep the costs in check, while liberal politicians facing pressure from labor unions, and those not supporting trade agreements, would tend to weigh more heavily the gains of those socio-economic groups who lose. Again this seldom is the case as the alignment of the elites doesn't follow a straight logic. Personal factors such as the capture of political power create strange bedfellows. Eventually the TAA failed to be approved by the US Congress.

34   R. Pablo Guerrero O.

Tramontano (2016) summarizes as follows "The current heated debate over international trade is the outcome of a flawed public policy and political framework. All participants in the debate are responsible for the flawed framework. The pro-trade advocates want only to focus on the gains and ignore the losses, while the anti-trade advocates want only to showcase the losses, deny any gains, and refuse to accept any remediation or compensation for the losses."

What can evaluation contribute?

Can evaluation elucidate on a case-by-case basis who gains and who loses from a public policy such as free trade? In our case, can evaluation help answer the Pareto question? The answer is likely yes. By relying on the principles of straightforward social cost-benefit analysis, and not necessarily just focusing just on quantifiable flows, it can help answer the primary conceptual question—whether a public policy generates more benefits than costs for the nation. Do the investments and public expenditures generated by a free-trade agreement generate greater economic returns to outweigh the outflow?

If this doesn't happen, and this would have to be taken sector by sector, then the secondary question of whether the losers with the policy can be compensated to ensure that they are not worse off becomes essential. This would help demystify the underlying rationale for populism—a catchall expression capturing the perceptions of the disaffected. A comprehensive evaluation completed in 2002 found that those who received TAA benefits had lower earnings than those who were able to get regular unemployment benefits (Social Policy Research Associates 2002). This study also showed that retraining programs boosted the earnings of younger workers but not older workers.

Evaluation cannot be done easily or conceptually at the national level. Studies of Free Trade impact focus on specific industries, not on aggregate socio-economic activity. The complexity is enormous, as Burns and Epstein (1972) show in their study of two industries. Evaluation of public policy is very different and more demanding than evaluation of public investments. But in principle the questions are similar, that is, what are the costs of implementing the policy, and what are the benefits. In the case of free trade, one must study the incidence of costs and benefits for the different socio-economic groups. According to Sen (2002), this is the most challenging and missing component of cost-benefit analysis. If one examines the welfare gains or surplus, one gets closer to knowing which group is benefiting. For example, consumers who derive benefits from lower prices for the goods they consume—the consumer surplus. On the cost side, one needs to examine who bears the costs of free trade when, say the auto industry, shuts down production in the country resulting in often structural unemployment conditions, that is, when labor is displaced and cannot find alternative employment.

An evaluation approach such as this is needed to identify the flows of costs and benefits and determine who bears them or enjoys them. Returning to the earlier argument about compensation, an evaluation framework would be able to determine whether the gains exceed the costs of the policy, and how the gains are distributed between investors and consumers. Returns to capital, labor, and technology are elucidated. Policy sponsor governments use fiscal tools to tax the returns and to channel compensation to those who bear the costs. But as mentioned earlier the direction of compensation follows different paths more closely aligned with political support than with burden incidence. It has been shown that in the USA there is a myriad of programs to subsidize the losers. Many of these programs are too small to compensate or too disparate to provide a cogent recompense. They are a nightmare to administer and many become entitlements without reason, creating more disincentives than incentives to engage in economic activity. The examples are too numerous to explore, but most well-known are farm subsidies, or food stamps, and many others. Some may get untied cash transfers for a while. An evaluation approach of free-trade includes a breakdown of the winners and losers (Pettinger 2018). On the winning side are the exporters with competitive advantage, workers who gain jobs in export industries, consumers who benefit from cheaper import prices, domestic firms who experience increases in income due to higher consumer demand due to cheaper imports, and a net economic welfare gain for society as a whole. On the losing side are domestic firms who are uncompetitive due to cheaper imports, workers who lose jobs in uncompetitive industries, and regions that host these losers. A useful evaluation approach would quantify these gains and losses and determine whether net gains are sufficient to compensate for the losses. A derivative issue is whether the losers are actually compensated or not, and where the burden of compensation falls, e.g., on general or specific taxes. Pettinger suggests that a big issue is that the losers will express their opposition to free trade internalizing the potential cost.

Summing up

Free-trade policies and agreements are controversial for the reasons discussed. To avert the negative consequences policymakers must thoroughly evaluate the incidence of costs and benefits of free trade at the micro level, and identify the gainers and losers. Furthermore, such an evaluation must demonstrate not only that the overall benefits of the policy exceed the costs in aggregate, but that those who lose get compensated. If the age structure of the losers is such that being displaced by the direct effects of free trade leaves them without recourse to employment, then the compensation mechanism must necessarily be long-term, like permanent unemployment insurance, until pensions kick in to fill the gap.

We have also discussed that this plight of the displaced leads to justified dissatisfaction and disaffection with the political class that supports free trade as a matter of ideology. This is the truth and not an alternative fact that explains the rise in populism. Evaluation done by experts at the right time can help support intelligent policymaking, public resources allocation, and would help abate discontent and a breakdown of social consensus.

36 R. Pablo Guerrero O.

Note

1. US Presidential Candidate Hillary Clinton perhaps lost her election to Donald Trump when she decried her opponents as a "basket of deplorables," describing them as xenophobic among other labels. It turns out that this socio-economic group—the deplorables—stepped up their political participation and against all odds may have swayed enough voters to affect the election. Candidate Clinton had chosen to ignore the plight of many who had lost their jobs and seen no gains from free-trade policies.

Bibliography

Burns, Duncan and Epstein, Barbara (1972), *Realities of Free Trade – Two Industry Studies*, University of Toronto Press.

Cohen, D., Stephen, P., Joel, R. and Blecker, R. A. (1996), *Fundamentals of U.S. Foreign Trade Policy*, Routledge -Taylor & Francis Group.

Clinton, Hillary (2016), https://en.wikipedia.org/wiki/Basket_of_deplorables.

Heller, R. H. (1973), *International Trade – Theory and Empirical Evidence*, Prentice Hall Inc.

McIntyre, Lee (2018), *Post-Truth*, The MIT Press.

Misak, Cheryl (2020), *Frank Ramsey – A Sheer Excess of Powers*, Oxford University Press.

Mishan, E. J. (1973), *Economics for Social Decisions*, Prager University Press.

Moran, Dominic (2020), *Truth Is in the Eye of the Beholder in the Mis-Information Age*, Ascendant Nature: Medium.

Paul, Joel Richard (2015), "The Cost of Free Trade", In *Brown Journal of World Affairs*, Vol. 22, No. 1 Fall/Winter 2015). University of California.

Pettinger, Tejvan (2018), *Who are the Winners and Losers from Free Trade*, economicshelp.org.

Ramsey, Frank P. (1926), "Truth and Probability", In *The Foundations of Mathematics and other Logical Essays, 1931*, Brace and Company Edited by R. B. Braithwaite, Routledge and Kegan Paul Ltd.

Rodrik, Dani (2018), *Straight Talk on Trade*, Princeton University Press.

Scott, Robert E. (2003), *The High Price of Free Trade*, Briefing Paper, Economic Policy Institute.

Sen, Amartya (2002), *Rationality and Freedom*, Harvard University Press.

Social Policy Research Associates (2002), *Estimated Impacts for Participants in the Trade Adjustment Assistance (TAA) Program Under the 2002 Amendments – Evaluation of the TAA Program*, Mathematica Policy Research.

Timiraos, Nick (1999), "5 Questions on Trade Adjustment Assistance", https://blogs.wsj.com/ briefly/2015/06/15/5-questions-on-trade-adjustment-assistance/.

Tramontano, Karen A. (2016), *Tearing Up Trade Agreements Won't Help Workers: A More Responsible Approach May*, Pell Center, Salve Regina University.

3 Evidence as enlightenment versus evidence as certainty

Appropriate uses of evaluative information to inform policy in a post-truth world

Richard Boyle and Sean Redmond

Introduction

There have traditionally been a number of scientific truths that have acted as key reference points for the development of many areas of public policy. Truth here is referred to in the same way as Kuhn (2012) refers to paradigms: a given state at any one point in time where the generation of theory and evidence appear to fit a particular "truth" or normative belief. However, the problem with all such scientific truths is that they are not good at dealing with the *complex* in policy development and implementation. Their eventual and inevitable overturn leaves an opening for those who decry expertise to downplay the role of experts and evidence.

In this chapter, we have a particular interest in the role of evaluative information in providing evidence when dealing with complex "wicked" policy problems in a post-truth world. By evaluative information, we mean any type of data (quantitative and qualitative) used in the assessment of the merit, worth, or value of a policy or program. This information can be found in a number of forms including evaluation, performance reporting, and performance auditing (Schwartz and Mayne, 2005). An important takeaway from this chapter is identifying ways in which evaluative information is created, validated, and used in complex policy environments. Complex and wicked policy issues present challenges for evaluators. Truth is contested and evidence may be derided, or often lacking. Ambiguity is the norm, and value disagreements prevalent. Fertile ground for post-truth protagonists wishing to contradict expertise and scientific evidence. In these circumstances as noted by Head and Alford "[t]here are not only cognitive-analytical challenges but also communicative, political, and institutional challenges to building a more shared understanding" (2015: 718). How evidence and knowledge is generated, shared, and disseminated is central to the degree of success in the recursive review of implementation experiences in different contexts (Sabel and Zeitlin, 2012).

How then to promote the use of evaluative information in dealing with "wicked" problems? The chapter pairs a policy scenario (creeping enlightenment) with an evaluation strategy (deliberative, collaborative, multifaceted research designs). This approach fits closely with a developing thesis in

DOI: 10.4324/9781032719979-4

38   *Richard Boyle and Sean Redmond*

evaluation research, namely that the days of one-off evaluations of one-off programmes are gone. What is needed are "streams" of evaluative information (Rist and Stame, 2006). We argue that the caution and incrementalism often practiced by policy officials and sometimes referred to pejoratively as "muddling through" (Lindblom, 1959) can actually offer an effective route toward creeping enlightenment. This is particularly the case we argue, when supported by a shared approach to the generation, dissemination, and use of evaluative information by evaluators, policymakers, stakeholders, and the public.

In carrying out this exploration, we first set out a theoretical framework for the examination of complex "wicked" problems. We then look at two policy areas in Ireland where approaches to the use of evaluative information are being developed focused more on incrementalism and creeping enlightenment. These two areas are:

- Youth justice, in particular the complex world of organized crime networks, where the blending of craft knowledge and experiential knowledge is generating hybrid forms of evaluative knowledge. Specially developed enquiry tools and methods are presented which are capable of generating new insights into complex and dangerous social-ecosystems.
- Water governance, where an experimental governance approach is being taken to addressing the wicked problem of improving water quality. Collaborative governance structures and networks will be examined and their generation and use of evaluative information in this context explored.

Finally, we reflect on the implications of this "creeping enlightenment" approach for the evaluation of complex policy problems for both evaluators and policymakers. We identify some important lessons around how to bring together the craft knowledge held by practitioners and policymakers, the experiential knowledge of stakeholders, and the evidential knowledge of evaluators to best effect. In terms of the questions raised by the editors in the Introduction, to some extent this chapter raises issues related to all three questions. The chapter focuses on complex policy issues and how evaluators can best interact with other stakeholders to build trust, and hence improve the shared knowledge base available for policymakers to both conceptualize and operationalize responses to the problems. In doing this it addresses the relationship between expertise, policy stakeholders, and decision-makers. The complexities inherent in the wicked problems examined have implications for the complexity of the evaluative process itself. We suggest that there is a need for a patient, multifaceted examination of the problem, and for experts who are willing to co-create evidence with other stakeholders.

Wicked problems

The term "Wicked Problem" was first described by Horst Rittel and Melvin Webber in an article in *Policy Sciences* (Rittel and Webber 1973). The paper,

Evidence as enlightenment versus evidence 39

which deals ostensibly with urban planning has since found resonances with complex problems of modernity in multiple domains; environmental threat and sustainable use of natural resources, urban planning, and human services including child protection, interventions for risk behaviors e.g., drugs and alcohol misuse, and concentrated cross-generational disadvantage, for example indigenous communities (Head 2008) (p.107).

It is important to note the backdrop to Rittel and Webber's article in the United States in the early 1970s. In the 1960s, scientific ingenuity and effort had put a man on the moon. In the decade before this "the quasi-sociological literature was predicting a Mass Society" of shared values and beliefs (Rittel and Webber 1973) (p.167). However, in the early years of the 1970s framed by increased cultural heterogeneity and societal tension, Rittel and Webber observe that the scientific and professional institutions were experiencing a significant depletion in public confidence and certainly an intolerance of planning being solely the preserve of the expert (p.156). A sense of ambivalence and skepticism toward the expert observed by Rittel and Webber in 1970s America bounces back as a threat to rational policy-making in the 21st century. The wicked problem with its intrinsic skeptical knottiness, conflating political values with science, presents as a useful frame to examine our current "post-truth" evaluation challenges.

One of Rittel and Webber's key formulations is his dichotomization of tame and wicked problems. Tame problems they assert are those where the nature of a problem is consensually agreed and definable. If a problem is so bounded it means that success in overcoming the problem is reasonably easy to evidence with a standard toolbox of measurement instruments. As a consequence of tame problems being essentially drawing board problems, much of the focus of the expert is on successive efficiency.

By contrast wicked problems lack precise definition. Indeed the nature and causes of the problem may be the subject of significant conflict. Disagreements on the causes of a wicked problem occur on evidential grounds but also critically, on the basis of competing world views or values by stakeholders. The splicing of values and science offer further opportunities for discord in articulating the discrepancy between the current situation and a desired state of affairs which will inevitably complicate the process of agreeing remedial actions. Wicked problems are difficult to rein in and because the reasons for their existence are likely to be contested, then so is the task of identifying the necessary conditions for success. Finally Rittel and Webber remind us that for planners and decision-makers in the real world, a bad result from trying to deal with a wicked problem, may be judged as a human failure and not a learning opportunity. This is far from the idealized virtuous circle of hypothesis-refutation-re-hypothesis, of the textbook scientific method of knowledge creation where both positive and negative results are equally cherished.

40 *Richard Boyle and Sean Redmond*

Rittel and Webber's proposition is nuanced. Complicated problems do not necessarily equate to wicked problems. Golden Gate Bridge in San Francisco and the Pyramids at Giza are complicated structures and wondrous examples of problem-solving and project management by talented engineers. However, both projects are clearly bounded in scope and so could be adequately described as tame. Other problems mundane by comparison, such as locating a drug treatment service or specialist residential supports for resettling prisoners in a neighborhood best suited to their needs, or the level of phosphorus in fertilizer that a farmer applies to a particular field, may be inherently contested and wicked.

Presented in the form of a matrix, Head (Head 2008) identifies wicked problems with the following properties: (a) complexity, (b) uncertainty, and (c) divergence (Figure 3.1). Each property offers additional descriptor options of low, moderate, and high intended for application to real-life contexts and indicating (left to right) evidence of escalating wickedness along the three criteria.

Firstly, we apply Head's matrix to the youth justice and water governance examples to establish and profile their wickedness. Secondly, we describe methodological and governance innovations developed in Ireland to improve capacity for understanding the selected wicked problem examples, facilitate the production of reliable evidence, and inform judgments about options for resolution.

Youth justice

We do not contend that "youth crime" as a policy domain is itself inherently wicked. Indeed in keeping with Rittel and Webber's general observations about scientific output, much is known internationally about predicting youthful

Complexity of elements, sub-systems and interdependencies	Low	Moderate	High
Uncertainty in relation to risks, consequences of action, and changing patterns	Low	Moderate	High
Divergence and fragmentation in viewpoints, values, strategic intentions	Low	Moderate	High

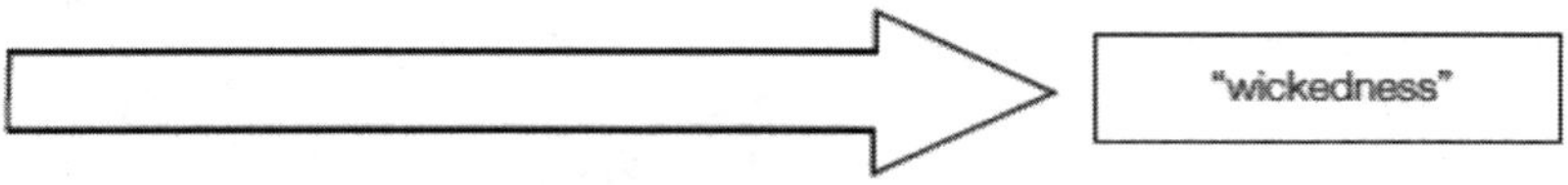

"wickedness"

Figure 3.1 Complexity, uncertainty, and divergence.

Source: Reproduced from Head 2008 p.103.

Evidence as enlightenment versus evidence 41

criminal behavior which makes it an area of tame as well as wicked scientific endeavor. As a consequence of efforts over the years, a large body of evidence now exists to understand and predict the onset of youth criminal behavior. This accumulated knowledge also provides intervention solutions using evidence-based programs with "permissible operations" (Rittel and Webber 1973) (p.164) and known efficacy (Farrington and Welsh 2008) that can confidently recommend reductions in prison-building requirements in favor of robust community programs (Aos, Miller, Drake, 2006). In Ireland overall patterns of youth offending can be discerned reasonably accurately from administrative data (PULSE) importantly identifying trends toward ageing out of crime, the so-called age/crime curve (Redmond 2020) (p.7).

Within the youth crime policy area the example we choose to examine is what has been referred to "the right hand tail" (Loeber and Farrington 2012) (p.137) of the age/crime curve. These children are involved in serious crime. Far less is known about them, demanding "special theories" (Loeber and Farrington 2012) (p.140) to explain their situations. Our case refers to approximately 1,000 young people in Ireland who are estimated to be involved with or at risk of being involved with criminal networks (Naughton and Redmond 2020). Though small in number (approximately 0.25% of the 12–18 years population in Ireland), this group of young people distributed in pockets across Ireland (Naughton and Redmond 2020) are responsible for a significantly disproportionate amount of crime (Redmond 2020) (p.56) and so are of national policy concern.[1]

Young people in Ireland involved in criminal networks meet Head's three general criteria for indicating wickedness (Head 2008). In terms of *complexity,* they constitute a hidden problem or "invisible harm" (Sparrow 2008) (p.181–198) which spans multiple policy and agency remits. In terms of *uncertainty,* the young people identified are immersed in toxic ecosystems and subject to the capricious whims of influential network actors in their neighborhoods (Redmond 2020). In terms of *divergence* of opinion; causation, discrepancy, and solutions are marked by perspectives which view the young people involved as dangerous criminals in the making and those which view the young people as victims of adult criminal exploitation and in need of state (child) protection.

Orthodox means of assembling useable evidence for this group of young people provide at best partial disclosure of the problem and a limited repertoire of intervention programs with limited efficacy. Administrative data held by the police relating to youth crime in Ireland refers in the main to detections. Young people involved in serious crime may be elusive to detection given that witnesses may be reluctant to report crime in the first place due to fear of reprisal. In terms of solutions, off-the-peg evidence-based gang programs which provide conclusive results from randomized control trials certainly exist. However, the majority of programs have been developed in the United States and United Kingdom which it has been plausibly argued (Hourigan 2011) (p.79) have iterations of "gang" fundamentally different from Ireland

42 *Richard Boyle and Sean Redmond*

which has a more southern European flavor where "family is at the core." The potential evidence mismatch does not refer only to different hues of gang anatomy. Family and kinship crime groups develop close relational bonds super-strengthened by *trust* in addition to transactional ties for economic gain found in many other types of crime network. The resilience of such relationships to external shocks or policy nudges raise significant operational consequences for law enforcement (Redmond 2015) (p.16–17).

Introducing greentown

The Greentown[2] Programme commenced in Ireland in 2016. Its mission was to investigate the context and phenomenon of youth involvement in adult criminal networks in Ireland. Evidence to assist in the task of problem definition involves; an original case study focusing on Greentown (Redmond 2020), two replication studies; Redtown (Naughton, Redmond et al. 2020), Bluetown (O'Meara Daly, Redmond et al. 2020), a national prevalence study (Naughton and Redmond 2020), and a comparative examination of the three initial case studies (2022). More recently, the program has engaged in intervention program design and field trials.

Consistent with Rittel and Webber's caution that an important condition of dealing satisfactorily with wicked problems is "the art of not knowing too early which type of solution to apply" (Rittel and Webber 1973) (p.164), the first general contribution that the Greentown Programme makes to improve the evidence yield in the face of complexity is to brood patiently over detailed and multifaceted examination of the problem. The second contribution from the Greentown Programme that we advance is inclusive deliberative design. Inclusive in this sense refers to create the conditions for functional collaborations between scientists and frontline practitioners.

Social network analysis strengthened by practice wisdom

To assist in *capturing the whole*, social network analysis provided a useful tool for moving beyond more usual focus on individual offender behavior. Social network analysis surfaces patterns of connections, flows of information and using constructs of centrality and between-ness, inferences regarding hierarchical status, and strategic positioning of network nodes. The Greentown network (illustrated) was created by police analysts using administrative crime data linking co-offending individuals in the Greentown area detected for burglary and drugs sales 2010–2011. The portrayal of crime data as a picture of real criminal *relationships* in their local area (as opposed for example to tables of numbers) was received supportively by frontline officers who rated it on average 7.5 out of 10 in terms of accurateness of their experience (Redmond 2015) (p. 94) when consulted.

Evidence as enlightenment versus evidence 43

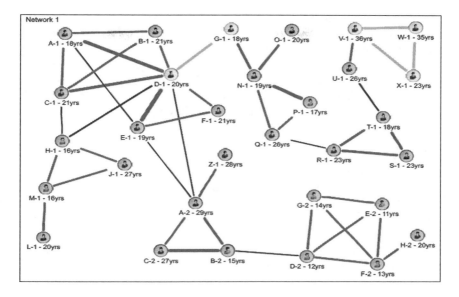

Of course a key weakness in the assumptions underpinning the construction of the network was the use of detection data which, as already stated, has significant limitations with this particular cohort of youths involved in crime. To add texture and depth to the map and its story, the Greentown study innovated "Twinsight" (Redmond 2020) (p.23–24) to elicit systematic collection of data from frontline police officers, especially selected for their knowledge of network actors. Twinsight was a data collection method using two network illustrations; one used by the researcher with a unique reference number for each network node (individual) identifying gender and age and one used by police officers, which in addition to unique reference numbers, tied these anonymized markers to the actual names of the actors. This innovation and associated choreography which physically positioned researcher and police officer in the same room but out of each other's eye-shot permitted researchers to co-navigate the network with 16 police officers in individual interviews. Officers were encouraged to support opinions about individuals shown in the network with references to actual events that could be corroborated, amended or contested by other police officers in interviews so that thick narratives could be stacked, providing evidence drawn from their community observations. Open coding of interviews and a detailed process of bottom-up distillation provided a clear audit trail demonstrating stepwise rationale for the trajectory of initial codes to resultant themes and findings. A subsequent sense-checking session with the group of police officer respondents indicated that the picture of the problem supported by the evidence collected by the Greentown research resonated with their collective real-life experiences.

44   Richard Boyle and Sean Redmond

Repeating Twinsight in two further locations, Redtown and Bluetown provided further evidence of wicked problem properties; in this case, the essential uniqueness of each problem encountered (Rittel and Webber 1973 p.164). Evidence presented in Bluetown and Redtown studies echo Pawson's claims that "individual estates have their own criminal careers" (Pawson and Tilley 1997) (p.97), demonstrating that within one locality, *Bluetown*, four separate networks existed, each with distinctive features of operational relevance to policy and program intervention.

Deliberative problem examination and design

In parallel to the replication studies, we convened a group of 26 international and national experts in organised crime, criminal networks, youth and child welfare (2017–2019). This group participated in a two-day problem solving workshop.[3] Our initial request of experts was an external sense-check and validation of the analysis and the findings of the Greentown study in terms of evidence quality.[4] Experts were required to use the Greentown network as the point of reference for deliberation, to discourage any bias toward theoretical abstractions of the problem of youth crime more generally. We believed that by bounding the problem of youth involvement in crime networks using Greentown as the whole exhibit, we were more likely to ensure that all experts were *examining the same patient*.

By providing reasonably strict "grounding" rules for harnessing expert examination of the problem we aimed to mitigate the effects of another feature of wicked problems, the tendency for solutions to be crafted by second-guessing myriad perceptions of discrepancy between the "is" and the "ought" (Rittel and Webber 1973) (p.161). This is not to say that there was easy consensus between experts' opinions regarding the current and desired state. Indeed encouraging dissent "strengthens collective intelligence" (Camillus 2008) (p.4) and is key to mobilizing support for engaging wicked problems. Our point is simply that fixing the wicked problem concept to a specific case example provides assurance that differences in perceptions of what needs to be done (*the discrepancy*) at least refers to the same problem meaning that individual strategies to bridge the gap between "is" and "ought" can be tested equally for relative merit.

A second function of deliberative design utilized the skills and knowledge held by frontline practitioners in Ireland. Here we engaged the support of 62 experienced youth professionals, police officers, probation officers, and child protection social workers in separate discipline-specific workshops totaling approximately 600 hours of expert input. The specific purpose of this process, cognizant that "the social planner has no right to be wrong" (Rittel and Webber 1973) (p.166–167), was to create safe space to stress test our "discovery driven assumptions" (Camillus 2008) (p.7) generated by deliberative program design in table-top real scenarios. In a reverse tactic to generalizing from the specific, which we aimed to achieve with our international and national-level collaborators, here we sought to ground high-level assumptions and solutions to street-level scrutiny.

The focus of our youth justice case example refers to the process of novel evidence generation as opposed to program design. Nevertheless, it is important to note that the core features for a new intervention emerged from this deliberative process. Where internationally theoretical and program solutions have focused on "pulling levers" to disrupt networks (Braga, Kennedy et al. 2001), improved community efficacy, specific interventions for families (US Department of Justice, Programs 2018) and individualized routes out of gang involvement for youth "knifing off" from their criminal pasts toward redemptive pathways (Maruna and Roy 2007), the Greentown Programme collapsed what we believed to be hitherto partial solutions into a program whole that responded to the specific problem analysis in Ireland.[5]

Work to do

A further level of deliberative design is, at the time of writing, currently in tow. This third process refers to local actors in the field, involving local crafting, implementation, and risk management. In 2022, the Greentown Programme is being trialed in two locations in Ireland. The output of the Greentown studies and the deliberative processes discussed above were intended only to deliver an approximation of a program, or a bounded evidence-informed *mission* as opposed to an intervention directed by strict operational rules and procedures. This means that there is an explicit assumption that specific tactics for operations would be further fashioned by program providers and local state agencies with governance responsibilities. Current work involves the co-design and production of a theory of change for the whole program, providing a plausible account of the intended contribution of the program to overall objectives of (a) reducing network influence on young people in terms of recruitment, and (b) providing practical exit solutions for young people already embedded in the network. The task of this specific deliberative process is to signpost where *north* is (Geyer and Cairney 2015) (p.176–178), to compose plausible change narratives to describe the journey north and scan for "weak signals" (p.7 Camillus) to manage the risk of short-term interruptions requiring remedial "whack-a-mole" responses (Sparrow 2008) (p.144–145).

Evidence as enlightenment—combining craft and experiential knowledge in pursuit of improved water quality

The pursuit of good water quality is a wicked problem that displays all three of the attributes identified by Head (2008) —complexity, uncertainty, and divergence—to a high degree. As with the youth justice example, not all aspects of addressing water quality problems are wicked in nature, but the issue taken as a whole is certainly wicked. Population and economic change, coupled with increased pollution of scarce freshwater sources and climate change, creates a complex environment for water managers. No one has a precise answer as to how to improve water quality, with initiatives often resulting in unknown and uncertain hydrological and ecological outcomes. The local context is key. Stakeholder groups diverge in their perspectives on the challenges faced. Farmers, for example, are incentivized to increase production through a growing use of fertilizers which can cause river pollution. Angling groups want clean waters in which fish can thrive. The challenges are ones where the different units and levels of government (international, national, regional, and local) have to coordinate with each other and with non-government actors in civil society and the private sector. Often, they have to collaborate to do something that they cannot precisely define or agree on in advance.

To try to address these challenges, governance arrangements have been put in place in Ireland to support a more cohesive and coordinated approach to policy and practice development in water quality which display a number of characteristics of experimental governance. The findings examined here are selected from a two-year research study of the water governance arrangements funded by the Irish Environmental Protection Agency (Boyle et al. 2021a). Sabel and Zeitlin (2012) coined the term "experimental governance" to describe one way in which collaborative governance arrangements have evolved in the face of wicked problems. Key aspects of an experimental governance approach are that broad framework goals are set, there is freedom to experiment and innovate solutions at the local level, and in return for this freedom, participants must regularly report on their performance. Learning from this, the framework goals, metrics, and procedures are themselves periodically revised by the actors who initially established them, often augmented by new participants whose knowledge and cooperation are seen as indispensable.

Here we focus on two aspects of the experimental governance arrangements that address some of the challenges for the provision of evaluative information in a post-truth world. One is how the governance arrangements are supporting the production and acceptance of craft knowledge generated at the local level. The other is how governance arrangements support the combination of such craft knowledge with experiential knowledge.

Evolving and validating craft knowledge

Promisingly, there is evidence of new data emerging locally that is helping to inform policy and practice (Boyle et al., 2021). Examples here include:

- New understanding of hydromorphology impact. Sediment has been identified as a bigger problem than was initially expected.
- Studies of behavioral and attitudinal change with respect to Ireland's water resources aim to provide important evidence of the effect of engagement with communities and farmers.

Evidence as enlightenment versus evidence 47

From an experimental governance perspective, it is important that as this new craft knowledge emerges from experts engaging in local monitoring and evaluation, there are fora in place to help determine the validity and usefulness of this information regionally and nationally. It is also important that these fora address both the interests of experts themselves and also wider stakeholders, to help ensure learning across organizations and across interest groups. This is one way of mitigating the possibilities of individuals or groups dominating the policy agenda with their own "post-truth" take on the situation.

Two such fora are particularly important in water governance in Ireland. One, the National Technical Implementation Group (NTIG), brings together experts to validate evaluative information and ensure evidence feeds through to inform policy-making at the national level. The other is the Water Forum, which is a stakeholder representative forum.

The National Technical Implementation Group (NTIG) brings together experts from across government departments, local government, and state agencies. It reviews progress, and provides updates to a policy coordination group on the implementation and effectiveness of measures. NTIG is seen as working well (Boyle et al. 2021a). By and large, it is seen as having the right people involved, with good attendance, good energy and discussion, and awareness raising. While in the initial stages it tended to focus more on updates and briefings, it has evolved so that people are now tabling more substantive issues for discussion and debate.

One interviewee noted the benefits collaborative arrangements among the experts producing the evidential knowledge have brought in terms of promoting flexibility in adapting to changing circumstances:

> So say in terms of the pressures that were identified at the beginning, like say nutrients and maybe sediment as well, things like hydromorphology are coming up so there has to be that flexibility as the investigations go on and they find issues that maybe weren't on the radar beforehand or issues that were on the radar are actually a bigger issue on the ground than they might have previously been thought of.
>
> (Boyle et al. 2021a)

The Water Forum is a statutory body that was set up to facilitate stakeholder engagement in water quality issues, and be representative of stakeholders with an interest in the quality of Ireland's water bodies. It consists of 26 members including representatives from a wide range of organizations with direct connections to issues relating to water quality and also public water consumers. The Forum has proved particularly valuable in a situation where there is stakeholder contestation about the nature of the problems and solutions to address them. In particular, historically there has been a wide divide between agricultural

48   *Richard Boyle and Sean Redmond*

interests and environmental groups as to the nature of the problems and solutions to address water quality. In these situations, as Conklin (2006: 5) identifies: "You don't so much 'solve' a wicked problem as you help stakeholders negotiate shared understanding and shared meaning about the problem and its possible solutions. The objective of the work is coherent action, not final solution."

Through debating the relevance and usefulness of evaluative information in the Water Forum, it has developed as an important forum for mutual learning, the sharing of information, and for keeping stakeholders up-to-date. Forum members emphasized the willingness of members to listen to others and understand where they are coming from (Boyle et al. 2021b). Members feel more informed, that their knowledge of water issues has increased, and that it has strengthened relationships with others in the group. With regard to being more informed and enhancing their knowledge base, this aspect of the work of the Water Forum reflects the importance of social learning as an emerging governance mechanism to promote collaborative action among stakeholders to improve water governance (Collins and Ison, 2009).

Participants have established network contacts with other actors interested in the same issue that they may not normally have had dialogue with, and this has helped establish trust, one of the potential benefits of forums noted by Lubell (2007). However, it is not a panacea, and limitations with regard to the degree of consensus building is an issue. Also, while the emphasis on consensus building is generally seen as a positive, some members noted that it could also be a limitation. It could mean that the more contentious issues are not addressed as thoroughly as they might, with more of a focus on information-sharing than on problem-solving, avoiding the really challenging issues. This highlights the need to ensure that dissenting knowledge is incorporated in any deliberations to ensure that the diversity of voices and views is heard. In the case of the Water Forum, the role of the chair was highlighted as crucial, and the fact that they were independent and facilitative seen as a strong positive in this regard.

Combining craft knowledge with experiential knowledge

As Gertler and Wolfe (2004: 50) note:

> shared or networked learning assumes that neither the public sector nor individual private enterprises are the source of all knowledge; rather, the process of innovation and institutional adaptation is an interactive one in which the means for establishing supportive social relations and of communicating insights and knowledge in all its various forms are crucial to the outcomes. The goal, then, is to establish effective systems for social knowledge management at the local and regional scale.

The Agricultural Sustainability and Advisory Programme (ASSAP) provides one example of combining expert craft knowledge with knowledge gained from experience to promote shared learning. ASSAP employs experts in developing solutions to water quality problems to work with farmers in areas where river pollution is high. As well as the technical skills required, ASSAP advisors have increasingly identified soft skills as a vital capacity issue and a benefit, recognizing the importance of gaining farmer trust and understanding. As one advisor noted in relation to the work with farmers:

> If they [farmers] can understand why, they will be more interested in the measures. You might recommend on average six items and they rank them in order of how impactful they are and focus on those, farmers are more likely to do two to three things for you. You give alternatives for solving the problem and negotiate and find something he will do. It's a complex negotiation and relationship; soft people skills need to be very good, as it works differently with different farmers.

A further example, but this time working with the broader local community, is provided by the inter-relationship between the Rivers Trusts (community-led charities, started by local people to care for their local rivers) and experts in the generation and use of evaluative information at the local level in Ireland. The development of these links to produce local evaluative information on approaches to improving water quality shows both the benefits and the challenges of joined-up thinking with regard to catchment management at the local level. This supports Schorr's contention that "communities will be able to act most effectively when they can combine local wisdom and their understanding of local circumstances with accumulated knowledge, drawn from research, theory, and practice, about what has worked elsewhere, what is working now, and what appears promising" (Schorr, 2003: 10).

The Moy River Trust, for example, has sought to combine their local community knowledge of the River Moy with "expert" knowledge to produce better outcomes. As described by a director of the Trust:

> We have learned a lot about the environment. This work has been a transition. People can educate themselves, whereas in the past it was left to someone who was an expert, a guru. We have started to align ourselves with people who can deliver and to increase our knowledge base. We are working with the Green Restoration Ireland group, a cooperative that was established "to help bring climate solutions closer to home"; they come in and survey the riverbank and advise us. We have engaged with farmers on local projects like bog restoration. Local communication is central to getting the farmers on board.

50   *Richard Boyle and Sean Redmond*

In a similar vein the Inishowen River Trust has commissioned experts from Trinity College Dublin to carry out a detailed study on "The Opportunity for Natural Water Retention Measures in Inishowen" (Bourke et al., 2020). The team conducted a detailed analysis of the flood risk in areas around Inishowen, examining data and sourcing information from landowners affected by recent floods. Information and knowledge from the community was also an important part of the project and the Trust developed a short ten-question survey to gather information from landowners. This is a good example of the local community working with experts to support generation and sharing of knowledge to produce better outcomes.

Conclusions

We started this chapter by noting that the resilience of scientific truths is limited in the face of wicked problems. Post-truth opinions often flourish in such an environment. What, then can be done to create the conditions where evaluative information can play a role in informing policy and practice, and where experts such as evaluators and scientists are seen as valuable contributors of knowledge? Here, we summarize four lessons learned from our examination of the two cases we examined, where the "death of the expert" and of the promises of the evidence hierarchy give way to balancing the craft knowledge held by practitioners and policymakers, the experiential knowledge of stakeholders, and the evidential knowledge of evaluators.

Lesson 1: The need for patient and multifaceted examination of the problem rather than promoting universal solutions and truth

Scientific and technical experts, whose subject knowledge have high status, can have a tendency to assume their viewpoint of interpretation of evaluative information is the "correct" one. Different scientific disciplines, like the social and natural sciences, can have diverging perspectives and values, and be equally convinced they are correct. However, our experience suggests that a willingness to engage with varying perspectives and assess the context in developing and using evaluative information is needed.

Our youth justice example, the Greentown Programme, centers on the minority of children who are involved in serious and persistent crime. This group could be illustrative of many other complex sub-groups in healthcare, justice, and education systems. In such systems big data in terms of diagnostic capability and planning, assure confidence, courtesy of the law of large numbers. However, as we have seen, evidence produced by orthodox criminology has largely failed to account for *the right hand tail*, who from a policy perspective have huge vulnerabilities, are responsible for significantly disproportionate amount of crime and equally disproportionate government expenditure. Surfacing useable evidence for this group demands different tools, approaches, and mind-set.

Evidence as enlightenment versus evidence 51

In a post-truth environment, connecting different viewpoints cannot be achieved by some rational appeal to simple policy solutions. Rather there is a need for contestation, exploration, and negotiation of different viewpoints on what insights are to be gained from any evaluative information being produced. Inevitably this takes time, but it is time that is needed to ensure the wicked problem is examined in detail and from different perspectives.

Lesson 2: The need for inclusive deliberative design

What our case examples show is that in an uncertain environment, experts need to be willing to "co-create" the evidence base with others, both other experts and diverse stakeholder groups. This requires a different skill set for experts, including evaluators. As Dewulf et al. (2005) note "Experience, insight and skills for dealing with ambiguity in multiparty negotiations are then to be considered an important requirement for scientific experts, policy makers, administrators and specific interest groups alike, if they want to reach integrated, adaptive and sustainable management of complex environments."

Both the Greentown Programme and the water quality case highlight the need for inclusive deliberative design. Inclusive in this sense refers to creating the conditions for functional collaborations between scientists, frontline practitioners, and stakeholder groups applied to specific local contexts.

Using social network analysis to engage frontline police officers in the convincing capture of *whole problems* in their "natural size and shape" (Sparrow 2008) (p.85–86) as opposed to fractions of problems viewed through the lens of specific expert disciplines, offered opportunities for police officers to become stakeholders and scientists in a joint meaningful endeavor. Experts working with local communities through Rivers Trusts has brought together community knowledge and expert knowledge to improve river water quality. Moreover, we believe that public confidence is strengthened by the ability to be fully conversant with multiple features of a problem at different levels of granularity, given that with wicked problems "every specification of the problem is a specification of the direction in which the treatment is considered" (Rittel and Webber 1973) (p.161). Exhaustive approaches to problem analysis with wicked problems at the very least improves transparency, and facilitates potential scaling-out of lessons learned.

Lesson 3: Understanding the necessity for specifying context and the value of multi-stakeholder problem-solving

As Rittel and Webber point out, maximizing value in wicked problem resolution requires the identification of the sweet spot between obvious local benefit, predictive of community mobilization, and more general and meaningful knowledge creation:

52   *Richard Boyle and Sean Redmond*

the higher the level of a problem's formulation, the broader and more general it becomes: and the more difficult it becomes to do something about it. On the other hand, one should not try to cure symptoms: and therefore one should try to settle the problem on as high a level as possible.

(Rittel and Webber 1973) (p. 165)

Cognizant of the "essential uniqueness" of each wicked problem, theoretical reference points built from the experience of one wicked problem can still inform subsequent approaches to other wicked problems presenting with thematic similarities; if only as start-points for new hypothesis.

In a similar *right-sizing* vein Sparrow adds that picking the right size problems to work on means achieving a balance, "a crush test" which carries strategic risks as well as the potential benefits of higher levels of stakeholder investment in muddling through resolutions

If practitioners bite off too much, chances are they will choke. Bite off too little, and nobody will much care.

(Sparrow 2008) (p.84)

The lesson we are drawing here is that achieving the right balance in terms of sizing a problem and adopting procedures informed by what we know about resolving wicked problems influences stakeholder buy-in. We ask tentatively therefore whether such research missions with experts working cheek by jowl with practitioners and invested community members could also improve trust; given what we know about the esprit de corps that can develop from teams being involved in task centered problem-solving. This more theoretical assertion regarding trust-building obviously needs to be tested empirically but is core to the tension that this book is attempting to examine.

Scientific knowledge can expose local phenomena such as the existence of crime networks to an international body of evidence built on theory and high standard empirical research and evaluation. Frontline practitioners in the youth domain can use their accumulated craft knowledge and practice wisdom to add important layers and nuance to problem analysis based on direct observation of the phenomena in its context as well as the adequacy of existing and proposed tools for dealing with the problem.

In the Greentown example qualitative evidence gathered using the same procedures from multiple case studies is being re-analyzed to generate more general theoretical propositions, albeit provisional and tentative, about the contexts and mechanisms that sustain crime networks' abilities to recruit and retain children to commit crime.

Experts from the Agricultural Sustainability and Advisory Programme working with farmers to reduce river pollution from farms have learned the benefits of working with farmers rather than imposing ready-made solutions. Combining

Evidence as enlightenment versus evidence 53

the expertise of the advisor with the local knowledge of the farmer can produce a better solution than an imposed "one size fits all" solution which does not win local support.

Experts need to co-create "truth" with other stakeholders where there is a lack of, or ambiguity regarding the validity of, evidence. Experts such as evaluators and policymakers have an important role to play in generating evaluative information. Other stakeholders often are good at identifying and reading "weak" signals that may suggest the need for further investigation or mid-course correction of a particular policy direction.

Lesson 4: The value of fora to validate craft knowledge

Schön and Rein (1994) argue that there is a need for reflection within policy practice, particularly when dealing with intractable challenges. In particular, they promote the concept of frame reflection. Their thesis is that real-life situations are often complex, vague, ambiguous, and indeterminate. In order to make sense of such situations, people and organizations select certain features which help them create a story which explains the situation. The authors refer to this selection process as the process of "naming and framing." In a post-truth environment, such frames can often be extremely partial, without an evidential base, and self-reinforcing within the group.

Frame reflection involves the stakeholders engaging to review and revise their frames of reference and through this process "constructing a shared narrative that recognizes multiple voices, teases out the implications of these value preferences, and seeks to resolve conflicts. This activity is partly analytical and partly discursive" (Head and Alford, 2015: 723). Dewulf et al. (2005) note that frame reflection involves not only looking at the extent to which the goals and metrics themselves change and evolve but also the extent to which stakeholders' frames of reference are influenced through the process.

The fora examined here, such as the workshops used in the youth justice case to provide plausible narratives for the route north and the more formal governance arrangement of the Water Forum and NTIG in the water governance case provided good examples where frame reflection occurred and stakeholders reviewed their own position and value preferences and what weight should be given to different evidence fragments. Working with and making the best use of such deliberative fora to validate craft knowledge is an important part of the evaluator's toolkit in generative evaluative information for use in helping address wicked problems.

Final thoughts

Of course, the means we have examined here to combine craft and experiential knowledge are not a panacea for addressing how evaluators and evaluative information can prosper in a post-truth world when dealing with wicked problems. Those determined to reject evidence and expertise and pursue their own goals regardless will continue to do so. In addition, taking a deliberative and reflexive approach to evaluation in policy domains where policymakers demand urgent responses can be problematic, when things just need to get done. However, even here we believe that our lessons have currency in designing and testing out new innovations in complex environments with potential efficiencies in bringing collaborators together deriving from new on-line technologies where usage has become routine due to the Covid-19 pandemic. Such real-life challenges demand agility from the scientific community in terms of quickly assembling evidence and being comfortable to be in the trenches alongside decision-makers where evidence is less than conclusive but decisions still have to be made. Evaluators, scientific experts and policy makers need to recognize that they are often not a welcome voice in a complex web of interests. But there are many people out there who can be persuaded to engage more effectively with evaluative information, and combine their own knowledge and experience with that of experts to inform policy and practice. We see this as developing a collaborative and deliberative approach toward creeping enlightenment.

Notes

1 See http://justice.ie/en/JELR/Pages/PR21000015 link provided 12:56 06/04/21.
2 References to locations have been anonymized in all studies.
3 Senior management and designers from two evidence-based programs, Multi-Systemic Therapy and Functional Family Therapy were engaged. These evidence-based programs have been subjected to randomized control trials and demonstrated some efficacy in working with gang-engaged youth. Importantly, the pool of off-the-peg evidence-based programs operating in the area is very small.
4 At this point, only the Greentown study had been completed and published. We nevertheless believed that expert responses and reactions to the study were of value in their own right and once documented, could in any event be compared to the two replication studies that were underway [Bluetown and Redtown] at a later stage.
5 https://eucpn.org/document/ireland-the-greentown-project

References

Aos, S., Miller, M. and Drake, E. (2006), 'Evidence-based public policy options to reduce future prison construction, criminal justice costs, and crime rates', *Federal Sentencing Reporter*, 19: 275.
Bourke, M. C., Halpin, R., Brady, F. and Quinn, P. (2020), 'The opportunity for natural water retention measures in Inishowen, Ireland', A report prepared for the Inishowen Rivers Trust, Consult Trinity, Dublin.
Boyle, R., O'Riordan, J., O'Leary, F. and Shannon, L. (2021a), *Using an Experimental Governance Lens to Examine Governance of the River Basin Management Plan for Ireland 2018–2021*, Wexford: Environmental Protection Agency.

Evidence as enlightenment versus evidence 55

Boyle, R., O'Riordan, J., Shannon, L. and O'Leary, F. (2021b), *An Fóram Uisce (The Water Forum) as an Example of Stakeholder Engagement in Governance*, Dublin: Institute of Public Administration.

Braga, A. A., et al. (2001), 'Problem-oriented policing, deterrence, and youth violence: An evaluation of Boston's operation ceasefire', *Journal of Research in Crime and Delinquency*, 38 (3): 195–225.

Camillus, J. C. (2008), 'Strategy as a wicked problem', *Harvard Business Review*. https://hbr.org/2008/05/strategy-as-a-wicked-problem.

Collins, K. and Ison, R. (2009), 'Jumping off Arnstein's ladder: Social learning as a new policy paradigm for climate change adaptation', *Environmental Policy and Governance*, 19 (6): 358–373. doi:10.1002/eet.v19:6.

Conklin, J. (2006), 'Wicked problems and social complexity', in J. Conklin (ed.), *Dialogue Mapping: Building Shared Understanding of Wicked Problems*, Chichester: John Wiley: 3–40.

Dewulf, A., Craps, M., Bouwen, R., Taillieu, T. and Pahl-Wostl, C. (2005), 'Integrated management of natural resources: Dealing with ambiguous issues, multiple actors and diverging frames', *Water, Science & Technology*, 52 (6): 115–124.

Farrington, D. P. and Welsh, B. C. (2008), *Saving Children from a Life of Crime: Early Risk Factors and Effective Interventions*, Oxford: Oxford University Press.

Gertler, M. and Wolfe, D. (2004), 'Local social knowledge management: Community actors, institutions and multilevel governance in regional foresight exercises', *Futures*, 36: 45–65.

Geyer, R. and Cairney, P. (2015), *Handbook on Complexity and Public Policy*, Cheltenham, UK, Northampton, MA, USA: Edward Elgar Publishing.

Head, B. W. (2008), 'Wicked problems in public policy', *Public Policy*, 3 (2): 101–118.

Head, B. W. and Alford, J. (2015), 'Wicked problems: Implications for public policy and management', *Administration & Society*, 47 (6): 711–739.

Hourigan, N. (2011), *Understanding Limerick: Social Exclusion and Change*, Cork: Cork University Press.

Kuhn, T. (2012), *The Structure of Scientific Revolutions*, Chicago: The University of Chicago Press.

Lindblom, C. (1959), 'The science of "muddling through"', *Public Administration Review*, 19 (2): 79–88.

Loeber, R. and Farrington, D. P. (2012), *From Juvenile Delinquency to Adult Crime: Criminal Careers, Justice Policy, and Prevention*, Oxford: Oxford University Press.

Lubell, M. (2007), 'Familiarity breeds trust: Collective action in a policy domain', *Journal of Politics*, 69: 237–250.

Maruna, S. and Roy, K. (2007), 'Amputation or reconstruction? Notes on the concept of "knifing off" and desistance from crime', *Journal of Contemporary Criminal Justice*, 23 (1): 104–124.

National Institute of Justice (NIJ), US Department of Justice, Office of Justice Programs and United States of America, 2018. Tailored Functional Family Therapy Program Shows Promise for Reducing Subsequent Criminal Activity in a Population at High Risk for Joining Gangs. Washington.

Naughton, C. M. and Redmond, S. (2020), *National Prevalence Study: Do the Findings from the Greentown Study of Children's Involvement in a Criminal Network Extend Beyond Greentown?* Department of Justice, Dublin, Ireland.

56 *Richard Boyle and Sean Redmond*

Naughton, C. M., et al. (2020), *Lifting the Lid on Redtown: A Replication Case Study, Which Investigates the Contribution of Engagement in a Local Criminal Network to Young People's More Serious and Persistent Offending Patterns.* Department of Justice, Dublin, Ireland.

O'Meara Daly, E., et al. (2020), *Lifting the Lid on Bluetown: A Replication Case Study, Which Investigates the Contribution of Engagement in a Local Criminal Network to Young People's More Serious and Persistent Offending Patterns.* Department of Justice, Dublin, Ireland.

Pawson, R. and Tilley, N. (1997), *Realistic Evaluation*, London: Sage.

Redmond, S. (2015), *Examining the Role of Criminal Networks in Causing Children to Develop Longer and More Serious Crime Trajectories "Greentown"-a Case Study*, Queen's University Belfast.

Redmond, S. (2020), *Lifting the Lid on Greentown Version 2 – Why We Should Be Concerned about the Influence Criminal Networks Have on Children's Offending Behaviour in Ireland.* Department of Justice, Dublin, Ireland.

Rist, S. and Stame, N. (2006), *From Studies to Streams: Managing Evaluative Systems*, New York: Routledge.

Rittel, H. W. and Webber, M. M. (1973), 'Dilemmas in a general theory of planning', *Policy Sciences*, 4 (2): 155–169.

Sabel, C. and Zeitlin, J. (2012), 'Experimentalist governance', in D. Levi-Faur (ed.), *The Oxford Handbook of Governance*, Oxford: Oxford University Press.

Schön, D. A. and Rein, M. (1994), *Frame Reflection: Toward the Resolution of Intractable Policy Controversies*, New York: Basic Books.

Schorr, L. B. (2003), *Determining "What Works" in Social Programs and Social Policies: Toward a More Inclusive Knowledge Base*, Washington, DC: Brookings Institution.

Schwartz, R. and Mayne, J. (2005), 'Assuring the quality of evaluative information: Theory and practice', *Evaluation and Program Planning*, Elsevier, 28 (1): 1–14.

Sparrow, M. K. (2008), *The Character of Harms: Operational Challenges in Control*, Cambridge: Cambridge University Press.

4 Lies and politics

Until death do us part …

Steve Jacob and Jeanne Milot-Poulin

Introduction

Due to the recent rise of populism around the world and the concomitant increase in the use of "alternative facts"[1] by politicians, the manipulation of the truth in politics has become a major concern in numerous countries. Many populist politicians use easily refutable statements to promote their political agenda (Barrera et al., 2020). During his inauguration as 46th President of the United States, Joe Biden expressed concern about this phenomenon: "[…] we must reject a culture in which facts themselves are manipulated and even manufactured. […] Recent weeks and months have taught us a painful lesson. There is truth and there are lies. Lies told for power and profit. And each of us has a duty and responsibility, as citizens, as Americans and especially as leaders—leaders who are pledged to honor our Constitution and protect our nation—to defend the truth and to defeat the lies" (Biden, 2021).

Through his advocacy of the truth, President Biden echoes the apprehensions of our time. Indeed, deception of all kinds in the political world is of concern to citizens and has been attracting the attention of both journalists and researchers alike. Despite the fact that "electoral" lies, such as promises that are intended to be broken or lies aimed at enhancing a candidate's image, are the first that come to mind when we think about lying in politics, public policy is also affected by this changing political environment. This phenomenon is particularly evident in the field of foreign policy, with, for example, the production of false information to justify wars, as was the case with the alleged presence of weapons of mass destruction in Iraq by the Bush Administration or with the war in Vietnam as revealed by the Pentagon Papers (Hartnett and Stengrim, 2004).

Although this chapter focuses on lying in politics, the conclusions developed herein can apply to the entire policymaking process, from the initial stages of recognizing and defining a problem to justify the elaboration of public policy to its evaluation and reformulation. Indeed, "[l]ies affect the distribution of power in society. Lies add to the power of the liar and reduce the power of those who have been deceived by altering their choices. Lies may misinform us by eliminating some of our objectives or making certain objectives seem unattainable or no longer desirable. Lies may also eliminate necessary alternatives or lead us to believe that there are more alternatives than there really are" (Brennen, 2017: 180). Ultimately, lies may also mislead evaluators during their work.

DOI: 10.4324/9781032719979-5

58   *Steve Jacob and Jeanne Milot-Poulin*

While the truth is considered by most to be an essential condition of democracy, deception is still very much present in today's political sphere. This observation leads us to examine, in this chapter, the moral dimension of truth and lies in politics. The first section explores the relationship between politics and lying, through a history of political lying and the definition of central concepts. The second section focuses on moral theories applied to lying in politics, namely utilitarianism, virtue politics, and deontology. Finally, the third section examines instruments for restoring public trust, through regulation, but also through mechanisms ranging from watchdogging to fact-checking. We conclude this chapter with some reflections on evaluation in the age of deception.

Lies and politics: A perfect match?

According to Machiavelli, politics inevitably requires deception. Accordingly, telling the truth should be seen as only one of the possible means available to rulers to achieve a desired and beneficial result. In his chapter "How should Princes keep their word?", Machiavelli invites rulers not to burden themselves with promises that, if kept, are no longer favorable to them: "A sagacious prince then cannot and should not fulfil his pledges when their observance is contrary to his interest, and when the causes that induced him to pledge his faith no longer exist" (Machiavelli, 2005 [1532], Ch. XVIII). It should be noted that Machiavelli does not consider "political lying" as necessarily contradictory to the interests of the people. His realist view separates politics from ethics and is therefore rejected by those who consider that moral principles should apply to politics such as Kant and Augustine (Mearsheimer, 2011: 10). However, the alternative to the Machiavellian political lie as proposed by Kant, for whom lying is "the greatest violation of man's duty to himself" (quoted in Mearsheimer, 2011: 10–11) and who rejects "political lying" under any circumstances, does not represent the only way to understand the application of morality to politics.

This opposition between philosophers is a testament to the fact that the discussion of lies and truth in politics has a long history. In the following section, we briefly look back at the 20th century to better understand the current landscape.

Political tricks in history

The 20th century witnessed different "trends" of "political lying." During World War I, several governments created "Propaganda Services" wherein the objective was to wage psychological warfare by demoralizing the populations of enemy countries through the dissemination of rumors and false news. Subsequently, political propaganda served the authoritarian regimes of the far left and the far right that emerged in the interwar period. The political discourse in these countries was manufactured to appeal to emotion and arouse passions rather than to elicit reason. We need only think of Nazi and Soviet propaganda, which sought "to manipulate the masses through violent and aggressive rhetoric"

(Schwartzenberg, 1998: 16, our translation). Hitler unabashedly condoned lying by stating the following: "in the big lie there is always a certain force of credibility; because the broad masses of a nation are always more easily corrupted in the deeper strata of their emotional nature than consciously or voluntarily; and thus in the primitive simplicity of their minds they more readily fall victims to the big lie than the small lie" (Hitler, 1925, Ch. X, translated by Murphy). A symbol of totalitarian regimes, propaganda did not end with the death of Goebbels, Hitler, or Stalin. This crude form of "political lying" remains a common communication tool used by contemporary autocratic regimes.

In Western countries, the 1960s–1980s period bore witness to the emergence of a new mode of mass communication based on the subtle balance between sincerity and deception. With political advertising, the objective is no longer to coerce but to charm. Seduction is achieved through political communication techniques inspired by Hollywood movies, relying largely on affectivity rather than logical and rational argumentation. The emergence of political marketing initially developed in the United States made it possible to create brand images that did not conform to reality in order to "sell" a candidate on the electoral market (Schwartzenberg, 1998). Political communication based on advertising and marketing embellishes political lies with illusionary devices, eventually replacing the brutal propaganda employed during the first half of the 20th century. Two criteria mark the distinction between political communication and propaganda: the first is media plurality and the free flow of information and the second is the consideration of public opinion by the speaker or issuer of the communication (Ollivier-Yaniv, 2010).

With the success of "new media," the media revolution of the 1980s introduced the concept of infotainment, a contraction of the words "information" and "entertainment," which designates any form of information that seeks to entertain rather than illuminate the truth surrounding real issues. Here, "political lying" takes the form of omission, an attempt to deliberately divert voters' attention from the main issues. In the 1990s, traditional political demagogy was combined with modern television, resulting in the advent of telepopulism. The proximity between the political and media spheres allowed media owners, such as Silvio Berlusconi in Italy, to disguise reality to serve their political interests (Schwartzenberg, 1998). The strategy pursued is to divert the attention of the voters through decoys and thereby filter and embellish the realities presented to them.

These historical examples demonstrate that there are nuances in the use of deception in politics. Given the diversity of practices, outright lies exist alongside various forms of deception that are not deliberately contrary to the truth. It is, therefore, necessary to clarify the term "political lying." The following section presents definitions of the different types of lies utilized in politics and makes distinctions between "truth," "deception," "lies," "spinning concealment," and "disinformation."

60 *Steve Jacob and Jeanne Milot-Poulin*

I never lie but ...

At first glance, the opposition between truth and lies is not as straightforward as one might assume. "In our complex world, many things can misinform us, but only some of them are intended to deceive us. If I give you inaccurate information but have no intention to mislead you, that is not deception. Deception is a person, news report, or video that intentionally deflects, withholds, or distorts information" (Brennen, 2017: 180). For politicians, the term "lie" has a much greater negative connotation than other forms of deception. A political journalist once reported: "Politicians are willing to concede that they misrepresent facts, that they hide information, that they always present their actions in a favourable light, that they do not want to see the other side of the coin. But to admit that they lie, never! The word 'lie' is reserved for crude behaviour" (Pratte, 1997: 13, our translation).

In light of these nuances in the realm of "political lying," what is considered a lie, and what is considered a form of deception? Lying is a variant of deception, but not all deception is lying. Other forms of deception include concealment and "spinning." "Unlike lying, neither involves making a false statement or telling a story with a false bottom line" (Mearsheimer, 2011: 9).

When observing the different nuances of "political lying," the opposition that emerges between deception and truth-telling is more inclusive than the opposition between truth and lies. Truth-telling refers to a situation in which "an individual does his best to state the facts and tell a story in a straightforward and honest way. [...] A truth-teller makes a serious effort to overcome any biases or selfish interests that he might have and report the relevant facts in an as fair-minded way as he can" (Mearsheimer, 2011: 15). Similarly, deception is a deliberate act. The objective is, however, the opposite of truth-telling. "Deception, in contrast, is where an individual purposely takes steps that are designed to prevent others from knowing the full truth [...] about a particular matter" (Mearsheimer, 2011: 15).

Although not generally considered an outright lie, spinning is also a form of deception. Spinning "can be characterized more as a process than an event," which is partly the reason why, in the spur of the moment, it is more difficult to detect than a lie (Gaber, 2000). The absence of an outright false statement also helps to disguise spinning: "Spinning is when a person telling a story emphasizes certain facts and links them together in ways that play to his advantage, while, at the same time, downplaying or ignoring inconvenient facts" (Mearsheimer, 2011: 16). Especially in a political context, spinning represents "the exploitation by governments of their dominant position as news providers for partisan purposes" (Garland, 2017: 172). For Gaber (2000), political parties also participate in spinning by employing "spin doctors," who present themselves as communication and political marketing consultants.

Concealment can be defined as deception by omission: "withholding information that might undermine or weaken one's position. [...] The individual simply remains silent about the evidence, because he wants to hide it from others" (Mearsheimer, 2011: 17). While most people consider lying to be a deplorable behavior, the gravity of spinning and concealment is perceived as lesser, even though they are equally deceptive behaviors.

In short, when a politician spins or conceals, he or she is not necessarily lying but is not being completely honest either. A lie is told when someone "makes a statement that he knows to be false in the hope that others will think it is true. A lie is a positive action designed to deceive the target audience" (Mearsheimer, 2011: 16). A lie can, moreover, consist of the invention of false information, but also the purposeful denial of facts. A distinction can be made between strategic lies, which are told by political leaders to help the State survive in the tempestuous game of interstate relations, and selfish lies, which have nothing to do with the national interest, but rather serve to protect the personal interests of leaders and their relatives (Mearsheimer, 2011). There are also what are known as "white lies" about unimportant matters with minimal consequences. While these are very much present, even necessary, in interpersonal relationships, their existence is contested in the political arena. In a democracy, where politicians are accountable to the electorate, white lies that have no harmful consequences are similar in effect to strategic lies that aim to uphold the common good. Lies remain one of the ways of attempting deception that doesn't necessarily succeed because they are not always believed by the audience. Lying is an intention, while deceiving implies success in making people believe false information (Faulkner, 2013).

The spread of false information is also amplified by the phenomenon of misinformation that has taken shape with the rise of social media in recent years. "Fake news" is "false, often sensational, information disseminated under the guise of news reporting" (Ha et al., 2021: 291). When fake news is massively relayed on social media, it is referred to as misinformation. Misinformation is defined as "false information that is spread, regardless of whether there is intent to mislead" (Ha et al., 2021: 291). The Cambridge Analytica and Facebook scandal in March 2018 drew worldwide attention to the political issues that arise when the micro-targeting of users is combined with the spread of fake news, thereby creating a situation of epistemic chaos (Zuboff, 2021). In the past, large social networks have been reluctant to make changes in their policies to minimize this kind of epistemic chaos. In September 2019, for example, Facebook stated that political advertising would not be subject to fact-checking (Zuboff, 2021). We will return to the issue of fact-checking later in this chapter.

In the political realm, we recognize that several practices range along the continuum between truth and falsehood. In the next section, we will draw on moral theories to better understand the perspectives that value truth and those that justify the use of lies in politics.

62 *Steve Jacob and Jeanne Milot-Poulin*

Moral theories on lying in politics

In his book, *La politique mensonge [Lying Politics]*, the French jurist Roger-Gérard Schwartzenberg distinguishes two conceptions of politics:

> [The first conception of politics] is confused with ethics; it is the application of morality to the conduct of societies. For others, the more or less conscious followers of Machiavelli, politics is a game of cunning and trickery, an exercise in pretense and posturing. The first tradition, also known as "truthful politics," is based on the sincerity of speech and respect for the citizen. Probity, loyalty, rigor. In this tradition, democracy is, first and foremost, a moral code. There can be no politics without ethics. Seneca or Montesquieu are not far from this line of thinking. The second conception, known as "lying politics," is its exact antithesis. Here, power is taken and exercised through deception and deceit. In other words, the complete opposite of common morality. In order to win and to govern, it is no longer a matter of convincing through the frankness of one's words and the rectitude of one's arguments, but of abuse. The ability to lure. Much as if public life were to become a parade of seduction or a business of illusions. This second vision prevails today. Within this system, politics transforms into a game of artifice. Sometimes it is an exercise in impostorism. Words, images, and devices: everything seems to combine to better deceive the public.
>
> (1998: 8, our translation)

Following the contradicting visions of politics proposed by Schwartzenberg, one moral and the other amoral, it seems that "political lying" resides exclusively in the camp of lying politics. Several authors interested in the issue of "political lying" support Schwartzenberg in stating that Machiavelli's theory, as set out in his famous book *The Prince*, is the starting point for this particular conception of politics. (Pasquerella and Killilea, 2005; Young-Bruehl and Kohn, 2007). In short, Machiavelli argues that leaders who seek to accomplish anything must contend with so many forces aligned against change that they cannot afford to follow the ethical rules that apply in the private sphere.

Beyond the political-truth/political-lie dichotomy, other moral theories allow us to consider the issue of "political lying" differently: utilitarianism, virtue ethics, and deontology. These three theories will be presented in the following sections and shall be sequenced in such a way as to present the theory that is most tolerant of "political lying" to the one that is most averse.

Utilitarianism

Utilitarianism stems from the writings of English philosopher, Jeremy Bentham. This theory proposes to solve moral dilemmas by relying on two principles: impartiality, which stipulates that no individual is intrinsically more valuable than another, and the maximization of well-being, which also implies the minimization of suffering. When a moral dilemma arises, one must make a "utilitarian" calculation to determine the consequences arising from various possible outcomes and evaluate their impact on the "level" of the well-being of all the individuals involved, whether closely or remotely. The action whose consequences generate the greatest well-being must therefore be chosen and considered as the most moral. As such, utilitarian theory is an undeniably consequentialist theory, as it is only interested in the effects, or repercussions, of an action. Since it is the consequences of an action that determine whether said action is moral, an act cannot be moral "in itself." Transposed to the issue of lying in politics, the utilitarian theory proposes to anticipate the consequences of lying and the consequences of telling the truth. The option whose consequences would lead to the maximum well-being, or the least suffering, for the population as a whole must be preferred. If by resorting to lying, a politician can generate more well-being than if that same politician chose to reveal the truth, then it becomes moral to lie. By lying to the American people about the attack on the USS *Greer* destroyer by the German Navy in August 1941, President Franklin Roosevelt brought the United States closer to direct participation in World War II (Mearsheimer, 2011: 12–13). Considering that the overall effects of the United States' participation in the war were more positive than negative, Roosevelt's lie could be justified by a utilitarian calculation. There is, however, an important limitation to the utilitarian theory. Performing the utilitarian calculus requires the ability to accurately predict the effects of any action. Given the complexities of modern politics, it seems illusory to think that a politician possesses all the necessary information to make an informed prediction about the consequences of a lie. Here, we can think of the effects of discrediting the political class, which is extremely difficult to evaluate. Moreover, the consequentialist perspective does not adequately address the tension between short-term gains and long-term effects. In some situations, the benefits of lying may be greater in the short run than in the long run, further complicating the utilitarian calculus. One can also question the rationality of rulers in a utilitarian calculus—which calls for perfect rationality—as well as the legitimacy of a single individual's conception of what well-being is. In short, while the utilitarian theory may present certain advantages, the extent to which the theory is "practically" applicable to human beings in situations as complex as the conduct of societies raises questions. This leads us to the second moral theory: virtue ethics.

Virtue ethics

Rather than behaving according to likely consequences, virtue ethics proposes to behave as a "virtuous person" would when faced with a moral dilemma. A person must model oneself on people who are distinguished by desirable character traits, such as sincerity, benevolence, or, courage. The challenge is then to define which virtuous people should be used as models. It may seem here that in the absence of a consensus on the model of virtue, this theory remains indeterminate and therefore difficult to apply impartially. Virtue ethics, however, offers an answer to this objection. There is no single "right" moral answer to moral dilemmas, which may indeed be confusing, but does not necessarily prevent the application of virtue ethics to concrete problems. The relative indeterminacy of virtue theory can also be seen as its strength since it accepts the possibility that two different answers to an ethical question do not contradict the virtuous character of others. As opposed to utilitarianism, the theory of virtue ethics is far less reliant on the implementation of a rational thought process. It assumes that a person can behave morally, only by imitating examples of morality and does not require this individual to understand the reasons that guide his or her actions. Applied to the issue of "political lying," this moral theory suggests that a politician should act as a person with virtuous traits would act. One can therefore assume that "political lying" would be very rarely encouraged because virtuous people are typically associated with traits such as honesty and good faith. It is conceivable, however, that a virtuous person might lie in extreme situations, for example when human lives are at stake. Consequently, "political lying" remains acceptable in particular situations. It is also possible to imagine situations wherein the decision to lie or to tell the truth would be two potentially virtuous reactions, depending on the model that guides the behavior. The fact remains that the absence of a clear definition of what makes a person "virtuous" constitutes a major limitation of virtue ethics. The last moral theory, deontology, on the other hand, makes it possible to clearly identify virtuous people.

Deontology

The philosopher Immanuel Kant is the leading exponent of deontological moral theory. The central thesis of deontologism is that acting morally means respecting established norms or duties such as "Thou shalt not kill." To determine these norms, Kant proposes a categorical imperative: "Act only according to that maxim whereby you can, at the same time, will that it should become a universal law" (Kant, 1785 quoted in Korsgaard, 1985: 1) The principle of an act must therefore be universalizable for the action in question to be moral and therefore represent a duty. When an individual undertakes an action whose maxim he does not believe should become a universal law, he is acting immorally. Here, well-being and happiness are completely dissociated. The morality of an action depends on its intention, or motivation, rather than its result. If the intention is moral, the action is moral, regardless of its consequences. On the matter of lying, one must only concede that lying should not be made into a universal law to recognize that individuals must not lie under any circumstances. Consequently, deontology formally prohibits all lies. This moral theory presents the advantage of providing an explicit guide to what constitutes a moral action. It is an action that is aligned with norms and duties that are universalizable. Since lying is not a universalizable principle, it is our duty not to lie. Deontology, however, poses an important limitation. In a situation where lying could prevent a great misfortune, lying remains immoral. The benefits that may arise from the lie itself are not even considered.

To conclude this section, Table 4.1 summarizes the main concepts presented in this chapter, in order to distinguish the (sometimes subtle) nuances between the different definitions.

Table 4.1 Many shades of truth or lie

Truth	Truth-telling refers to a situation in which "an individual does his best to state the facts and tell a story in a straightforward and honest way. […] A truth-teller makes a serious effort to overcome any biases or selfish interests that he might have and report the relevant facts in an as fair-minded way as he can" (Mearsheimer, 2011: 15).
Lies	A lie is told when someone "makes a statement that he knows to be false in the hope that others will think it is true. A lie is a positive action designed to deceive the target audience" (Mearsheimer, 2011: 16). A lie can, moreover, consist of the invention of false information, but also the purposeful denial of facts.
Deception	Deception is "where an individual purposely takes steps that are designed to prevent others from knowing the full truth […] about a particular matter" (Mearsheimer, 2011: 15). Lying is a variant of deception, but not all deception is lying. Other forms of deception include concealment and "spinning." "Unlike lying, neither involves making a false statement or telling a story with a false bottom line" (Mearsheimer, 2011: 9).
Spinning	"Spinning is when a person telling a story emphasizes certain facts and links them together in ways that play to his advantage, while, at the same time, downplaying or ignoring inconvenient facts" (Mearsheimer, 2011: 16). Spinning "can be characterized more as a process than an event" (Gaber, 2000).
Concealment	Concealment can be defined as deception by omission: "withholding information that might undermine or weaken one's position. […] The individual simply remains silent about the evidence, because he wants to hide it from others" (Mearsheimer, 2011: 17).
Fake news	"Fake news" is "false, often sensational, information disseminated under the guise of news reporting" (Ha et al., 2021: 291).
Misinformation	Misinformation is defined as "false information that is spread, regardless of whether there is intent to mislead" (Ha et al., 2021: 291). When fake news is massively relayed on social media, it is referred to as misinformation.

Instruments to restore public trust

In this section, we will describe different mechanisms aimed at restoring truth and limiting the growing phenomenon of "political lying".

For several decades, the erosion of citizens' trust in their leaders has been studied in Western societies. The general trend observed involves a decline in trust in governments. In the United States, trust in government institutions fell drastically in the 1960s and 1970s and fluctuated in the following decades, reaching an all-time low during Donald Trump's presidency (Pew Res. Cent., 2017). This shift in citizens' trust in government over the past 50 years is not specific to the United States. The majority of advanced industrial societies exhibit a loss of trust in their institutions, including Australia, the United Kingdom, and even the Nordic countries of Finland and Norway (Citrin and Stoker, 2018). Indeed, in the 21st century, new manifestations of distrust, including a rise in populism in both Europe and the United States, have emerged and have challenged the foundations of liberal democracy. At the root of populism, at least on the political right, are feelings of economic and cultural loss, with established and distant authorities perceived as the ones responsible for said loss, suggesting that "the foci of distrust should be broadened to include popular feelings about seemingly established institutional arrangements" (Citrin and Stoker, 2018: 63). Thus, the view that citizens' declining trust in their leaders is solely attributed to political lies and deception must be nuanced. Since political trust plays a crucial role in maintaining a stable regime (Zmerli and Hooghe, 2011), it remains important for democracies to put mechanisms in place to restore trust.

Beyond trust, the use of lies in politics has repercussions on democratic principles. As the objective of democracy is to let all individuals decide on their collective destiny, through voting, for instance, citizens must have access to truthful information in order to make informed choices. The presence of lies and deception in an electoral campaign prevents voters from truly deciding their own future (Schwartzenberg, 1998). When citizens no longer possess the information they need to make decisions, their power to choose how and by whom the collective is governed is usurped (Pratte, 1997). As Demosthenes, one of the great orators of ancient Greece, observed "a man can do you no greater injustice than tell lies. For in a political system based on speeches, how can it be safely administered if the speeches are not true?" (quoted in Spicer, 2020: 1491). On the other hand, when elected officials or governments resort to lies, they "extract from the people a share of power that would not have been given up voluntarily" (Pratte, 1997: 26, our translation). In short, a democracy cannot function if the people are kept in the dark and are not entitled to the truth. Lying in politics is harmful to democracy because it constitutes a breach of trust and a breach of the social contract (Pratte, 1997). In order to restrain the negative effects of lying in politics, recent initiatives have been implemented by elected officials, the media, researchers, and citizens' organizations.

Regulation

Increased transparency has often been presented as a solution to overturn the loss of trust citizens feel toward their institutions and representatives (Bovens, 2012). However, according to a study on the effects and impacts of transparency over the past 25 years, it was found that while transparency is effective in achieving certain outcomes, such as increasing participation, improving financial management, and reducing corruption, transparency is reportedly less effective in generating trust in governments and improving their legitimacy (Cucciniello et al., 2017). Regardless, transparency is still recognized in modern societies as an essential dimension of rationality, progress, and good governance. With this idea in mind, many countries have put in place several mechanisms to ensure greater transparency in the functioning of public administrations. In the past few decades, this shift toward transparency was emblematized through the Access to Public Information Act. In the United States, the Freedom of Information Act (FOIA), which came into force in 1967, allows easier access to government documents by requiring federal agencies to hand over their documents to anyone who requests them (Feinberg, 1986). In France, an independent administrative authority, the Commission d'accès aux documents administratifs (CADA), has been responsible for facilitating and monitoring private access to administrative documents since 1978 (Leclerc, 2011). By 2006, nearly 70 countries had adopted freedom of information laws to facilitate access to documents held by public bodies, while another 50 had made progress in the same direction (Banisar, 2006: 6). Article 19 of the Universal Declaration of Human Rights and the International Covenant on Civil and Political Rights states that everyone has the right "to free expression and to seek and impart information" and it is increasingly recognized that this right includes freedom of information (Banisar, 2006: 9). These access to information laws aim to provide citizens with information about government activities and policies to bolster their participation in the democratic process. The New Zealand Commission that led to the passage of the Official Information Act 1982 found that: "greater freedom of information could not be expected to end all differences of opinion within the community or to resolve major political issues. If applied systematically, however, with due regard for the balance between divergent issues [the changes] should hold narrow differences of opinion, increase the effectiveness of policies adopted and strengthen public confidence in the system" (Banisar, 2006: 7).

Another turning point came around the year 2000 with the adoption of various codes of ethics for elected officials, the contents of which required them to publicly declare their income, the gifts they received, or the lobbyists they met (Jacob and Montigny, 2022). For example, in most Western parliaments today, elected officials and their family members are required to register their financial interests with MPs in order to promote transparency and prevent conflicts of interest (Bovend'Eert, 2020). These codes emphasize the importance of values

68   *Steve Jacob and Jeanne Milot-Poulin*

such as integrity in the behavior of elected officials. Through the analysis of 14 national codes of conduct, researchers found that the most common public values were public interest, regime dignity, transparency, neutrality, impartiality, effectiveness, accountability, and legality (Beck Jørgensen and Sørensen, 2012). While misconduct by elected officials can seriously damage the reputation and authority of a parliament's democratic institutions, the codes of conduct can be effective if compliance is properly monitored (Bovend'Eert, 2020). Because "the existence of a code of conduct promotes awareness among MPs and citizens concerning the duties of MPs, gives a perception of what unethical behaviour entails, and gives insight into what is appropriate and what is not" (Bovend'Eert, 2020: 319–320), it can be argued that a code of ethics should become a standard rule for parliaments.

More recently, specific measures to counter misinformation have been set in motion by governments. In Canada, the Elections Act (2018) prohibits the use of false or misleading statements about an electoral candidate's personal attributes during the election period with the intent of affecting the results of the election. The impersonation of politicians, other than for parody or satirical purposes, or false statements regarding a candidate's withdrawal from the election are also prohibited. While these types of statements are undoubtedly protected speech under the Canadian Charter of Rights and Freedoms (the Canadian equivalent of the First Amendment), "Canada considers preserving the election process from disinformation as a sufficiently pressing and substantial goal that under a proportionality test, the benefits of such limits to freedom of expression outweigh its drawbacks in the context of a free and democratic society" (Gaumond, 2020). It should be noted, however, that no one has been charged under the Elections Act thus far. A Premier candidate in the 2019 election, Andrew Scheer (Conservative Party of Canada), actually lied about his professional qualifications by claiming to have been a licensed insurance broker before entering public life. The media's revelation of this potentially sanctionable conduct under the Elections Act a month before the election did not result in any legal consequences.

From watchdogging to fact-checking

The media have traditionally acted as a watchdog, making it "possible to confront the official truth with the actual truth" (Schwartzenberg, 1998: 32, our translation). The Watergate scandal, which led to the resignation of US President Richard Nixon in 1974 to avoid impeachment, is presented as one of the best-known episodes of "watchdogging" (Francke, 1995). The revelations, published by Bob Woodward and Carl Bernstein of the *Washington Post*, regarding the connections between the 1972 burglary of the Democratic Party offices and the Presidency, as well as the irregular financing of Richard Nixon's campaign were at the heart of this political scandal. This type of investigative journalism, the exposure of wrongdoing, injustice, and abuse of power, perfectly illustrates the "traditional watchdog role of the press and the emergence of the Fourth Estate function, where the press served as a check on the three branches of government. The press, by informing the public about the government, keeps the government accountable for its actions or inactions and plays an important role in the democratic system" (Reid and Alexander, 2005).

The media's tendency to follow government consensus, however, reveals a strong media bias in favor of the official line (White, 2005). In the wake of the US-led "War on Terror," itself a response to the terrorist attacks of September 11, 2001, the failure of the US news channels to oppose the "spin" and dishonesty of the White House information machine has challenged the media's watchdog function. The world's most constitutionally free media system failed to challenge the falsehood that Saddam Hussein possessed weapons of mass destruction and that his regime was linked to al Qaeda, prompting a reassessment of the media's ability to move beyond government consensus to expose the truth (White, 2005).

Today, the media have lost their monopoly on fact-checking, and new instruments for establishing the truth have gained in popularity in the 21st century. To conclude this section, we will present two of these tools, the campaign pledge evaluation tool (CPET) and fact-checking platforms. Both initiatives are potential solutions to curb the negative impacts of lying in politics.

A campaign pledge evaluation tool (CPET) tracks the fulfillment, or breakage, of electoral promises made by politicians. They are "platforms that allow for the systematic tracking, assessment, and communication of political pledge fulfillment" (Tremblay-Antoine et al., 2020: 306). The Obameter, launched in 2009, is considered to be the very first CPET. The number of CPETs available on the internet has steadily increased over time. A recent study identified at least 26 unique CPETs worldwide (Tremblay-Antoine et al., 2020). Non-profit organizations, media organizations, and academics are the most common developers of CPETs.

CPETs operate according to a common framework. They consist largely of websites that list and make freely available all the promises made by the party in power during the election campaign. The tracking of promises is conducted according to a classification system that divides the promises into different categories: broken, partially kept, kept, in progress, or not yet rated (Polimeter, 2021).

CPETs are based on the premise that the fulfillment of electoral promises by elected officials is a central element of representative democracy. Therefore, it is important that promises made during the election campaign be consistent with policies implemented after the election. CPETs are therefore opportunities for voters to learn more about the policy positions of parties and candidates, as well as government performance, and to develop their understanding of key social issues, government priorities, and policy actions. Although the effects of CPETs on citizens' attitudes and knowledge have yet to be evaluated, promise trackers could potentially affect citizen trust and government accountability (Tremblay-Antoine et al., 2020). In an effort to restore truth, CPETs can be "used and promoted as tools to reinforce transparency and accountability between elections" (Tremblay-Antoine et al., 2020: 371).

Gaining in popularity since the early 2000s, fact-checking is a technique used to verify the veracity of statements presented by politicians. Changes in media regulation, the professionalization of election campaigns, and evolving media technologies have hampered the ability, or even the motivation, of traditional journalists to fact-check, creating a growing void in the mainstream media landscape (Poulsen and Young, 2018). Digital platforms that assess the accuracy of elected officials' statements, such as Politifact and FactCheck in the United States, are examples of fact-checking initiatives that have filled this void. Fact-checking is defined as "the practice of systematically publishing assessments of the validity of claims made by public officials and institutions with an explicit attempt to identify whether a claim is factual" (Walter et al., 2020). These new actors among the potential antidotes to misinformation are described as "nonpartisan, nonprofit consumer advocate[s] for voters that aim[s] to reduce the level of deception and confusion in U.S. politics" (FactCheck, 2024). Fact-checking platforms can be distinguished from other organizations by their exclusive focus on factual statements made by key political actors in debates, speeches, interviews, and press releases, limiting topics to claims that can be definitively proven or disproven (Amazeen, 2016). While a significant portion of the population appears to be interested in fact-checking, research shows that individuals are, however, more interested in seeing views that differ from their own be corrected than having their personal views corrected, thereby exposing the risk of cognitive dissonance (Poulsen and Young, 2018).

Although recent research provides evidence that fact-checking's corrective messages can be effective in promoting accurate beliefs after exposure to false information (Flynn et al., 2017; Wood and Porter, 2019), the academic literature remains divided on the effectiveness of fact-checking mechanisms, even despite the exceptional rise of fact-checking (Weeks and Gil de Zúñiga, 2019; Walter et al., 2020). The overall acceptance of the movement, however, does not dissipate political divides, and those least likely to trust fact-checking mechanisms may be the most vulnerable to misinformation that targets those divides, thereby leading to a spiral of cynicism (Lyons et al., 2020). Although fact-checking is an activity that employs a form of scientific objectivity, fact-checking platforms are perceived by the public as partisan actors in a divided media system (Robertson et al., 2020). Moreover, while people use political personalities as a heuristic device to guide the assessment of what is true or false, they do not necessarily insist on veracity as a prerequisite for supporting political candidates (Swire et al., 2017). Similarly, the ability to correct political misinformation through fact-checking is significantly attenuated by participants' pre-existing beliefs, ideology, and knowledge (Walter et al., 2020).

While some argue that fact-checking has a significantly positive overall influence on political beliefs, the effects of fact-checking gradually weaken when using "truth scales," that is refuting only parts of a claim, and verifying campaign-related statements. There are also potential "backlash" effects from the use of fact-checking., for when people are told they are wrong, their trust in the media decreases (Ha et al., 2021). Furthermore, while fact-checking improve voters' factual knowledge, it does not affect policy conclusions or candidate support. In fact, the salience mechanism could explain the ineffectiveness of fact-checking (Barrera et al., 2020). Moreover, it is very difficult to provide objective information about the honesty of candidates, as suggested by the surprisingly low rate of agreement among different fact-checkers when evaluating the same statements (Lim, 2018). Subtle forms of carefully crafted deceptive statements are indeed more complicated to classify, as opposed to blatant falsehoods or obvious truths.

To address these difficulties in correcting political misperceptions, Weeks and Gil de Zúñiga (2019) propose thinking differently about fact-checking strategies. For messages correcting false, but highly persuasive, information to be effective, they must equally be influential and persuasive. However, the notion of influence within corrective messages is at odds with the ethics of the journalists who produce these messages, who often reject the idea that their messages should be influential. But this passivity may not be enough to correct erroneous beliefs, and a potential solution might be to think of corrective messages as a form of persuasion or social influence.

Evaluation in the age of deception

Our evaluation of the moral dimension of truth and lies in politics and our overview of the existing mechanisms that help limit lies in politics lead us to view this phenomenon as not entirely fatalistic. Although the hope of completely eliminating lies from political life remains utopian, it is still possible to unmask the lies of politicians. Neither science nor philosophy holds the absolute truth, those who doubt the existence of truth should remember that "science and philosophy teach us something about the truth: the truth responds to our need to understand reality objectively and our desire to access universal knowledge that is shareable" (Rizzerio, 2021: our translation).

Evaluators have a role to play in the efforts toward restoring confidence. In this chapter, we have seen that politics is geared more toward results than the truth. However, evaluation is about both results AND truth.

Speaking truth to power has been a challenge for evaluators for many decades. This challenge is exacerbated by the rise of populism and fake news which further blur the boundary between truth and lies. This problem is not limited to the political sphere but has permeated society as a whole. For instance, permissive moral attitudes toward the acceptability of cheating in the

72   Steve Jacob and Jeanne Milot-Poulin

workplace have increased (Gangadharan et al., 2020; Leavitt and Sluss, 2015). In this context, evaluators may be confronted with more pressure to misrepresent findings. The dissemination and practice of ethical standards by all key stakeholders involved in the evaluation process are necessary to "engage a meaningful and frank discussion of misrepresentation pressure. [...] Although this conversation might be a difficult one, most evaluators would probably agree that it is better to have a moderately challenging interaction early in the relationship than a much more awkward and painful one later on" (Morris and Clark, 2012: 67).

The production of credible evaluative evidence is also more difficult to attain within a context wherein information is less reliable. The work of evaluators is often dependent on the quality of the information provided by the various stakeholders involved in the evaluation process. These stakeholders include politicians, civil servants, program managers, and beneficiaries. Each of these actors may be tempted to steer the evaluation results in a direction that is more beneficial to them. This strategic use of evaluation is a potent reminder that evaluation is not only a scientific exercise but a political endeavor as well (Eliadis et al., 2011; Varone et al., 2023). Consequently, the conclusions and recommendations will be flawed if they are based on false assumptions, use inaccurate information, or apply faulty research methods. To address this risk, it is important to develop critical thinking skills when conducting evaluations and to ask whether each piece of information reflects reality. To assess the credibility of a source, evaluators can ask themselves the same question as fact-checkers: "Is this C.R.A.P.?".[2]

Although there is no absolute truth, it is feasible to strive for truth, a truth that is shared by all members of society. In order to do this, it is necessary to identify and correct the lies that are present in political life.

Notes

1 Alternative facts are statements that directly or indirectly contradict facts.
2 The CRAP test is a list of questions for assessing information and evaluating sources on five dimensions: Currency (Is it current enough?), Reliability (Can we trust the source/author?), Authority (Who is the author of the work, and what are his/her credentials?) and Purpose (What is the purpose of this source?).

References

Amazeen, M. A. (2016). Checking the Fact-Checkers in 2008: Predicting Political Ad Scrutiny and Assessing Consistency. *Journal of Political Marketing*, *15*(4), 433–464. https://doi.org/10.1080/15377857.2014.959691

Banisar, D. (2006). *Freedom of Information Around the World 2006: A Global Survey of Access to Government Information Laws* (SSRN Scholarly Paper ID 1707336). Social Science Research Network. https://doi.org/10.2139/ssrn.1707336

Lies and politics 73

Barrera, O., Guriev, S., Henry, E., & Zhuravskaya, E. (2020). Facts, Alternative Facts, and Fact Checking in Times of Post-Truth Politics. *Journal of Public Economics, 182*, 104123. https://doi.org/10.1016/j.jpubeco.2019.104123

Biden, J. R. (2021, January 20). *Inaugural Address*. https://www.whitehouse.gov/briefing-room/speeches-remarks/2021/01/20/inaugural-address-by-president-joseph-r-biden-jr/

Bovend'Eert, P. (2020). Public Office and Public Trust: Standards of Conduct in Parliament: A Comparative Analysis of Rules of Conduct in Three Parliaments. *Parliamentary Affairs, 73*(2), 296–322. https://doi.org/10.1093/pa/gsy048

Bovens, M. (2012). Two Concepts of Accountability: Accountability as a Virtue and as a Mechanism. In *Accountability and European Governance* (pp. 28–49). Routledge. https://doi.org/10.4324/9781315879390-7

Brennen. (2017). Making Sense of Lies, Deceptive Propaganda, and Fake News. *Journal of Media Ethics, 32*(3), 179–181.

Citrin, J., & Stoker, L. (2018). Political Trust in a Cynical Age. *Annual Review of Political Science, 21*(1), 49–70. https://doi.org/10.1146/annurev-polisci-050316-092550

Cucciniello, M., Porumbescu, G. A., & Grimmelikhuijsen, S. (2017). 25 Years of Transparency Research: Evidence and Future Directions. *Public Administration Review, 77*(1), 32–44. https://doi.org/10.1111/puar.12685

Eliadis, P., Furubo, J.-E., & Jacob, S. (Eds.). (2011). *Evaluation: Seeking Truth or Power?*. Transaction Publishers.

FactCheck. (2024). *FactCheck*. The Annenberg Public Policy Center of the University of Pennsylvania. https://www.factcheck.org/

Faulkner, P. (2013). Lying and Deceit. In *International Encyclopedia of Ethics*. American Cancer Society. https://doi.org/10.1002/9781444367072.wbiee482

Feinberg, L. E. (1986). Managing the Freedom of Information Act and Federal Information Policy. *Public Administration Review, 46*(6), 615–621. https://doi.org/10.2307/976227

Flynn, D. J., Nyhan, B., & Reifler, J. (2017). The Nature and Origins of Misperceptions: Understanding False and Unsupported Beliefs About Politics: Nature and Origins of Misperceptions. *Political Psychology, 38*, 127–150. https://doi.org/10.1111/pops.12394

Francke, W. (1995). The Evolving Watchdog: The Media's Role in Government Ethics. *The ANNALS of the American Academy of Political and Social Science, 537*(1), 109–121. https://doi.org/10.1177/0002716295537000010

Gaber, I. (2000). Lies, Damn Lies... And Political Spin. *British Journalism Review, 11*(1), 60–70. https://doi.org/10.1177/095647480001100111

Gangadharan, L., Grossman, P. L., & Vecci, J. (2020). Antisocial Behavior in the Workplace. In K. F. Zimmermann (Ed.), *Handbook of Labor, Human Resources and Population Economics* (pp. 1–26). Springer.

Garland, R. (2017). Between Mediatisation and Politicization: The Changing Role and Position of Whitehall Press Officers in the Age of Political Spin. *Public Relations Inquiry,6*(2), 171–189. https://doi.org/10.1177/2046147X17695365

Gaumond, E. (2020, décembre 11). Is Canadian Law Better Equipped to Handle Disinformation? *Lawfare*. https://www.lawfareblog.com/canadian-law-better-equipped-handle-disinformation

Ha, L., Andreu Perez, L., & Ray, R. (2021). Mapping Recent Development in Scholarship on Fake News and Misinformation, 2008 to 2017: Disciplinary Contribution, Topics, and Impact. *American Behavioral Scientist, 65*(2), 290–315. https://doi.org/10.1177/0002764219869402

Hartnett, S. J., & Stengrim, L. A. (2004). "The Whole Operation of Deception": Reconstructing President Bush's Rhetoric of Weapons of Mass Destruction. *Cultural Studies Critical Methodologies, 4*(2), 152–197. https://doi.org/10.1177/1532708603262787

Hitler, A. (1925). *Mein Kampf* (J. Murphy Trad, Vol. 1). Eher-Verlag.

Jacob, S., & Montigny, I. (2022). *C'est pas un cadeau. Plongée au cœur de l'éthique parlementaire.* Presses de l'Université Laval.

Jørgensen, T. B., & Sørensen, D.-L. (2012). Codes of Good Governance. *Public Integrity, 15*(1), 71–96. https://doi.org/10.2753/PIN1099-9922150104

Kant, I., & Wood, A. W. (1996). Groundwork of the metaphysics of morals (1785). In M. J. Gregor (Ed.), *Practical Philosophy.* The Cambridge Edition of the Works of Immanuel Kant (pp. 37–108). Cambridge: Cambridge University Press. https://doi.org/10.1017/CBO9780511813306.007

Korsgaard, C. (1985). Kant's Formula of Universal Law. *Pacific Philosophical Quarterly.* https://dash.harvard.edu/handle/1/3201869

Leavitt, K., & Sluss, D. M. (2015). Lying for Who We Are: An Identity-Based Model of Workplace Dishonesty. *The Academy of Management Review, 40*(4), 587–610.

Leclerc, J.-P. (2011). Le rôle de la commission d'accès aux documents administratifs. *Revue française d'administration publique, 137–138*(1), 171–179.

Lim, C. (2018). Checking How Fact-Checkers Check. *Research & Politics, 5*(3). https://doi.org/10.1177/2053168018786848

Lyons, B., Merola, V., Reifler, J., & Stoeckel, F. (2020). How Politics Shape Views Toward Fact-Checking: Evidence from Six European Countries. *The International Journal of Press/Politics, 25.* https://doi.org/10.1177/1940161220921732

Machiavelli, N. (2005). *Prince.* Oxford University Press.

Mearsheimer, J. J. (2011). *Why Leaders Lie: The Truth About Lying in International Politics.* Oxford University Press.

Morris, M., & Clark, B. (2012). You Want Me to Do What? Evaluators and the Pressure to Misrepresent Findings. *American Journal of Evaluation, 34*(1), 57–70.

Ollivier-Yaniv, C. (2010). Discours politiques, propagande, communication, manipulation. *Mots. Les langages du politique, 94,* 31–37. https://doi.org/10.4000/mots.19857

Pasquerella, L., & Killilea, A. G. (2005). The Ethics of Lying in the Public Interest. *Public Integrity, 7*(3), 261–273.

Pew Research Center. (2017). *Public Trust in Government Remains Near Historic Lows as Partisan Attitudes Shift.* Pew Research Center.

Polimeter. (2021). *Polimeter.* Vox Pop Labs.

Poulsen, S., & Young, D. G. (2018). A History of Fact Checking in U.S. Politics and Election Context. In B. G. Southwell, E. A. Thorson, & L. Sheble (Éds.), *Misinformation and Mass Audiences* (pp. 232–248). University of Texas Press.

Pratte, A. (1997). *Le syndrome de Pinocchio.* Les Éditions du Boréal.

Reid, A. S., & Alexander, L. B. (2005). A Test Case for Newsgathering: The Effects of September 11, 2001 on the Changing Watchdog Role of the Press. *Loyola of Los Angeles Entertainment Law Review, 25,* 357.

Rizzerio, L. (2021, février 13). Pourquoi aspirons-nous tant à la « vérité »? *La Libre*. https://www.lalibre.be/debats/opinions/ce-bien-que-la-verite-nous-fait-6026c1bc997 8e2610a8ca460

Robertson, C., Mourao, R., & Thorson, E. (2020). Who Uses Fact-Checking Sites? The Impact of Demographics, Political Antecedents, and Media Use on Fact-Checking Site Awareness, Attitudes, and Behavior. *The International Journal of Press/Politics*, *25*. https://doi.org/10.1177/1940161219898055

Schwartzenberg, R.-G. (1998). *La politique mensonge*. Éditions Odile Jacob.

Spicer, M. (2020). "Who's Been Fooling Who?" Reflections on Truth and Deception in Politics and Their Implications for Public Administration. *Administration & Society*, 1–25. https://doi.org/10.1177/0095399720907800

Swire, B., Berinsky, A. J., Lewandowsky, S., & Ecker, U. K. H. (2017). Processing Political Misinformation: Comprehending the Trump Phenomenon. *Royal Society Open Science*, *4*(3), 160802. https://doi.org/10.1098/rsos.160802

Tremblay-Antoine, C., Côté, G., Dufresne, Y., & Birch, L. (2020). What Do We Know About Campaign Pledge Evaluation Tools? *Journal of Information Technology & Politics*, *17*(3), 304–320. https://doi.org/10.1080/19331681.2020.1761505

Varone, F., Jacob, S., & Bundi, P. (Eds.). (2023). *Handbook of Public Policy Evaluation*. Edward Elgar.

Walter, N., Cohen, J., Holbert, R., & Morag, Y. (2020). Fact-Checking: A Meta-Analysis of What Works and for Whom. *Political Communication*, *37*, 1–26. https://doi.org/10 .1080/10584609.2019.1668894

Weeks, B., & Gil de Zúñiga, H. (2019). What's Next? Six Observations for the Future of Political Misinformation Research. *American Behavioral Scientist*, *65*. https://doi.org /10.1177/0002764219878236

White, A. (2005). Truth, Honesty and Spin. *Democratization*, *12*(5), 651–667. https://doi .org/10.1080/13510340500322017

Wood, T., & Porter, E. (2019). The Elusive Backfire Effect: Mass Attitudes' Steadfast Factual Adherence. *Political Behavior*, *41*. https://doi.org/10.1007/s11109-018 -9443-y

Young-Bruehl, E., & Kohn, J. (2007). Truth, Lies, and Politics: A Conversation. *Social Research: An International Quarterly*, *74*(4), 1045–1070.

Zmerli, S., & Hooghe, M. (2011). *Political Trust: Why Context Matters*. ECPR Press.

Zuboff, S. (2021, janvier 29). The Coup We Are Not Talking About. *The New York Times*. https://www.nytimes.com/2021/01/29/opinion/sunday/facebook-surveillance-society -technology.html?action=click&module=Opinion&pgtype=Homepage

5 Heuristics and biases in the post-truth era—a piece of advice for policy-makers

Jakub Krawiec and Paweł Śliwowski

Introduction

Almost 65 years ago Herbert Simon stated that decision-making is at the core of administrative activities, therefore theories of administrative processes should be derived from the psychology of human choice (Simon, 2013). However, Simon concluded that theoretical and empirical connections between psychological science and policy science are scarce. After 65 years, researchers underline that this diagnosis remains valid, although there is a growing interest in infusing knowledge from psychological sciences into research on public policy, public management, and administration (Olsen, 2015; Tummers, 2020; Grimmelikhuijsen et al., 2017).

More than a decade ago some innovation-oriented administrations (UK, Netherlands, New Zealand, Canada) started to use behavioral sciences toolkit to achieve their goals more effectively. Also the UN, WHO, World Bank, OECD, and the European Commission established their behavioral insights units and promote the use of the psychological and cognitive knowledge in the public sector. Behavioral sciences provide novel and empirically tested knowledge on how different factors, i.e. neurobiology, cognitive mechanisms, motivation and emotions, habits, time, situational context, and social mechanisms influence human decision-making and other behaviors. Although these factors had been previously overlooked in standard economic, legal or policy analyses, there is now a growing body of literature produced by policy scholars who use psychological or behavioral conceptual toolkit to analyze public administration domain or policy work (Jones et al., 2013; Marra, 2021; Olejniczak et al., 2019). The emerging body of literature could be divided into two strands. Firstly, *behavioral public policy* (BPP) focuses on the use of policy instruments designed with the use of behavioral insights and tested with experimental approaches (Straßheim, 2020). In this strand, behaviors and decisions of policy targets, e.g. citizens, firms, etc. are the dominant area of interest. On the other hand, there is an expanding subfield of *behavioral public administration* (BPA), which aim to connect important political-administrative concepts with theories and research agendas from psychology (Tummers, 2020). In this strand, behaviors and decisions of policy actors, e.g. politicians, policy experts, bureaucrats are important

DOI: 10.4324/9781032719979-6

research topic. Some scholars propose to merge concepts from both BPP and BPA and to develop *behavioral governance* discipline (BG), which concerns the cognitive and decision processes through which decision-makers, implementing actors and target populations both shape and react to public policies and to each other (Gofen et al., 2021).

In the following chapter we try to apply this third, integrative approach to demonstrate that the scientific discourse on decision-making in public policy, especially in the times of the Post-Truth, is another important domain, in which policy research could benefit from using the input from psychological science. Psychological science offers explanations on how people acquire and process information, how they build their understanding of what is true and false, how they distinguish between facts and fake-news. It helps understand phenomena like distrust in experts or skepticism toward scientific evidence. Moreover, it demonstrates the role of values, ideologies, worldviews and political orientation in constructing beliefs about and attitudes toward pressing policy challenges (climate change, inequalities, migration, vaccine hesitation) (Hornsey et al., 2016). By doing so, psychological science could be helpful not only in understanding how and why particular decision-makers may fail to make a rational decision, but also in suggesting solutions on how best to counter emotions, social influence, or cognitive constraints which affect our reasoning, i.e. how to use evidence-informed policy tools to create decision-supporting environments (Thaler & Sunstein, 2008; Hertwig & Grüne-Yanoff, 2017).

In the following work we therefore elaborate the taxonomy or catalogue of psychological determinants and try to show what are the main cognitive traps, a decision-maker in the roles of policy-maker and policy-taker can fell in. We believe that awareness of these processes is the first step to counter the detrimental influence of biases, and in fact, reduce to some extent Post-Truth processes. To some extent, we see uncontrolled heuristics and biases as potential antecedents of Post-Truth (Flyvbjerg et al., 2019). Moreover, we hope that this chapter will help to develop more coherent toolbox for evaluators, as the next pages provide concise knowledge about cognitive constrains a decision-maker may be exposed to. The knowledge gathered here from behavioral sciences can support evaluation practice, especially in the wake of two out of three main challenges it faces nowadays (Olejniczak et al., 2020): explaining why solutions work (or not) and transferring research findings into policy actions. By being aware of existing psychological processes, evaluators can gain a much deeper understanding of the processes involved and offer recommendations that may, in the future, prevent the disastrous effects of heuristics and cognitive errors on the functioning of decision-makers. In our view, it applies both to policy-makers and policy-addressees. As it is suggested by Kahneman (2011), the psychological mechanisms described below are universal to all people, whether regulators or ordinary citizens. What differs, however, is the potential scale of problems

78 Jakub Krawiec and Paweł Śliwowski

that can be caused if, for example, a policy-maker is affected by confirmation bias and, in constructing public policy, interprets the results of new research to be as consistent as possible with his a priori thesis (Thaler & Sunstein, 2008). Then, his decisions may affect not only himself or his close family members, but also a large part of society.

Additionally, this chapter attempts to answer the second question posed by the editors of this book: "What is the relationship between expertise and decision-making in today's political circumstances?" In our view, this relationship may be moderated precisely by heuristics and biases. Although research shows that people who have more domain knowledge, i.e., are experts in a given field, may be slightly more resistant to cognitive biases (Kahneman, 2011), we believe that awareness of the described psychological processes is crucial to tame them. The more we are aware of the psychological processes taking place, the less negative impact they will have on the relationship between decision-makers' experience and their decisions.

The remainder of this chapter is structured as follows. The "Psychological determinants of policy work" section presents the analysis of how bounded rationality influence policymakers and policy targets. Then, presents selected psychological determinants of decision-making in the public policy domain. The next section "Debiasing and tackling down cognitive biases" discusses about debiasing strategies and good practices alleviating the effects of biases and heuristics. The chapter closes with conclusions summarizing enlisted arguments and theses.

Psychological determinants of policy work

Reflections on the decision-making processes of policymakers cannot be done without recalling the concept of bounded rationality. It claims that policymakers and ordinary citizens possess cognitive architecture limiting their rational reasoning and operations (Simon, 1972). Notably, in this discussion, the difference between policymakers and citizens is that the decisions made by the former may have a considerable impact on the latter. According to researchers, it may occur at least in two different ways: policymakers may implement a policy which will directly change the state of citizens' possession, or create a decision-making situation in which citizens ought to choose which option they prefer (Dudley & Xie, 2020b). The second way is of particular interest in the behavioral economics domain, which as a crossroad between psychology and economics studies, studies how people make decisions. The famous duo of the leading behavioral economists, Richard Thaler and Cass Sunstein, captured the world's attention when, in their seminal book, *Nudge: Improving Decisions about Health, Wealth, and Happiness*, they pointed out that behavioral science has enormous potential for the use in social policy. The central concept defining the core of their book—nudging—refers to "any aspect of the choice situation architecture that

Heuristics and biases in the post-truth era   79

predictably changes behavior, without prohibiting any options, or significantly changing economic benefits" (Thaler & Sunstein, 2008). Describing nudging and other behavioral tools, they highlighted how nudging could effectively and inexpensively increase human well-being, health, and finances on a large scale. As representatives of the Heuristics & Biases school, like Kahneman and Tversky, they appealed directly to the cognitive biases, or systematic errors in thinking occurring during processing information, that we should consider when analyzing how people make decisions (Thaler & Sunstein, 2008).

Furthermore, Thaler & Sunstein were the ones who popularized the "choice architecture" term, which refers to the design of a situation where an individual is deciding between at least two different alternatives (Thaler & Sunstein, 2008). For the last decade, the interest in nudging and behavioral interventions has grown enormously, which was a starting point for establishing agencies implementing these tools in public policy, such as Behavioral Insights Team in the UK or Behavioural Economics Team the Australian Government. Most of these efforts used behavioral insights to harness the bounded rationality to create more effective policies such as tax payments (Hallsworth et al., 2017) or enrollment into pension plans (Thaler & Benartzi, 2004).

One of the most recent trends stemming from these research programs is how bounded rationality concepts apply to supporting decision-makers such as politicians, regulators, or government employees. Most of these attempts, try to utilize knowledge about cognitive heuristics and biases to avoid systematic errors policymakers may fall in. This means a lot of work is involved in transferring knowledge from the domain of psychology to more practical public policy situations (Dudley & Xie, 2020b). Researchers representing Heuristics & Biases school, have established a long list of cognitive biases, one can fall in. In the literature, there are at least a few attempts to gather possibly complete catalog of systematic errors we should pay attention to (Kaufmann et al., 2010; Stanovich et al., 2008); however, it is mostly psychological literature, which may appear not so useful for policy practitioners. A systematic approach to study heuristics and biases in public policy is still a new trend, especially when it comes to research concerning not the decision-making processes of citizens, but of policy regulators or politicians. As many authors have recognized, the effects of systematic errors impose great risk especially when they can affect choice architects (Dudley & Xie, 2020a; Kuran & Sunstein, 1998; Münscher et al., 2016). So far we can enlist only a few attempts to gather heuristics and biases important in predicting citizens' (Battaglio et al., 2019) or policymakers' decision processes (Battaglio et al., 2019; Dudley & Xie, 2020a, 2020; BIT, 2018). Among them, appear more and less complex approaches to synthesize previous research, adding new dimensions to more effectively differentiate between studied categories. Battaglio et al. (2019), tries to identify latent cognitive causes standing behind particular observable cognitive biases. For example, as a latent cognitive cause underlying anchoring or availability biases, he proposes a latent

80   *Jakub Krawiec and Paweł Śliwowski*

cause called "accessibility" (Battaglio et al., 2019). Although new with reference to classical psychology literature in this subject, the invention of such additional dimension may undoubtedly help to look at the problem from a different perspective, and—hopefully—help to create effective tools such as public policy interventions. Furthermore, the taxonomy provided by Battaglio et al. (2019) is a complex attempt to summarize entire research done within the behavioral public policy area—including both studies concerning how do citizens and policymakers fall into cognitive biases. Therefore, here we propose to start building the toolbox targeting policy makers' decision-making routes by starting with more concise taxonomy which was developed by Dudley and Xie (2020). In this paper, researchers argue that the most widespread heuristics and biases identified so far by researchers studying the decision-making routes undertaken by policymakers are actually five well-grounded in psychology cognitive traps: availability heuristics, myopia, overconfidence, loss aversion, and confirmation bias (Dudley & Xie, 2020). Not only concise and covering diversified grounds, this list largely overlap with the model proposed by Behavioural Insights Team (2018), which focused on eight touchpoints or processes where it is important to support policymakers: framing, confirmation bias, allocation of attention, group reinforcement, illusion of similarity, inter-group opposition, optimism bias, illusion of control. Model proposed by BIT (2018) includes not only cognitive biases mentioned by Dudley and Xie (2020) but also more general influences a system may impose on policy actors. It makes this model much more broader and falls beyond the scope of our review, which aims at cataloging cognitive heuristics and biases, a policymaker may be prone to. Because of that, in order to provide versatile but concise taxonomy of cognitive heuristics and biases frequently identified in the policy makers' contexts, we built upon the five biases mentioned by Dudley and Xie (2020), adding three more: anchoring bias, bandwagon effect (Cantarelli et al., 2020) and salience effect (Tiefenbeck et al., 2016). Both biases appear in the most recent literature and concern slightly different psychological phenomena than the five mentioned by Dudley and Xie (2020), which we outline below in detail. The description of chosen biases and heuristics is provided in Table 5.1. In our view, these eight cognitive constraints together summarize existing literature on the usage of cognitive biases in behavioral public policy and cover various research threads that seem to be continued in future studies and may help support policymakers. In the below sections, we describe eight heuristics and biases regarding the public policy domain.

Availability heuristic

In 1974, Amos Tversky and Daniel Kahneman described the availability heuristic as "a cognitive rule of thumb in which probability of events is judged based on how readily they come to mind" (Tversky & Kahneman, 1973). The accessibility heuristic is based on the idea that if something can be recalled,

Heuristics and biases in the post-truth era 81

Table 5.1 Eight cognitive constraints which may affect the decision-making process of policymakers and policy addressees

Name of cognitive constraint	Description
Availability heuristic	Individuals tend to weight their judgments toward more recent information, causing new opinions to be skewed toward the most recent news (Tversky & Kahneman, 1974)
Anchoring bias	Individuals relies (anchors) on some information and then modifies (adapts to) it to answer a question or make a judgment (Tversky & Kahneman, 1973)
Bandwagon effect	Refers to the phenomenon when individuals often believe certain things or do them only because many other people do (Howard, 2019)
Confirmation bias	A tendency to seek or interpret evidence in a way that supports existing beliefs (Lord et al., 1979)
Loss aversion	People are able to put more effort into avoiding a certain amount of loss than they would put into gaining a reward of similar magnitude (Kahneman, 2011)
Myopia	General tendency to ignore part of the information available to evaluate a situation properly (Cooper & Kovacic, 2012)
Overconfidence	Overconfidence or optimism bias is a person's tendency to overestimate their abilities, the quality of their plans, and the likelihood of future success (Hallsworth et al., 2018)
Salience effect	Individuals' tendency to focus on the prominent and immediate aspects of the situation (Tiefenbeck et al., 2018; Schenk, 2011)

it must be important or more important than alternatives that are not as easily recalled (Schwarz et al., 1991). As a result, following the accessibility heuristic, individuals tend to give more importance to information that they have received recently, leading to a bias toward the most recent news and potentially affecting their opinions. A common question is given as an example that illustrates well the operation of the availability heuristic is what is recorded more in the United States each year: homicides or suicides? Typically, most of us would think that the number of recorded homicides far exceeds the number of suicides. The facts say otherwise: there are far more suicides. The researchers who first asked about this in their study, Lichtenstein, Slovic et al. (1978), mention that this is the influence of the greater availability of homicide-related information than suicide-related information. Mass media, television, radio, or newspapers are much more likely to report homicides that were spectacular. The availability heuristic leads to an increase in the influence exerted on our judgments by easily

82   Jakub Krawiec and Paweł Śliwowski

recalled events. We more readily recall dramatic, specific, vivid, recent, or more frequently discussed initially in the media and then in social groups.

As one might imagine, policymakers, as other individuals maybe, are also susceptible to availability heuristics, especially in relation to agenda setting. In this regard, availability heuristics is one of the most important psychological mechanisms responsible for the strong impact of "focusing events" (Birkland, 1998) on policymaking. One of the most striking recent examples is the discussion about nuclear plant safety after Fukushima disaster. Although available evidence show that nuclear plants are one of the safest energy sources, after the natural disaster in Japan large anti-nuclear protests occurred in many countries, leading to fundamental policy shift in some of them. For example, in Germany, federal government announced that it would close all of its nuclear power plants by 2022 and subsequently eight of the seventeen operating reactors in Germany were permanently shut down following Fukushima. One study found that the nuclear phase-out caused $12 billion in social costs per year, primarily due to increases in mortality due to exposure to pollution from fossil fuels (Jarvis et al., 2019).

Particularly these days, with more and more talk of information bubbles (Pariser, 2011), choice architects can find it particularly easy to cite as the most valid arguments to justify their actions arguments heard from the media or repeatedly repeated information around them (McCaughey & Bruning, 2010). It was particularly evident during the COVID-19 pandemic, when policymakers tended to overreact in response to rapidly changing information about the virus and effective mitigation strategies. In these recent months, availability heuristic was playing important role during decision-making and implementation phases of policymaking.

What is interesting, on the other hand, some research suggests that policy regulators may sometimes seem less prone to "information cascades," which some perceive as a cause of availability heuristic (Kuran & Sunstein, 1998). This finding is explained by the amount of specific knowledge one possesses in a particular domain—the more experienced and knowledgeable a regulator is, the less will be influenced by the most vivid or recent events (Kuran & Sunstein, 1998).

Anchoring bias

Although the anchoring was firstly described by Sherif et al. (1958), the first conceptualization of this process as a cognitive bias was described by Tversky and Kahneman in 1974. It involves estimating starting values and adjusting them to arrive at a final value, whereby the starting point may be suggested in the problem formulation or may result from incomplete calculations (Tversky & Kahneman, 1974). In other words, a person relies (anchors) on some information and then modifies (adapts to) it to answer a question or make a judgment. Depending on the starting point, estimates can take on different levels

Heuristics and biases in the post-truth era 83

related to the initial value (Tversky & Kahneman, 1974). Thus, in the first step, there is a cognitive anchoring of the value to the anchor level, and in the next step, further adjustment measurements take place and away from the preconceived anchor.

As researchers underline, the anchoring bias may be highly pervasive, influencing the judgments of potential shop customers by manipulating promotional offers (setting anchor of the previous price) and even influencing the judgment of court judges (Enough & Mussweiler, 2001). Due to its prevalence, there were already few attempts to study anchoring bias in samples of policymakers (Belle et al., 2017; Pandey & Marlowe, 2014) or public policy employees (Belle et al., 2017). However, due to its mixed outcomes (Battaglio et al., 2019; Pandey & Marlowe, 2014), it may be crucial to conduct more experiments testing whether policymakers are also vulnerable to anchoring bias to the same extent as ordinary citizens. One of the situations that may come to mind is visualizing situations when policymakers rely on anchors too much, maybe generalization of one report finding to, e.g., other social groups. Especially nowadays, when more researchers emphasize that one-size-fits-all solutions are usually not the best solution to target public policy problems (e.g., Thaler & Sunstein, 2008), it becomes essential to study individual differences underlying various policy problems (Sunstein et al., 2018).

Anchoring bias is particularly evident during policy formulation and decision-making processes. For example in Poland the government introduced the "Family 500+" child allowance. It is basically the universal benefit for kids (ca. 100 USD per one child in family). The amount—500 PLN—was not empirically elaborated. It is neither related to relative poverty measures in Poland nor indexed to the changes of minimal or medium income in country. It does not change with changing rates of inflation. The amount of benefit is more of symbol of new social or family policy paradigm in Poland and as such, anchors many of the current debates on the benefit systems reforms. Moreover, some of the local governments or introduce their own "500+" instruments, regardless of their local socio-economic conditions.

In relation to the "post-factual" society challenges or fake-news inference into policymaking, we can recall the example of the anchoring bias role in the Brexit debates in the United Kingdom. In 2016, Boris Johnson campaigned from a Vote Leave campaign bus, on which it was stated: "We send the EU £350 million a week. let's fund our NHS instead." In the reaction to this political campaign, Chair of the UK Statistics Authority, Sir David Norgrove wrote to then foreign minister B. Johnson, that "It is a clear misuse of official statistics." Nevertheless the figure deeply rooted itself in public opinion. A study conducted jointly by King's College London and Ipsos MORI found that 42 percent of people who had heard of the claim still believed it is true, even after sustained criticism of the false claim by the UK Statistics Authority and other authorities or experts and those perceptions remained mostly unchanged since before the referendum.

84 *Jakub Krawiec and Paweł Śliwowski*

Bandwagon effect

The bandwagon effect is when people often believe certain things or do them only because many other people do (Howard, 2019). Additionally, based on this bias, scholars argue that as an idea gains popularity, people are more likely to accept it. This is consistent with previous theories on heuristics and cognitive errors presented by Tversky and Kahneman (1974). The bandwagon effect can be seen as a heuristic, similar to other heuristics, allowing us to make quick decisions (Gigerenzer & Todd, 1999). It saves us the time and effort of making our own evaluations by relying on the decisions of others. Because a widely accepted idea or behavior indicates support from many people, we also adopt it. Another reason why we follow the group's behavior or ideas, which is more related to individual needs, is to avoid standing out and being excluded from the group.

Furthermore, the bandwagon effect has recently started to be claimed as an essential bias in the decision-making of medicine professionals (Howard, 2019; O'Connor & Clark, 2019). So far, there is a little bit of interest in studying this effect in the area of public policy administration (Bellé et al., 2019). However, isomorphism or parallel adoption of policies between entities is a widely described topic in the administration domain (Kallio & Kuoppakangas, 2013). A recent example of the COVID-19 pandemic has shown how quickly policymakers may adopt solutions from other countries (Nazif-Muñoz et al., 2021). This viralization of different policies to contain the spread of the COVID-19 viruses may also question to what extent policymakers were susceptible to the bandwagon effect, or they indeed analyzed various solutions on their own (Nazif-Muñoz et al., 2021).

In relation to policy cycle, bandwagon effect is especially visible during agenda setting. Growing body of evidence shows that this kind of mechanism play a key role in climate change denialism. The largest demographic correlate of climate change belief is political affiliation and political partisanship is an important predictor of accepting the reality of climate change in a number of countries (Hornsey et al., 2016). This has twofold consequences. It has impact on both politicians attitudes toward accepting the climate change science and acting accordingly. On the other hand, it has profound impact on policy acceptance by different groups of voters.

Confirmation bias

Confirmation bias refers to the "tendency to seek or interpret evidence in a way that supports existing beliefs" (Lord et al., 1979). The idea explains that individuals, when processing information, tend to prioritize information that confirms their pre-existing assumptions or beliefs, rather than objectively considering all information presented to them, and may overlook evidence that contradicts their viewpoint (Schulz-Hardt et al., 2000). Interestingly, confirmation bias is one of the effects already widely studied in the context of public policy and policymakers (Battaglio et al., 2019). For example, one study noted that political decision-makers, when they verify and process information, also tend to hold irrationally to their initial beliefs about policy choices (Cooper & Kovacic, 2012). As a result, policymakers may misinterpret available data supporting their prior beliefs and infer correlation or even causation even when none exists (Seidenfeld, 2001).

As some authors point out (Sunstein, 2009), the timing of decisions limits the time decision-makers have to analyze all available data, thus supporting policymakers to focus on information that supports their initial assumptions. What can further complicate situations is that like-minded individuals can reinforce confirmation bias (Sunstein, 2009).

Loss aversion

Loss aversion derives directly from prospect theory, coined by Kahneman and Tversky (1974). In simple terms, the theory refers to the tendency that people can put more effort into avoiding a certain amount of loss than they would put into gaining a reward of similar magnitude. Thus, it refers to a kind of imbalance between the perception of rewards and losses. Additionally, Kahneman argues that when loss aversion is induced, the prevalence of loss aversion or risk aversion is a "case of narrow framing." Narrow framing occurs when people passively accept how specific problems are framed and consider decisions in isolation from other choices (Kahneman, 2011). Decisions made under narrow framing deviate from viewing risk as neutral and lead to inconsistent choices and risk and loss aversion (Kahneman, 2011).

Significantly, human tendencies toward loss aversion can compound a degree of cognitive myopia—as research shows, the greater the expertise in a particular domain, the less cognitive flexibility in perceiving and solving problems (Dane, 2010). As the researchers point out, in some cases, policymakers may be short-sighted by focusing only on cost containment, e.g., in the area of energy. Additionally, such biases may be compounded by attitudes that consumers are irrational in foregoing the large benefits associated with fuel-efficient products (Gayer & Viscusi, 2013).

Myopia

Cognitive myopia refers to the general tendency to ignore part of the information available to evaluate a situation properly. Researchers distinguish specific types of myopia that can help to identify biased behaviors. One of them is temporal myopia, which describes the tendency to focus excessively on short-term considerations or policy benefits without considering long-term consequences (Cooper & Kovacic, 2012). Another form of myopia pertains to horizontal aspects, which indicate that policymakers may neglect to take into account objectives or consequences

86 *Jakub Krawiec and Paweł Śliwowski*

beyond their particular domains of interest and proficiency, as noted by Viscusi and Gayer (2015). As an illustration, Gayer and Viscusi (2013) analyze regulations pertaining to energy efficiency and contend that policymakers may exhibit myopia by concentrating solely on fuel and energy efficiency, disregarding other essential product characteristics that affect consumers' buying choices.

Overconfidence

Overconfidence or optimism bias is a person's tendency to overestimate their abilities, the quality of their plans, and the likelihood of future success. It can be associated with the illusion of control (Hallsworth et al., 2018). It refers to one's ability to understand problems and make judgments (Kahneman, 2011). Compared to other cognitive errors, overconfidence is "under-researched" in the behavioral public administration literature (Battaglio et al., 2019).

Similar to confirmation bias or myopia, overconfidence may lead to systematic ignorance of risk connected to decisions of policies. On the other hand, policymakers are often forced to appear confident decision-makers—without it, citizens or subordinates may start questioning the legitimacy of decisions taken. Nevertheless, in order to satisfy these demands, policymakers may attempt to present their evaluations with confidence instead of acknowledging any uncertainty.

Unfortunately, sometimes admitting uncertainty could encourage litigation by other socio-political groups adversely affected by a particular policy and decision. Consequently, this is an additional motivation for policymakers to defend their policy decisions at all costs. In view of this, the policymakers' analysis and how they make decisions must show that they understand the potential impact of their actions and decisions on the lives of citizens.

Salience bias

The concept of salience bias was firstly introduced by Kahneman and Tversky (1974). However, one can at first compare it to the availability heuristic, the salience bias is often described in the literature as a stand-alone phenomenon (Tiefenbeck et al., 2018) and can be defined as individuals' tendency to focus on the prominent and immediately visible aspects of the situation (Tiefenbeck et al., 2018; Bordalo et al., 2012). In their study, Fiske and Taylor (1975) have studied this concept by gathering participants around the couple, who chatted in the middle of the room. Afterward, participants were asked to rate the few aspects of the couple's interaction. Results have shown that participants who better saw the face of speaking person, have rated him/her as being more active during this situation. Researchers explained the results by salience effect—for participants the person who sat frontally toward them, was more prominent and visible.

In the real world, the salience effect may occur in various situations and contexts. One of the most ubiquitous nowadays is the attitude of the internet users toward privacy issues. Most of the individuals would declare that they strongly care about the extent they share own data. In practice, it usually turns out, that due to the convenience or perks of having particular mobile applications we are eager to give consent to most of the surveillance without merely reading through the terms of use (Kehr et al., 2015). Another example may be found in the business world. Managers may undervalue the costs of background processes such as administrative tasks, which may result in misguided decisions (Hirshleifer, 2008)

The salience effect may have further implications for more policy contexts. For example, Schenk (2011) has suggested that the effect provides great potential for tax policies. As the author explains, the exploitation of the salience bias in taxes, may turn out into low-salience taxes, not being recognized by the policy-addressees, but effectively yielding economic results for the government. Although democratically questionable, the author defends the thesis, by emphasizing low-salience taxes are also ethical due to their accessibility. Similarly to taxes such as VAT, they are readily accessible for individuals, but largely ignored (Schenk, 2011).

Debiasing and tackling down cognitive biases

Applying behavioral interventions

In the literature on how to debias human decision-making processes or in general how to avoid cognitive biases, one can identify at least two approaches: modifying the decision-maker and modifying the environment (Soll et al., 2014). First one of them relies on educating individuals about thinking strategies, rules of thumb, or more general decision aids one can implement to avoid biases. The second one concerns ways of altering the environment in order to provide aids for decision-makers that may encourage better thinking (Soll et al., 2014). The schools of design and behavioral interventions grow along this distinction. Behavioral interventions are interventions drawn from psychological processes that aim to change behavior without regard to punishment or monetary rewards. Particularly in the field of public policy, two behavioral intervention approaches have received the most attention: nudging and boosting. The first, nudging, promotes the choice of designated options without prohibiting or withdrawing them, and the second, boosting, focuses on empowering the decision-maker, who can thus make a more informed decision (Franklin et al., 2019). Currently, nudging and boosting are being increasingly applied worldwide (Hertwig & Grüne-Yanoff, 2017). Despite the extensive discussion around the potential applications of the two approaches (often juxtaposed as competing), the literature lacks a direct comparison of the effectiveness of the two categories of interventions, which is highlighted by many authors (Bradt, 2019; Franklin et al., 2019; Hertwig & Grüne-Yanoff, 2017), but some authors proposes to perceive these two categories of interventions as alternative in various situations, depending on the particular aims of choice architect (Hertwig & Grüne-Yanoff, 2017). Despite the promotion of the nudge approach as the most effective behavioral intervention for changing human behavior by manipulating decision-making environments (Sunstein, 2015), it is worth noting that the boost approach is a newer but equally promising category of behavioral interventions that are utilized in social policy.

It is worthy to point out that unlike nudges, which derive from Heuristics & Biases School (Thaler & Sunstein, 2008), the boost approach is based on the Simple Heuristics school, also called fast-and-frugal-heuristics (Grüne-Yanoff & Hertwig, 2016). While the main aspect of the impact of a nudge is the architecture of the decision situation, consequently influencing the decision-maker behavior, the main aim of the boost is to increase the competence of the decision-maker to make the best possible decisions according to his/her preferences (Hertwig & Grüne-Yanoff, 2017).

Applications of nudges and boosts can be observed in such social policy programs as Save More Tomorrow in the USA (Thaler & Benartzi, 2004). As a core of this program, one of the most prominent nudges might be identified—a default rule (Sunstein, 2014). It aims to nudge people toward a better choice from the perspective of a choice architect. Default affects individuals by the preselection of one option, which makes them more eager to select this particular option (Jachimowicz et al., 2019). Underlying a wide range of programs using automatic enrolment in education, health, and saving has been proved effective as the most practical nudge (Jachimowicz et al., 2019; Sunstein, 2014) and the most widely studied (Hummel & Maedche, 2019). Hummel and Maedche (2019) state that the second most researched types of nudges are warnings, which encompass various signals aimed at directing individuals' attention toward crucial information. Moreover, as the third most researched nudge, they point to social norms nudges. This intervention's main idea is to create a choice with reference to social context, i.e., emphasizing what other people do (Sunstein, 2014). One of the most effective social norm nudge uses was reported by (Hallsworth et al., 2017), where the main finding was an increased payment rate for overdue tax. It was possible thanks to the application of reminder letters containing messages using social norms. The most effective message contained a descriptive social norm, referring to the rules one should obey—in this context, paying taxes on time. Thanks to these changes in the environment, researchers were able to accelerate the additional 9.3 mln pounds within the first 23 days of the experiment.

On the other hand, as one of the most prominent boosts can be indicated inoculation strategies (Kozyreva et al., 2020; Roozenbeek & van der Linden, 2019), used to strengthen individuals' ability to recognize disinformation, such as online fake news. The intervention created by Roozenbeek and Van der Linden (2019) refers to the inoculation theory developed by McGuire and Papageorgis (1961).

Heuristics and biases in the post-truth era 89

Like the biological vaccine, they reckon that weakened versions of misinformation can empower individuals to be immune to fake news (Roozenbeek & van der Linden, 2019). Researchers went even further—in their newest research, they created a web browser game, allowing participants to experience fake news production from the inside. To get points, they have to use six techniques commonly used in misinformation: polarization, invoking emotions, spreading conspiracy theories, trolling people online, deflecting blame, and impersonating fake accounts. So far, the results have shown that after such training, participants are significantly better in recognition and resistance toward the fake news encountered after the gameplay (Roozenbeek & van der Linden, 2019).

Given the broad application of these behavioral interventions, it is important to examine their effectiveness and complementarity in the different policy contexts. A growing group of researchers in the field emphasize possible ways of using nudges and boosts interchangeably or complementary. However, a complete and coherent debiasing toolbox needs much further research (Hertwig & Grune-Yanoff, 2017, 2019; Kozyreva et al., 2020).

Good practices alleviating the effects of cognitive biases

As nudges and boosts may be perceived as stand-alone tools which debias cognitive processes from the environmental and decision-maker perspective, below we enlist short list of strategies or good practices recommended by various researchers and practitioners which may be seen as solutions to some extent alleviating the detrimental effects of cognitive shortcuts. Given that the discipline is still developing and a complete list of strategies still requires time and research, here are some practices that can prevent at least some of the cognitive biases mentioned above.

A general principle approach to unraveling cognitive biases can be drawn from Kahneman (2011). The author refers to the foundations of the Heuristics & Biases school, identifying two cognitive systems within which we operate when making decisions: System 1 and System 2. The former could be called an automated way of processing information and making decisions that are not only fast and effortless but also characterized by numerous, sometimes unconscious simplifications. System 2, on the other hand, could be called a kind of conscious "I," which is updated when to solve more complex and demanding problems or to learn a new activity or knowledge. As Kahneman mentions, many of our mistakes are because, by default, we approach most decisions using System 1, that is, processing information shallowly and quickly. Therefore, one of the first ways may be to make a particular task more difficult. Then, the decision-maker switches to a more conscious System 2 and thus processes information more accurately. This could be a solution to reduce at least availability heuristic and myopia bias, as the decision-maker would be forced to pay attention to the entire set of information, not just the most recent or selected one (Kahneman,

2011). Additionally, an effective solution in combating the availability heuristic in collective decision-making could potentially utilize a strategy well known to authors with a background in security or military science, namely red-teaming. This strategy involves selecting from among a group of decision-makers a person who will be the proverbial "devil's advocate" in a given situation and whose task will be to critique and challenge the prevailing opinions, no matter what their own opinions are (Kardos & Dexter, 2017).

Disrupting our used conditions and intentionally making information processing slightly more complex can also help combat confirmation bias. According to research, decreasing the fluency of the information being assimilated can increase cognitive effort and, therefore, process information more analytically (Hernandez & Preston, 2013; Diemand-Yauman et al., 2011). For example, in the paper by Diemand-Yauman and colleagues (2011), when students were provided with class materials written in a font that made processing fluency difficult (e.g., Comic Sans italicized), they scored higher on the test than students who learned from standardized materials. Similar results were obtained by Hernandez and Preston (2013). They showed that when individuals typically highly polarized on political issues were given an article written in a non-standard font (specifically formatted Haettenschweiler font), they could approach an issue in a more balanced and analytical manner.

Creating the conditions for analyzing information in a slightly more balanced way is also recommended by some researchers when overcoming cognitive biases such as anchoring bias, bandwagon effect, or overconfidence effect (Mussweiler et al., 2000; Rachlin, 2000; Bazerman & Moore, 2012). For example, as these authors point out, forcing decision-makers to create a list of arguments against a given "anchor," the option that seems most likely, or a list of arguments against the main option that most people follow, is an effective way to reduce bias toward those options. Additionally, a potentially good way to reduce the bandwagon effect may also be to cause the decision-maker to allocate more time to the decision and allow emotions to subside, decreasing the desire to follow the crowd (Rachlin, 2000).

The second to last practice worth mentioning is political bundling, which can be an effective technique to reduce surrendering to loss aversion in the case of public policies (Milkman et al., 2012). Since, according to prospect theory, losses tend to have greater subjective value than gains of the same magnitude (Kahneman, 2011), policies that involve significant costs (even if they objectively economically produce a net gain for society) may not garner sufficient support. Milkman et al. (2012) demonstrated that combining multiple bills into a single package can enhance the endorsement for bills that entail both costs and benefits, and that bundled bills are perceived as having greater worth than the individual bills would suggest. Additionally, in subsequent research, they showed that this relationship is due to less focus on losses and more focus on gains.

A final best practice worth mentioning is the issue of administering salience bias. For example, Tiefenbeck et al. (2018) show that giving decision-makers real-time attention to energy consumption can lead to a 22 percent reduction in environmental resource consumption. On the other hand, as Schenk (2011) points out, some policies may lead to unwanted attitudes when too visible. This was the case with implementing higher fuel surcharges, which had an immediate effect. In contrast, when the enacted price increase was deferred and was advertised to citizens as caring for the future of generations, far more people supported the change (Rogers & Bazerman, 2008).

Conclusions

As many researchers suggest, many of the mentioned cognitive errors, if uncontrolled, contribute to the current situation, which we can call the Post-Truth Era. They weaken understanding of the scientific facts presented, derail the process of arriving at objective truth, and can amplify herd effects. What is important, we recommend to look at heuristics and biases not as a sole cause of the current situation, but as potential factors moderating the relationship between expertise and decision-making in today's political circumstances. If we learn to distinguish these psychological processes and further control them, then we will not only be able to build effective actions based on the knowledge and experience of our experts, but also to limit the action of emotions or social processes.

We believe that nobody is actually safe from these cognitive shortcuts and awareness of the mechanisms is the first step to decrease our innate vulnerability. If we know about these constrains, we can use it as a starting point to avoid future misunderstandings. However, as we try to convince the reader, awareness is not the ultimate solution. Looking for such strategies as red-teaming, political bundling, or various behavioral interventions can strengthen our performance both on the individual and societal level.

Funding

This work was supported by the Ministry of Science and Higher Education in Poland under the 2019–2022 program "Regional Initiative of Excellence," project number 012/RID/2018/19.

References

Battaglio, Jr. R. P., Belardinelli, P., Bellé, N., & Cantarelli, P. (2019). Behavioral public administration ad fontes: A synthesis of research on bounded rationality, cognitive biases, and nudging in public organizations. *Public Administration Review, 79*(3), 304–320.

Bazerman, M. H., & Moore, D. A. (2012). *Judgment in managerial decision making.* John Wiley & Sons.

Bellé, N., Belardinelli, P., Cantarelli, P., & Mele, V. (2019). On iron cages and suboptimal choices: An experimental test of the micro-foundations of isomorphism in the public sector. *International Public Management Journal, 22*(2), 373–414. https://doi.org/10.1080/10967494.2018.1494066

Belle, N., Cantarelli, P., & Belardinelli, P. (2017). Cognitive biases in performance appraisal: Experimental evidence on anchoring and halo effects with public sector managers and employees. *Review of Public Personnel Administration, 37*(3), 275–294. https://doi.org/10.1177/0734371X17704891

Birkland, T. A. (1998). Focusing events, mobilization, and agenda setting. *Journal of Public Policy, 18*(1), 53–74.

BIT. (2018). *Behavioural government*. London: The Behavioural Insights Team. https://www.bi.team/publications/behavioural-government/

Bordalo, P., Gennaioli, N., & Shleifer, A. (2012). Salience theory of choice under risk. *The Quarterly Journal of Economics, 127*(3), 1243–1285.

Bradt, J. (2019). Comparing the effects of behaviorally informed interventions on flood insurance demand: An experimental analysis of 'boosts' and 'nudges.' *Behavioural Public Policy*, 1–31. https://doi.org/10.1017/bpp.2019.31

Cantarelli, P., Belle, N., & Belardinelli, P. (2020). Behavioral public HR: Experimental evidence on cognitive biases and debiasing interventions. *Review of Public Personnel Administration, 40*(1), 56–81. https://doi.org/10.1177/0734371X18778090

Cooper, J. C., & Kovacic, W. E. (2012). Erratum to: Behavioral economics: Implications for regulatory behavior. *Journal of Regulatory Economics, 41*(2), 292.

Dane, E. (2010). Reconsidering the trade-off between expertise and flexibility: A cognitive entrenchment perspective. *Academy of Management Review, 35*(4), 579–603.

Diemand-Yauman, C., Oppenheimer, D. M., & Vaughan, E. B. (2011). Fortune favors the: Effects of disfluency on educational outcomes. *Cognition, 118*(1), 111–115.

Dudley, S. E., & Xie, Z. (2020a). Designing a choice architecture for regulators. *Public Administration Review, 80*(1), 151–156.

Dudley, S. E., & Xie, Z. (2020b). Nudging the nudger: Toward a choice architecture for regulators. *Regulation & Governance, 16*, 261–273. https://doi.org/10.1111/rego.12329

Enough, B., & Mussweiler, T. (2001). Sentencing under uncertainty: Anchoring effects in the courtroom. *Journal of Applied Social Psychology, 31*(7), 1535–1551.

Flyvbjerg, B., Ansar, A., Budzier, A., Buhl, S., Cantarelli, C. C., Garbuio, M., Glenting, C., Holm, M., Lovallo, D., & Molin, E. J. E. (2019). On de-bunking 'Fake News' in the post-truth era: How to reduce statistical error in research. SSRN 3416731. https://papers.ssrn.com/sol3/papers.cfm?abstract_id=3416731

Franklin, M., Folke, T., & Ruggeri, K. (2019). Optimising nudges and boosts for financial decisions under uncertainty. *Palgrave Communications, 5*(1), 1–13.

Gayer, T., & Viscusi, W. K. (2013). Overriding consumer preferences with energy regulations. *Journal of Regulatory Economics, 43*(3), 248–264. https://doi.org/10.1007/s11149-013-9210-2

Gigerenzer, G.,Todd, P. M.& The ABC Research Group. (1999). *Simple heuristics that make us smart*, New York, NY: Oxford University Press.

Gofen, A., Moseley, A., Thomann, E., & Kent Weaver, R. (2021). Behavioural governance in the policy process: Introduction to the special issue. *Journal of European Public Policy, 28*(5), 633–657. https://doi.org/10.1080/13501763.2021.1912153

Grimmelikhuijsen, S., Jilke, S., Olsen, A. L., & Tummers, L. (2017). Behavioral public administration: Combining insights from public administration and psychology. *Public Administration Review*, *77*(1), 45–56. https://doi.org/10.1111/puar.12609

Grüne-Yanoff, T., & Hertwig, R. (2016). Nudge versus boost: How coherent are policy and theory? *Minds and Machines*, *26*(1–2). https://doi.org/10.1007/s11023-015-9367-9

Hallsworth, M., Egan, M., Rutter, J., & McCrae, J. (2018). *Behavioural government: Using behavioural science to improve how governments make decisions*, London: The Behavioural Insights Team.

Hallsworth, M., List, J. A., Metcalfe, R. D., & Vlaev, I. (2017). The behavioralist as tax collector: Using natural field experiments to enhance tax compliance. *Journal of Public Economics*, *148*, 14–31. https://doi.org/10.1016/j.jpubeco.2017.02.003

Hernandez, I., & Preston, J. L. (2013). Disfluency disrupts the confirmation bias. *Journal of Experimental Social Psychology*, *49*(1), 178–182. https://doi.org/10.1016/j.jesp.2012.08.010

Hertwig, R., & Grüne-Yanoff, T. (2017). Nudging and boosting: Steering or empowering good decisions. *Perspectives on Psychological Science*, *12*(6). https://doi.org/10.1177/1745691617702496

Hertwig, R., & Grüne-Yanoff, T. (2019). Nudging and boosting financial decisions. *Bancaria: Journal of Italian Banking Association*, *73*(3), 2–19.

Hirshleifer, D. (2008). Psychological bias as a driver of financial regulation. *European Financial Management*, *14*(5), 856–874. https://doi.org/10.1111/j.1468-036X.2007.00437.x

Hornsey, M. J., Harris, E. A., Bain, P. G., & Fielding, K. S. (2016). Meta-analyses of the determinants and outcomes of belief in climate change. *Nature Climate Change*, *6*(6), 622–626.

Howard, J. (2019). *Cognitive Errors and Diagnostic Mistakes: A Case-Based Guide to Critical Thinking in Medicine,* Springer International Publishing. https://doi.org/10.1007/978-3-319-93224-8

Hummel, D., & Maedche, A. (2019). How effective is nudging? A quantitative review on the effect sizes and limits of empirical nudging studies. *Journal of Behavioral and Experimental Economics*, *80*, 47–58.

Jachimowicz, J. M., Duncan, S., Weber, E. U., & Johnson, E. J. (2019). When and why defaults influence decisions: A meta-analysis of default effects. *Behavioural Public Policy*, *3*(2), 159–186.

Jarvis, S., Deschenes, O., & Jha, A. (2019). *The private and external costs of Germany's nuclear phase-out (No. W26598; p. W26598)*. National Bureau of Economic Research. https://doi.org/10.3386/w26598

Jones, R., Pykett, J., & Whitehead, M. (2013). Psychological governance and behaviour change. *Policy & Politics*, *41*(2), 159–182.

Kahneman, D. (2011). *Thinking, fast and slow*. Macmillan.

Kallio, T. J., & Kuoppakangas, P. (2013). Bandwagoning municipal enterprises: Institutional isomorphism and the search for the third way. *Policy Studies*, *34*(1), 19–35. https://doi.org/10.1080/01442872.2012.731842

Kardos, M., & Dexter, P. (2017). *A simple handbook for non-traditional red teaming*. Defence Science and Technology Group Edinburgh, SA.

Kaufmann, L., Carter, C. R., & Buhrmann, C. (2010). Debiasing the supplier selection decision: A taxonomy and conceptualization. *International Journal of Physical Distribution & Logistics Management*, *40*(10), 792–821.

94 *Jakub Krawiec and Paweł Śliwowski*

Kehr, F., Kowatsch, T., Wentzel, D., & Fleisch, E. (2015). Blissfully ignorant: The effects of general privacy concerns, general institutional trust, and affect in the privacy calculus. *Information Systems Journal, 25*(6), 607–635. https://doi.org/10.1111/isj .12062

Kozyreva, A., Lewandowsky, S., & Hertwig, R. (2020). Citizens versus the internet: Confronting digital challenges with cognitive tools. *Psychological Science in the Public Interest, 21*(3). https://doi.org/10.1177/1529100620946707

Kuran, T., & Sunstein, C. R. (1998). Availability cascades and risk regulation. *Stanford Law Review, 51*, 683.

Lichtenstein, S., Slovic, P., Fischhoff, B., Layman, M., & Combs, B. (1978). Judged frequency of lethal events. *Journal of Experimental Psychology: Human Learning and Memory, 4*(6), 551.

Lord, C. G., Ross, L., & Lepper, M. R. (1979). Biased assimilation and attitude polarization: The effects of prior theories on subsequently considered evidence. In *Journal of Personality and Social Psychology* (Vol. 37, Issue 11, pp. 2098–2109). American Psychological Association. https://doi.org/10.1037/0022-3514.37.11.2098

Marra, M. (2021). A behavioral design to reform Italy's evaluation policy. *American Journal of Evaluation, 42*(4), 483–504. https://doi.org/10.1177/1098214020972791

McCaughey, D., & Bruning, N. S. (2010). Rationality versus reality: The challenges of evidence-based decision making for health policy makers. *Implementation Science, 5*(1), 39. https://doi.org/10.1186/1748-5908-5-39

McGuire, W. J., & Papageorgis, D. (1961). The relative efficacy of various types of prior belief-defense in producing immunity against persuasion. *The Journal of Abnormal and Social Psychology, 62*(2), 327.

Milkman, K. L., Mazza, M. C., Shu, L. L., Tsay, C. J., & Bazerman, M. H. (2012). Policy bundling to overcome loss aversion: A method for improving legislative outcomes. *Organizational Behavior and Human Decision Processes, 117*(1), 158–167.

Münscher, R., Vetter, M., & Scheuerle, T. (2016). A review and taxonomy of choice architecture techniques. *Journal of Behavioral Decision Making, 29*(5), 511–524.

Mussweiler, T., Strack, F., & Pfeiffer, T. (2000). Overcoming the inevitable anchoring effect: Considering the opposite compensates for selective accessibility. *Personality and Social Psychology Bulletin, 26*(9), 1142–1150.

Nazif-Muñoz, J. I., Peña, S., & Oulhote, Y. (2021). The global viralization of policies to contain the spreading of the COVID-19 pandemic: Analyses of school closures and first reported cases. *PLoS One, 16*(4), e0248828.

O'Connor, N., & Clark, S. (2019). Beware bandwagons! The bandwagon phenomenon in medicine, psychiatry and management. *Australasian Psychiatry, 27*(6), 603–606.

Olejniczak, K., Borkowska-Waszak, S., Domaradzka-Widła, A., & Park, Y. (2020). Policy labs: The next frontier of policy design and evaluation?. *Policy & Politics, 48*(1), 89–110.

Olejniczak, K., Śliwowski, P., & Roszczyńska-Kurasińska, M. (2019). Behaviour architects: A framework for employing behavioural insights in public policy practice. *Zarządzanie Publiczne/Public Governance, 1*(47), 18–32.

Olsen, A. L. (2015). The numerical psychology of performance information: Implications for citizens, managers, and policymakers. *Public Performance & Management Review, 39*(1), 100–115. https://doi.org/10.1080/15309576.2016.1071167

Heuristics and biases in the post-truth era 95

Pandey, S. K., & Marlowe, J. (2014). Assessing survey-based measurement of personnel red tape with anchoring vignettes. *Review of Public Personnel Administration*, *35*(3), 215–237. https://doi.org/10.1177/0734371X14531988

Pariser, E. (2011). *The filter bubble: What the Internet is hiding from you*. Penguin.

Rachlin, H. (2000). *The science of self-control*. Harvard University Press.

Rogers, T., & Bazerman, M. H. (2008). Future lock-in: Future implementation increases selection of "should" choices. *Organizational Behavior and Human Decision Processes*, *106*, 1–20.

Roozenbeek, J., & van der Linden, S. (2019). Fake news game confers psychological resistance against online misinformation. *Palgrave Communications*, *5*(1), 65. https://doi.org/10.1057/s41599-019-0279-9

Schenk, D. H. (2011). Exploiting the salience bias in designing taxes. *Yale Journal on Regulation*, *28*, 253.

Schulz-Hardt, S., Frey, D., Lüthgens, C., & Moscovici, S. (2000). Biased information search in group decision making. *Journal of Personality and Social Psychology*, *78*(4), 655.

Schwarz, N., Bless, H., Strack, F., Klumpp, G., Rittenauer-Schatka, H., & Simons, A. (1991). Ease of retrieval as information: Another look at the availability heuristic. *Journal of Personality and Social Psychology*, *61*(2), 195.

Seidenfeld, M. (2001). Cognitive loafing, social conformity, and judicial review of agency rulemaking. *Cornell Law Review*, *87*, 486.

Sherif, M., Taub, D., & Hovland, C. I. (1958). Assimilation and contrast effects of anchoring stimuli on judgments. *Journal of Experimental Psychology*, *55*(2), 150.

Simon, H. A. (1972). Theories of bounded rationality. *Decision and Organization*, *1*(1), 161–176.

Simon, H. A. (2013). *Administrative behavior* (4th ed.). Simon and Schuster.

Soll, J. B., Milkman, K. L., & Payne, J. W. (2014). *A user's guide to debiasing*.In Keren, Gideon & Wu, George (eds.) The Wiley Blackwell Handbook of Judgment and Decision Making (pp. 924–951). John Wiley & Sons, Ltd. https://doi.org/10.1002/9781118468333.ch33.

Stanovich, K. E., Toplak, M. E., & West, R. F. (2008). The development of rational thought: A taxonomy of heuristics and biases. In R. V. Kail (Ed.), *Advances in child development and behavior* (Vol. 36, pp. 251–285). Elsevier. JAI. https://doi.org/10.1016/S0065-2407(08)00006-2

Straßheim, H. (2020). The rise and spread of behavioral public policy: An opportunity for critical research and self-reflection. *International Review of Public Policy*, *2*(2:1), 115–128.

Sunstein, C. R. (2009). *Going to extremes: How like minds unite and divide*. Oxford University Press.

Sunstein, C. R. (2014). Nudging: A very short guide. *Journal of Consumer Policy*, *37*(4), 583–588.

Sunstein, C. R. (2015). Nudges do not undermine human agency. *Journal of Consumer Policy*, *38*(3), 207–210. https://doi.org/10.1007/s10603-015-9289-1

Sunstein, C. R., Reisch, L. A., & Rauber, J. (2018). A worldwide consensus on nudging? Not quite, but almost. *Regulation & Governance*, *12*(1), 3–22.

96 *Jakub Krawiec and Paweł Śliwowski*

Thaler, R. H., & Benartzi, S. (2004). Save more tomorrow™: Using behavioral economics to increase employee saving. *Journal of Political Economy, 112*(S1), S164–S187.

Thaler, R. H., & Sunstein, C. R. (2008). *Nudge: Improving decisions about health, wealth, and happiness.* Yale University Press.

Tiefenbeck, V., Goette, L., Degen, K., Tasic, V., Fleisch, E., Lalive, R., & Staake, T. (2018). Overcoming salience bias: How real-time feedback fosters resource conservation. *Management Science, 64*(3), 1458–1476.

Tummers, L. (2020, June 30). Behavioral public administration. *Oxford Research Encyclopedia of Politics.* Retrieved January 6, 2024, from https://oxfordre.com/politics/view/10.1093/acrefore/9780190228637.001.0001/acrefore-9780190228637-e-1443

Tversky, A., & Kahneman, D. (1973). Availability: A heuristic for judging frequency and probability. *Cognitive Psychology, 5*(2), 207–232.

Tversky, A., & Kahneman, D. (1974). Judgment under uncertainty: Heuristics and biases. *Science, 185*(4157), 1124–1131.

Viscusi, W. K., & Gayer, T. (2015). Behavioural public choice: The behavioral paradox of government policy. *Harvard Journal of Law and Public Policy, 38*(3), 973.

6 In search of effective communication with decision-makers for the post-truth era

Discourse strategies from pre-imperial China

Karol Olejniczak and Marcin Jacoby

Introduction

Evaluation, as a part of policy sciences, has been focusing on helping decision-makers undertake better-informed policy decisions (Chelimsky, 2006; Wildawsky, 1979). In practice, the transmission of knowledge between evaluators and decision-makers is rather limited. As literature indicates, there is a communication gap between the communities of researchers and decision-makers, and that gap hampers the flow of knowledge (Caplan, 1979). As C. Weiss (1980) pointed out, knowledge does not flow, it at best creeps into decision accretion. Thus, evaluation use remains a major challenge (Palenberg & Paulson, 2020). We understand evaluation use (also called utilization) as a process in which decision-makers use the findings of evaluations for strategic or operational decisions related to design and implementation of public policies.

The recent emergence of discourse strategies and persuasion tools of the post-truth era makes evaluation's mission even more challenging. In this chapter, we follow definition provided in an Introduction to this book. Post-truth is defined as denoting circumstances in which objective facts are less influential in shaping decision-making than appeals to emotions and personal beliefs (McIntyre, 2018). In this context decision-makers are even less capable of rational decisions, and more prone to bounded rationality and biases or even irrational perception of reality (Kavanagh & Rich, 2018).

Although the post-truth phenomenon, especially in its technological aspect, is new, the underlying mechanisms that drive it are, as discussed in the earlier chapters of this book, rooted in universal human nature and behavior patterns. In other words, this distortion of policy decision-making is a well-known phenomenon, and it is only its spread and scale which are different. Modern modes of social communication can be viewed only as radical ways of exploiting universal decision-making biases that have shaped human interaction regardless of time and place, and are deeply rooted in human mechanisms of bounded rationality (Bendor, 2015; McIntyre, 2018; Nichols, 2017). Thus, in search for new, effective decision-making strategies for the post-truth era, it is worth gaining a wider perspective, examining the heritage of global political thought and practice of the past, especially that which is rooted outside the Western civilization.

DOI: 10.4324/9781032719979-7

This chapter has been made available under a CC-BY-NC-ND 4.0 license.

98   *Karol Olejniczak and Marcin Jacoby*

In this chapter, we recognize the challenge of persuading decision-makers to listen attentively to what we—the evaluators have to say. We identify the need to search for effective ways of delivering our message so that it is genuinely considered in the decision-making process.

In search of inspiration about effective communication with decision-makers, we look outside the box of the evaluation practice and, more broadly, beyond the well-trodden paths of our own cultural and temporal context to explore the rich heritage of Asian cultures. Accordingly, we put forward the following question: **What specific persuasion strategies from Chinese pre-imperial political discourse could serve as a source of inspiration for our communication with decision-makers in the post-truth era?**

Our work is novel in two ways. Firstly, it reaches out beyond our Western cultural context. The evaluation practice, and more broadly public policy sciences, are grounded in American pragmatism (Lasswell, 1951), dominated by linear causality thinking. Research indicates that thinking and problem-solving patterns of other cultural traditions can differ from Westerners (Nisbett, 2004; Jullien, 2004). Thus, we want to explore a different human tradition of thinking about relations and causality, namely the Chinese tradition.

Secondly, we reach beyond our discipline. Evaluation is based in social sciences, but in this chapter we scout for ideas in the area of the humanities, and with the use of their analytical methods. It is a truism to say that literature is a vessel of human collective experience and wisdom. But recent publications add to confirming the power of narratives in grasping human attention (Fludernik, 2009; Phelan, 2020), and shaping understanding of socio-economic behaviors (Shiller, 2020). This indicates the worth of exploring communication strategies coded in the literature.

This chapter consists of three sections. In the first section we provide the rationale for choosing the specific historical period of the Chinese tradition (the Warring States Period, 453–221 BCE), and body of literature sources (*Zhanguoce, Zhuangzi*, and the *Lüshi Chunqiu*). We also briefly explain the approaches to text analysis in the humanistic paradigm. The core of the chapter is devoted to an in-depth analysis of the original Chinese sources. We discuss three main communication strategies that emerged from the analyzed texts. We illustrate them with narrative examples from original sources. In the closing part of the chapter we link those findings to the current literature on biases and failures in decision-making, and we consider possible applications for our evaluation craft in the post-truth era.

We hope that the chapter can be a valuable contribution to the research on evaluation, and more broadly, research on public policy decision-making, providing some inspiration in tackling the challenges of the post-truth era. We believe that this path has a potential for finding practical solutions and for advancing the theory and craft of evaluation, as well as building interdisciplinary research between evaluation and the humanities.

Scope and method of the analysis

In search of inspiration from China, we turn to primary literature sources from the Warring States Period (453–221 BCE), which immediately precedes the founding of the first imperial rule (Qin Dynasty, 221–206 BCE). This is a time of great social shifts and political upheaval (Yang Kuan, 2016). Deepening economic, political, and military rivalry between different Chinese states led to the rise of errand advisors, diplomats, strategists, and thinkers representing the new professional elites (the *shi* class) (Li Fulan & Li Yan, 1998). Rapid progress in political, strategic, and social thought of the period is reflected in its rich literary heritage, including some of the best known gems of Chinese culture, such as the *Laozi*, *Zhuangzi*, or *Sunzi's Art of War* (*Sunzi Bingfa*).

The Warring States Period, and more specifically, its second half (end of the 4th and the 3rd century BCE) is not only formative for Chinese culture as we know it today, but has numerous parallels with the modern VUCA world (short for volatility, uncertainty, complexity, and ambiguity) (Bennett & Lemoine, 2014). The changing geopolitical situation, technical progress, the threat of military conflict, and social unrest were some of the factors that shaped Chinese thought in the period, and which at the same time correspond closely to the challenges faced by expert communities today. Moreover, some 2,300 years ago in China, much like globally today, experts needed to compete for the attention of the decision-makers who were themselves under immense pressure. Advisors were often faced with the seemingly impossible task of trying to persuade rulers to listen to advice on complex, long-term diplomatic solutions, rather than heeding short-term, military gains. Just like today, informed and evidence-based advice had to compete with short-sighted, intuitive decision-making of the rulers (Yu Kai, 2015).

Due to the highly challenging political environment, the Warring States Period developed a unique, rich tradition of persuasive discourse. It naturally reflects the feudal, patriarchal society of the period, and the norms and values represented in this discourse, including social stratification and social roles of the sexes, are very different from the acceptable standard of modern society. Bearing in mind the above contextual limitations, we believe that these written works, just like classic European works of that time on politics and statehood, can still provide a source of inspiration for expert communities of today. Of special interest are historical anecdotes which recount dialogues of various persuaders with the rulers of Chinese states and other persons of authority. Despite the fact that the historical accuracy of these accounts is doubtful (Crump, 1964), the persuasive strategies they record can be subject to scholarly analysis. These narratives function in a specific cultural and historical context, which needs to be taken into account in any analysis. In order to ensure this, the methodological approach chosen in this study combines traditional Chinese hermeneutics with rhetorical narratology, and more specifically, the rhetorical analysis of

100 Karol Olejniczak and Marcin Jacoby

the narrative. Modern research in rhetoric narratology recognizes the persuasive value and effectiveness of the narrative (Phelan, 2020; Fludernik, 2009; Rowland, 2009). It also acknowledges the widespread use of persuasive narratives in ancient literature of various cultural traditions (Dinkler, 2016).

The corpus of extant texts of the Warring States Period includes hundreds of historical anecdotes. Only a certain proportion of them is in the form of narratives with direct dialogues. These are dated mostly between 4th and 3rd century BCE, some occur in later compilations. The four main sources of such Warring States Period narratives are: *Zhanguoce, Zhuangzi, Han Feizi*, and the *Lüshi Chunqiu* (Chen Puqing, 1992). Three of these texts form the basis of the present analysis. For reason of space and due to high level of proximity between the narratives in the last two texts, the *Han Feizi* is excluded from this analysis in favor of a lesser known, but equally fascinating work, the *Lüshi Chunqiu*.

Zhanguoce (ZGC) is a compilation of over 400 historical anecdotes which refer to times between 466 and 221 BCE (Wen Honglong, 2010). Most of their protagonists are political advisors, diplomats and strategists, especially the likes of Zhang Yi (?–310 BCE) and Su Qin (?–284 BCE). Anecdotes are organized in 33 chapters devoted to 12 warring states.

Zhuangzi (ZZ) is a famous oeuvre of Daoist philosophy and literature, attributed to the legendary thinker Zhuang Zhou (c. 369–286 BCE). It is also a compilation of various texts, similarly arranged in 33 chapters, which are further subdivided into sections. 70 percent of the total number of 249 sections of the book are in the form of philosophical anecdotes, parables, and fables. Many are devoted to the area of politics, most are strongly persuasive.

Lüshi Chunqiu (LSCQ) is the youngest of the three. It was compiled ca. 241–238 BCE (Zhu Yongjia & Su Mu, 1995; Knoblock & Riegel, 2000) by a group of philosophers, strategists, and experts in various fields, under the auspices of an influential merchant and politician active in the state of Qin—Lü Buwei (d. 235 BCE). This well-preserved but less researched work of political thought of pre-imperial China unites various philosophical schools of the period (Confucianism, Daoism, Legalism) to produce an almanac of practical, political recommendations for rulers of the future Empire (Wang Qicai, 2007; Knoblock & Riegel, 2000). It is divided into three parts and 26 chapters, and includes 298 narratives, used in various persuasive contexts.

In the present analysis, ZGC, ZZ, and LSCQ were chosen as text corpus, which was coded using four formal criteria of critical narrative analysis (Rowland, 2009):

i) **characters:** advisor/sage/expert/strategist/philosopher as the protagonist, and ruler of a state/aristocrat/another person representing power and authority as the antagonist;

ii) **setting:** court of the ruler or another setting where power dynamics are favorable for the person representing authority. Direct dialogue between the protagonist and the antagonist;

In search of effective communication   101

iii) **plot:** introductory, situational opening, direct dialogue between the protagonist and the antagonist, persuasive speech by the protagonist, reaction of the antagonist and/or result of the persuasion;

iv) **theme:** effective persuasion of the ruler/person of authority in a situation/ setting unfavorable for the protagonist. Showing the power/effectiveness of persuasive strategies.

Seven anecdotes from the text corpus were identified as best fulfilling the criteria of the formal analysis specified above. In the next step, the seven anecdotes were subject to functional analysis using both close text reading in the Chinese hermeneutical tradition (original text and commentaries), as well as thematic analysis from the toolbox of rhetoric narratology (Phelan, 2020). As a result, three distinct discourse strategies of persuasion were identified.

The coding in the formal analysis stage was conducted on source texts in classical Chinese (the original language of the corpus). The functional analysis was conducted on the seven selected anecdotes both in the original, as well as in translations into Modern Standard Chinese and into English. For convenience of the reader, only the English translations are quoted and commented on in the present analysis.

Discourse strategies from pre-imperial China

The focus of the functional analysis of the seven selected narratives was on strategies of persuasion employed by the protagonist in his (they all happened to be male) direct dialogue with the antagonist. As the formal conditions of each narrative were all similar, the analysis rendered results in the form of three, quite distinct discourse strategies. These strategies are briefly labeled below, followed by descriptions of their original context in the narratives where they were found. Most come from ZGC, as this text conforms best to the object of the present study.

Discourse strategy 1: overcoming negative bias of the ruler through initial accord

In this strategy, the protagonist faces the ruler who despises moral teachings, and is not interested in what the protagonist has to say. He attempts to secure the ruler's attention against this strong, initial negative bias. This is achieved in a roundabout way, utilizing the protagonist's knowledge of the ruler's preferences and interests. The protagonist moves gradually and cautiously from what the ruler thinks he will hear to what the protagonist actually wants to say.

---

102 *Karol Olejniczak and Marcin Jacoby*

> Anecdote 1.1. *Zhuangzi*, Chapter 30 (Huang et al., 2008:432–434; Mair, 1998:312–316)

In this unusually lengthy anecdote, the philosopher Zhuang Zhou (Zhuangzi) is summoned by the heir apparent of the Zhao state to try and convince the ruler, king Wen (King Huiwen, reigned 298–266 BCE), to abandon his love of swordsmanship, crude physical power and violence. The king surrounds himself solely with swordsmen for whom he organizes endless, bloody duels, and does not want to see anyone else. Zhuangzi secures his audience only by disguising as a warrior, and claiming that he comes with a very special weapon: "My sword cuts down one man every ten paces, and for a thousand tricents it doesn't pause in its march forward" (Mair, 1998:314). This secures the king's attention and creates space for Zhuangzi to use his power of persuasion. What follows is a story of three types of swords. When Zhuangzi finishes, the king realizes that the three swords are metaphors of different styles of leadership. The "sword of the son of heaven" means ruling using mastery of the elements, and mystic knowledge of the universe. The "sword of the feudal lord" means ruling using a well-selected group of noble, uncorrupt, and able officials. The "sword of the common man" is in fact a ruthless critique of what the king likes most: brutal, physical power that takes one nowhere. Zhuangzi concludes: "Now, your majesty occupies the position of the son of heaven, yet has the preference for the sword of the common man. I venture to deplore it on your behalf." The anecdote ends with a powerful statement on the effectiveness of the persuasion: "King Wen did not leave his palace for three months, and the swordsmen all committed suicide in their rooms" (Mair, 1998:316).

Zhuangzi sees the king at a huge personal risk and with not much chance of success. The king would not listen to any advice, and is completely engulfed in his obsession with swordsmanship. Zhuangzi initially seems to be offering him a new stimulus in his addiction, communicating as one of his kind. Using metaphors from the realm of martial arts that the king understands well, Zhuangzi manages to show him a world beyond the narrow horizons of his obsession.

> Anecdote 1.2: *Lüshi Chunqiu* (LSCQ) Views Chapter 3, "Smooth Persuasion" (Zhu & Su, 1995:557–558; Tang, 2010:170–172)

In a very similar setting and facing a similar antagonist, one Hui Ang from the family clan of the famous philosopher Huizi (incidentally, Zhuangzi's friend), comes to the court of the notorious King Kang of the state of Song. The king

In search of effective communication   103

appears in several other anecdotes of the Warring States Period as the epitome of a violent despot. He punishes by death left and right, loves war and makes rush, uninformed decisions.

In the story, Hui Ang comes to court with a task of teaching the king about two fundamental Confucian virtues: benevolence and righteousness. And this is how the conversation starts:

> ... the king stamped his feet and coughed when he said in a hurried voice, "What I like are men who are brave and powerful. What I do not like are men who profess benevolence and righteousness. What advise the guest can give me?"

> Hui Ang answered, "I have an art that can ward off a brave man's stab and a powerful man's strike. Is Your Majesty not interested in it?" The king said, "Good. That's what I want to hear."

> (Tang, 2010:170–171)

As in the previous story, the king soon learns that his visitor will not teach him how to ward off stabs and strikes at all. Hui Ang progresses from talking about defending against attack, to the main point of his persuasion: the best art of defense is simply becoming a person that others admire and have no intention of attacking. And of course, such mastery in the art of fighting without fighting can be achieved through no other than practicing benevolence and righteousness that King Kang despises so much. Benevolence and righteousness were two key concepts for the schools of Confucius (551–479 BCE) and Mo Di (Mozi, active ca. 430 BCE), and these are the two philosophers that Hui Ang brings forward:

> Confucius and Mo Di had no territories but were as honorable as rulers. They had no official positions but were respected as high officials. Men and women in the world all stretched their necks and stood on tiptoe to look at them and wished they were secure and successful.

> (Tang, 2010:171)

Again, as in the case of Zhuangzi, the king is overpowered by the persuasion:

> The king of the state of Song had nothing to say for an answer. When Hui Ang had departed, he said to those who were present, "An eloquent speaker! The guest has convinced me."

> (Tang, 2010:171)

Anecdote 1.3: *Zhanguoce* (ZGC), The Book of Zhao, no. 250 (Wen, 2010:499; Crump, 1996:303–304)

104 *Karol Olejniczak and Marcin Jacoby*

The third anecdote has the clever persuader and diplomat Su Qin as the protagonist. He demands audience with Li Dui who is an official at the court of King Wuling (reigned 325–299 BCE) of the state of Zhao. Su Qin hopes for an opportunity to show the depth of his knowledge "on affairs of the empire." If Li Dui is impressed by his advice, he should get a financial reward which would enable him to continue his journey to the state of Qin. However, Li Dui does not seem to be interested in hearing what Su Qin has to say. He agrees to meet him only under the condition that he speaks "the words of spirits, for I know all there is to know of the affairs of man" (Crump, 1996:303). This patronizing attitude does not discourage Su Qin, and after he promises that he will "use the words of spirits," the audience is granted.

His rhetoric strategy is similar to the previous two anecdotes: Su Qin starts exactly with what the antagonist wants to hear. This time, it is quite a strange fable about two sculptures used for religious purposes, one made of earth, and another made of wood. The earthen idol mocks the wooden one that it will be blown off easily by the wind or washed away by the rains, and end up in the sea. "In all the vast waters there would be no place for you to stay" (Crump, 1996:304). Su Qin moves quickly to explain the meaning of the fable: Li Dui is like a wooden idol, just about to be blown away from his position of power and influence by his enemies. Su has an idea how to save him, if only Li Dui cares to listen to his advice.

What happens later might seem surprising: Li Dui is not prepared to change his plans, and at the same time he knows that Su Qin is a powerful persuader. He therefore sits at the second audience with Su Qin with stops in his ears, so that he does not hear anything the persuader has to say. Just like Li Dui, we do not learn the content of Su Qin's speech. But Su Qin is still satisfied though, as he gets his money and can continue on his journey to the state of Qin.

The anecdote might not be the best example of a successful persuasion, but shows an effective way of overcoming initial reluctance of the antagonist to listen to what the protagonist has to say, consistent with the previous two examples.

Discourse strategy 2: securing the ruler's attention through unexpected behavior of the persuader

In this strategy, the protagonist presupposes that the ruler might not give him full attention. The protagonist is also aware of the fact that he will have very limited time to discuss complex issues with the ruler. Therefore, the persuader uses the device of surprise to intrigue the ruler before starting the delivery of the main line of argument.

In search of effective communication 105

Anecdote 2.1: *Zhanguoce* (ZGC), The Book of Yan, no. 445 (Wen, 2010:894–895; Crump, 1996:467–468)

The errand diplomat Su Qin is again the protagonist in the story on how to persuade the king of a state to do what at first seems utterly irrational. The historical setting of the story is quite dubious, and the dates and reigns of kings do not match. In the story, set in 332 BCE, Qi, one of the biggest and most powerful of the warring states occupying today's Shandong Province, attacked the weaker, Northern neighbor Yan (the area of today's Beijing and further North) and took over ten of Yan's towns. Su Qin, whose mission is to persuade the victorious King of Qi on Yan's behalf, begins his audience with the king from congratulations and condolences communicated almost instantly. He doesn't need to wait long for a reaction: "The king of Qi seized his dagger-ax and made Su Qin retreat: 'What mean these congratulations and condolences all in the same breath?' he cried" (Crump, 1996:467). Su Qin then proceeds to explain what he meant using a metaphor of a poisonous plant aconite: "When men are starving [...] the reason they will not eat deadly aconite is because it might fill their bellies but would be the death of them none the less. At this moment Yan is weak, but it is related by marriage to mighty Qin [a state even more powerful than Qi] [...] Qin is there to take advantage of the aftermath and to bring down upon you the most mettlesome troops in the empire. This is exactly like filling the belly with aconite" (ibid.). Su Qin then suggests to the king to return the newly accrued territory to Yan and to apologize solemnly to the state of Qin for attacking Yan. The king, to the reader's surprise, listens to the persuasion. He "returned the ten Yan towns, and offered a thousand ounces of gold in apology. He made a deep and humble obeisance on the bare earth and pleaded to become a fraternal state with Yan" (Crump, 1996:468). Su Qin accomplishes his task using a shocking effect and a persuasive metaphor of eating poisonous food when hungry. The opening of the anecdote is the key; Su Qin takes a big risk (remember the dagger-ax) and decides to shake the King of Qi out of his comfort zone in the very first sentence. After all, what would be more unnerving and irritating than listening to condolences after a military victory? The bet gives Su Qin a good return: the king is now focused on the conversation and is thus well-prepared to succumb to the persuasive power of the metaphor.

Anecdote 2.2: *Zhanguoce* (ZGC), The Book of Zhao, no. 287 (Wen, 2010:632–633; Crump, 1996:344)

106 *Karol Olejniczak and Marcin Jacoby*

A similar tactic is used by one Feng Ji in his audience with King Xiaocheng of the state of Zhao (reigned 265–245 BCE). Feng Ji appears several times in ZGC, but we know almost nothing about him apart from these narratives. In the story, he manages to secure a personal appointment with the king, but when the audience starts, refuses to say anything. He stands in silence "with hands clasped and hear bowed, wanting to speak but not daring to" (Crump, 1996:344). This prompts the king to inquire the reason for such a theatrical performance, upon which Feng Ji begins his rather lengthy speech. It includes one embedded, historical anecdote and two historical *exemplae*. All with one purpose in mind: to show that enlightened rulers of old were prepared to listen to advisors even though they did not know them well and had not established any meaningful relationship with them. Feng Ji is evidently a newcomer at the court of the Zhao king. The king might not, therefore, be quick to talk with him about important matters during the very first audience. But Feng Ji seems in a hurry to be heard. After his imaginative speech and the king's favorable response, the protagonist finally asks: "'Heretofore I have had very little intercourse with your majesty, but I do wish to speak of deep matters. Is it permitted?' 'I request your instructions' replied the king, and Feng Ji then spoke" (ibid.).

We do not learn what Feng Ji had to say, as the story ends here. It seems that for the compilers of ZGC, Feng Ji's words of wisdom for the king of Zhao did not seem as important as his persuasive strategies to secure the king's attention.

Both anecdotes show that for persuaders of the Warring States Period the first moment of the interaction with the ruler was of key importance. They needed to make an impact in order to be heard, and one of the devices they used was taking their listeners by surprise: through a potentially insulting statement or through a puzzling silence. It is also interesting to note that in both anecdotes, after the shock opening, the protagonists continue their speeches basing heavily on metaphors, historical *exemplae* and embedded narratives—all these are indirect tools of persuasion. These seem to be deemed much more effective than direct arguments. They come only later, after the indirect tools take their effect on the interlocutor.

Discourse strategy 3: Persuading the ruler through pragmatic reasoning against action which has already been decided and which is emotionally charged

In this strategy, the persuader faces the challenge of stopping the execution of a decision which has already been made and which is based on an emotional rationale. The persuader concentrates on building a pragmatic argument for changing the decision, counterweighing the emotional factors influencing the ruler.

In search of effective communication   107

> Anecdote 3.1: *Lushi Chunqiu* (LSCQ) Comments Chapter 1, "The Beginning of Spring" (Zhu & Su, 1995:897–898; Tang, 2010:284–285), same story also in *Zhanguoce* (ZGC), The Book of Wei, no. 308 (Crump, 1996:362–363)

In this quite long narrative, the son of the deceased King Hui from the state of Wei (reigned 370–318 BCE) wants to bury his father according to previously decided schedule despite very unfavorable weather conditions: high snow and biting cold. He refuses to change the schedule despite many pleas of his court officials. The heir feels that as a filial son, his obligation toward his dead father takes precedence over the comfort and safety of his subjects or the costs of the ceremony organized in such demanding weather conditions. Court officials turn to the sage Huizi (the protagonist of Anecdote 1.2) in their last hope to persuade the heir.

Huizi begins his persuasion with a story of how King Wen of Zhou (11th c. BCE) reacted when waters exposed the coffin of his father, buried on a hillside. King Wen, who was a model of loyalty and duty, was not in a hurry to rebury the coffin. Instead, he interpreted the event as allowing the dead king a chance to see his subjects again: "King Wen had the coffin dug up, put it behind a curtain and held court in front of it so that people could all come and see the former king. He had the coffin reburied three days later." Huizi draws a parallel between the natural exposure of the coffin of the father of King Wen, and the weather conditions forcing the postponement of the burial of King Hui of Wei. Both are unexpected and beyond human control. Both might be interpreted as resulting from actions of the spirits of the deceased rulers. The difference is in the way the living react. King Wen heeds the "call" of his dead father and holds ceremonial audiences for him. The heir of Wei wants to go on with the schedule of the funeral regardless the circumstances, and so might be turning a blind eye on his dead father's wish. Huizi then activates his main moral argument: "The deceased king must wish to stay a while longer to comfort the state and the people. That is why he has made the snow fall so heavily. If the funeral is postponed and the date is changed on this account, Your Highness will be performing the duty of King Wen. If Your Highness does not do so, it will mean that Your Highness does not want to follow the example of King Wen."

The heir of Wei now has a very different choice to make: stick to the original plan and risk being criticized as not filial to his father and not following the revered examples of sage kings of the past, or listen to Huizi, make the court officials happy, and go in the footsteps of the noble King Wen of Zhou. This makes him change his mind, and the funeral is postponed.

108 *Karol Olejniczak and Marcin Jacoby*

> Anecdote 3.2: *Zhanguoce* (ZGC), The Book of Qin, no. 98 (Wen, 2010:126; Crump, 1996:129)

The last anecdote is not only a great example of persuasion but also shows the pragmatic side of ancient Chinese ruling elites. This time, the antagonist is Queen Xuan of the state of Qin, mother of King Zhao (reigned 306–251). After she became a widow, she had a lover from the Wei state, called Chou. She was so fond of him that when she was on her deathbed, she ordered him to be killed and buried with her so that, in compliance with contemporary beliefs, he could accompany her in the afterlife. Understandably, Mr. Chou (or Wei Chou, as he is called in the text) was not too glad when he heard of the plan. His acquaintance Yong Rui made an attempt to speak to the dying queen on his behalf. Let's quote the entire dialogue:

> *"Does your highness believe that there is sentience after death?" he asked.*
> *"No, I do not," replied the queen.*
> *"Ah! Your highness's godlike intelligence clearly perceives that the dead feel nothing. Why then would you have one whom you loved alive buried with the dead who feel nothing? If the dead are sentient, your highness, then your husband, the deceased king, will have been harboring his anger against you for a long time now and you will scarce have time to make amends to him – and certainly no time left for further dalliance with Wei Chou."*
> *"True," said the queen and desisted.*
>
> (Crump, 1996:129)

Yong Rui shows to the queen that her order to bury her lover with her makes no logical sense. She seems not only intelligent, but also honest enough to admit this, accept the argument, and change her decision. Yong Rui's persuasion is successful, and Mr. Chou is saved.

These two anecdotes touch upon ancient Chinese beliefs in the afterlife, and both topics concern decisions which are directly connected with these beliefs. Persuaders do not appeal to these beliefs, nor to emotions, but to reasoning. Through clever construction of the argument, they show to their interlocutors that the only rational choice is to change their initial decisions.

Lessons for evaluation practice

In this section, we try to link the strategies from pre-imperial China with current developments in public policy and speculate about practical adaptations to evaluation craft. We want to clearly stress that we look for smart ways of closing the gap between decision-makers and evidence providers (in our case evaluators and policy advisors). This does not mean manipulating decision-makers, nor compromising the quality of evidence in order to fit listeners' ears. We look for effective discourse strategies that would allow us to keep the integrity of the message and at the same time reshape decision makers' mental models (causal thinking and understanding) in a constructive and effective way.

We have identified five lessons—the first two emerge from observations common to all analyzed Chinese narratives, while the remaining three lessons are linked to specific pre-imperial strategies. For each lesson we provide core conclusion coming from our analysis of Chinese sources, we link it with contemporary public policy research, and we discuss key implications and takeaways for evaluation practice.

Lesson 1: Understanding addressee's mental models

All strategies show deep understanding of the addressee of the message—the ruler or other person in the position of power. Advisors in those stories recognized the antagonist's way of thinking and his/her *modus operandi*. And then they align the communication strategy with it.

This observation corresponds with modern practices in service design. The inspiration from this field has major place in recent public policy (Peters, 2018). One of the key element of this practice is thinking in terms of users and their specific profiles (Kumar, 2012; Liedtka & Ogilvie, 2011; Martin & Hanington, 2012). It means understanding what drives specific group of users and under what circumstances they operate. From a method perspective it means developing, based in interview, observation and survey insights, profiles or, so-called, personas of users.

For the practice of evaluation we can think about our audience as specific group of knowledge users. Each type has different knowledge needs, communication preferences, and—what is most important—operates with a different mental model. Evaluators have to put an effort into understanding mental models driving the behaviors and decisions of specific knowledge users, and plugged-into specific *personas*.

This user-oriented approach is already emerging in evaluation practice—see: Learning Agendas and Knowledge Brokering practices emerging in the context of US federal agencies (Newcomer et al., 2021). They recognize different types of knowledge user, they acknowledge that users are engaged in different decision moments, and express different information needs as well as preferences for the form of communication. This does not mean distortion or compromising the integrity of evidence. It only means that the discussion should start with mental model/thinking pattern of the audience and gradually lead the audience to the evidence.

Lesson 2: Applying rhetoric strategies

All narratives use logical parallels, metaphors, historical *exemplae*, surprise, and curiosity as methods to grab the interlocutor's attention—often relating to obvious examples from everyday reality that is familiar and logical for the decision-maker. These are all rhetoric strategies that are well-known and thoroughly characterized in Western classical rhetoric (Jasinski, 2001; Plett, 2010) but seem to be often neglected in modern discourse.

The power of narrative and framing the issue is well recognized in the current public policy literature and, more broadly, in communication literature (Mulholland, 2005). Stories and metaphors are also effectively used to change behaviors and thinking patterns in Dialectical Behavioral Therapy (DBT) (Esmail, 2020).

So far in evaluation literature, the accent has been on building narratives with quantitative data (Evergreen, 2019). We think that there is a space for narratives of a more qualitative nature. We can put more attention on developing stories with data and Theories of Change that we reconstruct from the programs. Showing key decision-makers, program operators, and stakeholders the narrative (often incoherent) of hidden assumptions underlying the program can be most valuable. In fact, the idea that program "theories represent the stories that people tell about how problems arise and how they can be solved" has been put forward by classic evaluation literature (Weiss, 1995). The recent advancement focuses the stories more on actors and their behaviors, which can be even more straightforward in communication with decision-makers (Koleros et al., 2018; Olejniczak et al., 2020).

Lesson 3: Triggering cognitive dissonance

This lesson emerges from the first strategy identified in our analysis. Its mechanism is based on triggering cognitive dissonance. We first elevate the user's position, recognize his/her high profile, and then show the gap between (a) his/her aspirations/standard for the ruler/position and (b) his/her actual behavior. This discrepancy is usually a trigger for change in behavior or correction of beliefs.

This behavioral mechanism is on the shortlist of strategies applied in contemporary public policy interventions to convince the addressees to behavioral change and compliance. It has been specially promoted with the rise of nudges (Shafir, 2013; Gofen et al., 2021). However, the issue of cognitive dissonance can create a challenge for evaluators. People seek to avoid or reduce "cognitive dissonance" often by dismissing the evidence that is inconsistent with their worldview, beliefs, current understanding of the situation, or in general, their mental model (how things work and what to do to change things) (Sunstein, 2013). Thus, when using this strategy, evaluators have to recognize how determined their addressees are in holding certain propositions and how strong evidence or counterpoints must be used to shake the specific mental model.

Lesson 4: Enlightening about long-term implications

This lesson emerges from the second strategy identified in our analysis of Chinese texts. It is based on a surprise strategy for colliding short and long-term perspectives. The first story discussed in our exemplars switches perspective and contrasts short-term vs. long-term implications of decisions. That enlightens the addressee and allows him to see a more strategic perspective of his decisions.

In current public policy, literature myopia is identified as one of the shortcomings of performance measurement systems. The decision-makers' insufficient ideas about the system's behavior in time, with its delayed side-effects is often the reason for policy failures (Dörner, 1990). Recent evaluation literature started to explore approaches and methods for advocating a long-term perspective for policy evaluation and going beyond the typical short-term perspective that programs and evaluators usually operate with (Fross et al., 2021).

In our view, bringing "the future" to the current attention of decision-makers could require more advanced methods than just face-to-face communication. Thus, the folk wisdom that "experiencing is believing" directs our attention to experiential learning methods such as serious games and simulations. Games can be used as "time machines" that bring future implications into the current policy landscape of considerations. Decision-makers that engage in a simulation can experience first-hand longer-term consequences of their decisions, explore different scenarios of trickle-down effects, side-effects, and feedback loops, and assess the sustainability of their policy solutions (Olejniczak et al., 2020).

Lesson 5: Making argument visible

The final lesson emerges from the third strategy discussed in our analysis. It is based on reconstructing the argument and then finding and showing rebuttal based on inconsistency in the addressee's thinking.

The argument-building strategy is also grounded in the Western tradition. The recent reference in public discourse is Toulmin's model of argument building (Toulmin, 2003). The relevance of this is well acknowledged in public policy analysis literature (Dunn, 2017). It is also linked to economic reasoning on social issues that frame social problems in terms of trade-offs (Winter, 2013); only in this case do we develop two lines of arguments—for two competing decisions.

For evaluation practice, we can focus more on visualizing the main structure of the argument, putting side by side the logical connection and assumptions made by decision-makers, and confronting this with them. Thus, we propose to reconstruct policy argument and even provide a visual illustration of its structure for the decision-makers (see Figure 6.1). The visuals allow better to follow the narrative and show differences and gaps in the argumentation and body of evidence on which certain decision is built.

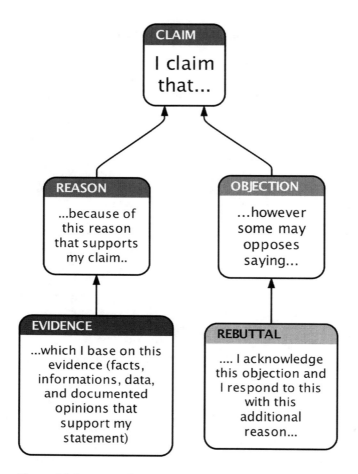

Figure 6.1 Structure of an argument

The exploration of the rich heritage of Chinese pre-imperial political discourse has provided us with specific strategies of persuasion that could be further explored for evaluation work with decision-makers in the post-truth era. With this conclusion, two reservations have to be made. First, our chapter focuses on suggestions for evaluators to better prepare for interaction with decision-makers and how to use various rhetorical strategies in actual communication purposefully. However, these persuasion strategies are just one of the elements in a complicated and dynamic relationship between evidence and decisions in the post-truth era.

Second, as all evaluators know, context matters. Naturally, the sources used in this chapter reflect the feudal, patriarchal society of the period, which is very different from modern society. However, we claim that while context changes, some core mechanisms often remain universal. After all, the works of both Shakespeare and Machiavelli still resonate with us.

The usefulness of employing elements of classical Chinese strategic thought in modern contexts is indicated by practice in politics and commerce. The successes of the People's Republic of China in engaging numerous other countries through a combination of commercial lures and forces dependencies rest heavily on ancient Chinese diplomatic tradition, as shown in the *Zhanguoce*. Servant leadership styles embracing Confucian values and Legalist approaches, as summarized in the *Lüshi Chunqiu*, have been widely employed by politicians all across East and South East Asia, going well beyond Chinese civilization's historical and cultural boundaries. The immense popularity of *Sunzi's Art of War* in Western business self-help literature shows, in turn, that military strategy from the Chinese Warring States Period can be successfully transferred to executive and business education of today. The tradition of the political discourse of the 4th and 3rd centuries BCE in China is very much alive, and despite all its restrictions and anchoring in the patriarchal value-system of old, it continues to be used in a variety of modern contexts not only in Asia.

Therefore, despite these reservations, we hope that the strategies discussed in this chapter can be a valuable inspiration to the ongoing efforts of evaluation practitioners in delivering messages that makes public policies smarter.

Funding

This work was supported by the Ministry of Science and Higher Education in Poland under the Interdisciplinary Projects at SWPS University.

References

Bendor, J. (2015). Bounded Rationality. In J. Wright (Ed.), *International Encyclopedia of the Social & Behavioral Sciences* (2nd Edition, pp. 773–776). Amsterdam: Elsevier.

Bennett, N., & Lemoine, J. (2014). What VUCA Really Means for You. *Harvard Business Review*, January–February.

Caplan, N. (1979). The Two-Communities Theory and Knowledge Utilization. *American Behavioral Scientist, 22*(3), 459–470.

Chelimsky, E. (2006). The Purposes of Evaluation in a Democratic Society. In I. Shaw, J. C. Greene, & M. M. Mark (Eds.), *Handbook of Evaluation. Policies, Programs and Practices* (pp. 33–55). Thousand Oaks, CA: Sage.

Chen, P. (1992). *Yuyan wenxue lilun. Lishi yu yingyong.* Taibei: Luotuo chubanshe.

Crump, J. I., Jr. (1964). *Intrigues. Studies of the Chan-kuo Ts'e.* Ann Arbor: The University of Michigan Press.

Crump, J. I., Jr. (1996). *Chan-kuo Ts'e.* Ann Arbor: Center for Chinese Studies, The University of Michigan Press.

114 *Karol Olejniczak and Marcin Jacoby*

Dinkler, M. B. (2016). New Testament Rhetorical Narratology: An Invitation toward Integration. *Biblical Interpretation, 24*(2), 203–228.

Dörner, D. (1990). The Logic of Failure. *Philosophical Transactions of the Royal Society of London. Series B, Biological Sciences, 327*(1241), 463–473.

Dunn, W. N. (2017). *Public Policy Analysis: An Integrated Approach* (6th Edition). New York: Routledge.

Esmail, J. J. (2020). *DBT Metaphors and Stories*. New York, NY: Routledge.

Evergreen, S. (2019). *Effective Data Visualization*. Thousand Oaks, CA: SAGE Publications.

Fludernik, M. (2009). *An Introduction to Narratology*. New York: Routledge.

Fross, K., Lindkvist, I., & McGillivray, M. (Eds.). (2021). *Long Term Perspectives in Evaluation. Increasing Relevance and Utility*. New York, NY: Routledge.

Gofen, A., Moseley, A., Thomann, E., & Weaver, K. (2021). Behavioural Governance in the Policy Process: Introduction to the Special Issue. *Journal of European Public Policy, 28*(5), 633–657. https://doi.org/10.1080/13501763.2021.1912153

Huang, J., Li, J., & Dai, M. (2008). *Xinyi Zhuangzi duben*. Taibei: Sanmin shuju.

Jasinski, J. (2001). *Sourcebook on Rhetoric. Key Concepts in Contemporary Rhetorical Studies*. Thousand Oaks, CA: Sage Publications.

Jullien, F. (2004). *Detour and Access: Strategies of Meaning in China and Greece*. New York: Zone Books.

Kavanagh, J., & Rich, M. D. (2018). *Truth Decay: An Initial Exploration of the Diminishing Role of Facts and Analysis in American Public Life*. Santa Monica, CA: RAND Corporation.

Knoblock, J., & Riegel, J. (2000). *The Annals of Lü Buwei: A Complete Translation and Study*. Stanford: Stanford University Press.

Koleros, A., Mulkerne, S., Oldenbeuving, M., & Stein, D. (2018). The Actor-Based Change Framework: A Pragmatic Approach to Developing Program Theory for Interventions in Complex Systems. *American Journal of Evaluation, 41*(1), 34–53. https://doi.org/10.1177/1098214018786462

Kumar, V. (2012). *101 Design Methods: A Structured Approach for Driving Innovation in Your Organization*. Hoboken, NJ: Wiley.

Lasswell, H. D. (1951). The Policy Orientation. In D. Lerner & H. Lasswell (Eds.), *The Policy Sciences. Recent Developments in Scope and Method.* (pp. 3–15). Stanford: Stanford University Press.

Li, F., & Li, Y. (1998). *Zhongguo gudai yuyan shi*. Xindian: Hanwei chubanshe.

Liedtka, J., & Ogilvie, T. (2011). *Designing for Growth: A Design Thinking Tool Kit for Managers*. New York, Chichester and West Sussex: Columbia University Press.

Mair, V. H. (1998). *Wandering on the Way. Early Taoist Tales and Parables of Chuang Tzu*. Honolulu: University of Hawai'i Press.

Martin, B., & Hanington, B. (2012). *Universal Methods of Design: 100 Ways to Research Complex Problems, Develop Innovative Ideas, and Design Effective Solutions*. Beverly, MA: Rockport Publishers.

McIntyre, L. C. (2018). *Post-truth*. Cambridge, MA: MIT Press.

Mulholland, J. (2005). *Handbook of Persuasive Tactics. A Practical Language Guide*. London: Routledge.

Newcomer, K., Olejniczak, K., & Hart, N. (2021). *Making Federal Agencies Evidence-Based: The Key Role of Learning Agendas*. Washington, DC: The IBM Center for

The Business of Government. http://www.businessofgovernment.org/report/making-federal-agencies-evidence-based-key-role-learning-agendas

Nichols, T. M. (2017). *The Death of Expertise: The Campaign Against Established Knowledge and Why it Matters*. New York, NY: Oxford University Press.

Nisbett, R. (2004). *The Geography of Thought: How Asians and Westerners Think Differently and Why*. New York, NY: Free Press.

Olejniczak, K., Newcomer, K., & Meijer, S. (2020). Advancing Evaluation Practice With Serious Games. *American Journal of Evaluation, 41*(3), 339–366. https://doi.org/10.1177/1098214020905897

Olejniczak, K., Śliwowski, P., & Leeuw, F. (2020). Comparing Behavioral Assumptions of Policy Tools: Framework for Policy Designers. *Journal of Comparative Policy Analysis, 22*(6), 498–520. https://doi.org/10.1080/13876988.2020.1808465

Palenberg, M., & Paulson, A. (Eds.). (2020). *The Realpolitik of Evaluation: Why Demand and Supply Rarely Intersect*. New York: Routledge.

Peters, B. G. (2018). *Policy Problems and Policy Design (New Horizons in Public Policy Series)*. Cheltenham and Northampton, MA: Edward Elgar Publishing.

Phelan, J. (2020). *Debating Rhetorical Narratology: On the Synthetic, Mimetic, and Thematic Aspects of Narrative*. Columbus: Ohio State University Press.

Plett, H. F. (2010). *Literary Rhetoric. Concepts—Structures—Analyses*. Leiden: Brill.

Rowland, R. (2009). The Narrative Perspective. In J. Kuypers (Ed.), *Rhetorical Criticism. Perspectives in Action* (pp. 117–142). Plymouth, MA: Lexington Books.

Shafir, E. (Ed.). (2013). *The Behavioral Foundations of Public Policy*. Princeton: Princeton University Press.

Shiller, R. (2020). *Narrative Economics: How Stories Go Viral and Drive Major Economic Events*. Princeton, NJ: Princeton University Press.

Sunstein, C. R. (2013). *How to Humble a Wingnut and Other Lessons from Behavioral Economics (Chicago Shorts)*. Chicago: University of Chicago Press.

Tang, B. (2010). *Lü's Commentaries of History*. Beijing: Foreign Languages Press.

Toulmin, S. E. (2003). *The Uses of Argument* (Updated Edition). Cambridge: Cambridge University Press.

Wang, Q. (2007). *Lüshi Chunqiu yanjiu*. Beijing: Xueyuan chunbanshe.

Weiss, C. H. (1980). Knowledge Creep and Decision Accretion. *Science Communication, 1*(3), 381–404.

Weiss, C. H. (1995). Nothing as Practical as Good Theory: Exploring Theory-Based Evaluation for Comprehensive Community Initiatives for Children and Families. In J. P. Connell, A. C. Kubisch, L. B. Schorr, & C. H. Weiss (Eds.), *New Approaches to Evaluating Community Initiatives: Concepts, Methods, and Contexts* (pp. 65–92). Washington, DC: Aspen Institute. http://www.aspenroundtable.org/vol1/index.htm

Wen, H. (2010). *Xinyi Zhanguo ce*. Taibei: Sanmin shuju.

Wildavsky, A. (1979). *The Art and Craft of Policy Analysis (2018 re-Edition)*. Berkeley, CA: Palgrave Macmillan.

Winter, H. (2013). *Trade-Offs. An Introduction to Economic Reasoning and Social Issues*. Chicago, IL: University of Chicago Press.

Yang, K. (2016). *Zhanguo shi*. Shanghai: Shanghai renmin chubanshe.

Yu, K. (2015). *Zhanguoshi*. Shanghai: Shanghai renmin chubanshe.

Zhu, Y., & Su, M. (1995). *Xinyi Lüshi chunqiu*. Taipei: Sanmin shuju.

7 Do citizens even want to hear the truth?

Public attitudes toward evidence-informed policymaking

Pirmin Bundi and Valérie Pattyn

Introduction

Evidence-based policymaking enjoys great popularity among governments and public administrations, who use this normative leitmotif in order to improve and justify public policies (Cairney, 2016; French, 2018; Head, 2016; Parsons, 2002). According to Radaelli (1995), reliable information and expert knowledge are an essential part of policy design and implementation. One source of evidence can be provided by evaluations. By relying on scientific procedures, evaluations systematically assess the impact of policy programs and make recommendations for policy-makers. For a long time, research on evaluation proclaimed the credo that truth should be spoken to power (Perkins, 1995; Wildavsky, 1989). In recent years, many evaluators apply a more pragmatic stance though (e.g. Hoppe, 1999), also faced with the often limited utilization of evaluation findings in the political arena (Eberli, 2018; Frey, 2012; Weiss, 1998). Accordingly, an increasing number of policy-makers and scholars, also in the evaluation field, now consistently talk about evidence *informed* policymaking as a more realistic ambition to strive for (Head, 2016). While evidence-informed policymaking can be conceived as taken for granted, at least in policy communities in democratic societies (see Sanderson, 2009), the same democratic principles also require us to consider what citizens themselves think of the use of evidence in policymaking processes.

As the case of COVID-19 has clearly shown, the involvement of experts and evidence has not been free from criticism and triggered fierce debate. Also scholars increasingly reflect about the challenging position of citizens vis-à-vis expert involvement in policymaking (Caramani, 2017; Dommett & Pearce, 2019; Pastorella, 2016). According to Bertsou (2021), governments face a conflicting dilemma when involving experts in political decisions, which in essence boils down to the classic discussion between input and output legitimacy (Scharpf, 1999). To put it in somewhat unnuanced terms, the inclusion of experts in the policymaking process can help ensuring effective public policies. Experts will follow their convictions to propose policy solutions that are based on the best available knowledge, and as such contribute to more effective policies that will benefit society. Also Bertsou and Caramani (2022) propagated that a regime can establish legitimacy on the basis of scientific knowledge, sector-specific experience, and unattached interests of its members only (output legitimacy). This approach

DOI: 10.4324/9781032719979-8

tends to be in tension, however, when highlighting governments' need for input legitimacy. The core democratic argument involves that governments rest on the foundation of public accountability. Citizens elect a political leadership, which subsequently pursues a political direction representing a substantial part of the population. Governments' performance can be rewarded or might be questioned again in the next elections, and, in the worst case, governments can even be voted out of office. The involvement of experts is said to challenge this accountability principle, as it by nature inhibits the risk of untransparent decision-making (Heldt & Herzog, 2021). It requires citizens to trust the procedures on which scientists rely, which are hard to understand and often not explained to the public (Bundi & Pattyn, 2022). Approaching it from this angle, the involvement of experts can also provoke distrust in governments. While both types of legitimacy are not unreconcilable per se, they do reflect different priorities. To put it in the well-known adagio of Scharpf (1999): Governing effective [or] democratic?

This contribution is situated against this background and probes into the complexity of evaluation in our institutional and political systems. More in particular, this chapter asks the following question: Are there differences in public attitudes toward evidence-informed policy and can these differences be attributed to political ideologies? Despite the increasing discussions on the topic, there is thus far little empirical knowledge on how citizens perceive the role of evidence in policymaking, let alone across countries. Addressing this question is pertinent, especially in the wake of the emerging post-truth phenomenon. According to Suiter (2016), many contemporary democracies witnessed this "combination of policy blunders" after having experienced a severe economic crisis and facing the consequences of our globalized world with a new hybrid media (bubble) system combining reality TV and social media. In a setting of post-truth politics, emotions are more dominant than actual facts. Moreover, as shown in the context of COVID-19, different groups with diverse political opinions often do not possess a common sets of facts. Marshall and Drieschova (2018) argue that post-truth politics has been made possible by two distinct conditions. One the one hand, traditional media (e.g., newspapers, television and radio) have lost their monopoly to provide information and disseminated them through new platforms that could be established due to technological innovations (Cosentino, 2020). On the other hand, and as empirically confirmed by other studies (Bundi & Pattyn, 2022; Gauchat, 2015), an increasing share of citizens distrust political elites, traditional media, and expert knowledge. This also drives people to rely on alternative sources of information, other than scientific evidence.

Knowing which citizen communities are more open or more skeptical about evidence in policymaking, can help us developing more targeted strategies overcoming this. The empirical corpus of this chapter revolves around the results of a cross-sectional survey conducted in Australia, Belgium, Canada, France, Switzerland, and the United States. The survey, measuring public attitudes toward evidence-based policymaking, was launched in

118 *Pirmin Bundi and Valérie Pattyn*

the middle of the COVID-19 pandemic (2020–2021). The selected countries reflect a most different case selection (Seawright & Gerring, 2008), covering both parliamentary and non-parliamentary democracies (Siaroff, 2003) and countries with different administrative systems (Meyer & Hammerschmid, 2010; Turgeon & Gagnon, 2013). Most crucially, our sample also provides variance for the post-truth discourse. Political observers particularly identified an increase of post-truth politics in Australia and the United States, while the other countries in the sample restrained from this. The results put empirical flesh on the theoretical discussion about how citizens value evidence-based policymaking. As we will show, support for evidence strongly varies across countries and across citizen profiles. In the post-truth countries of our sample, political polarization seems especially strongly related to attitudes toward using evidence in policymaking. The empirical results bring important implications for evaluators and future research on evaluation, which merit careful consideration.

The chapter is structured as following. In the next section, we further delve into the role of citizens in policymaking, which explains why we should care about public attitudes toward evidence, and evaluation in particular. Next, we present the major findings from our empirical study in the six countries surveyed. This sets the stage for a reflection about lessons for evaluation research and research on evaluation in particular. Our study can be read as a call for a more systematic research agenda on the topic.

Citizens and evidence-informed policymaking

Why care about citizen perceptions of evidence-informed policymaking? To start with, it is important to consider citizens' possible roles in the political process (Frederickson, 1991). Citizens can act as interest groups (pluralist), consumers (public choice), voters (legislative), and clients. They not only delegate their policy preferences to the political elites, as a restricted view on citizens would imply, but they can also be conceived as one of the most important stakeholders of public policy. Given their importance, the participation of citizens in the policymaking process increasingly gets attention in practice, in fact long after their involvement has been advocated in literature (Fung, 2015; Kim, 2008; Michels & De Graaf, 2017; Roberts, 2015). Citizen participation has been particularly conceived as an added value for policy design, which is a development activity for and with the populations (Smith & Ingram, 2002).

In the same line of thinking, citizen participation enjoys a reinvigorated popularity in the evaluation field. Almost 50 years ago, Caputo (1973) argued that citizens should take part in the evaluation of programs by organizing citizen assessments of policies, next to experts. Also, recent publications draw attention to the role of citizens in evaluation (Boyle et al., 2008; Bundi & Pattyn, 2021; Burton, 2009; Hanberger, 2018; N. Norris, 2015;

Do citizens even want to hear the truth? 119

Picciotto, 2017). Inspired by Fung (2015), it can be argued that citizen participation has much to offer for policy-makers: first, and echoing the above argument about input legitimacy, it offers the promise of improved legitimacy. Citizens who are not members of the political arena can represent interests that are shared by many other citizens and which do not necessarily reflect electoral incentives (Bäckstrand, 2006). Moreover, citizens may offer local knowledge embedded in a specific cultural and often practical context which evaluators may not be aware of (Juntti et al., 2009). More importantly, citizen involvement can provide epistemological benefits: citizens may be more open to new inputs and more knowledgeable about how public policy works in particular in social communities (Fischer, 2000). Second, citizen participation can foster effective governance, especially when dealing with wicked multisectoral problems (Mukherjee et al., 2021). Citizens, unlike political actors for example, may be well positioned to assess trade-offs between ethical or material values, or they may be able to frame a policy problem in a more feasible way than experts (Fung, 2015). Citizens can provide new perspectives that can promote the validity of certain policies (Juntti et al., 2009). Finally, citizen participation has the potential in principle to reduce social injustices that may occur through governance mechanisms (Fung, 2015). This argument does not automatically apply to all citizens, though Binnema and Michels (2021) have shown that deliberation forums often remain with an educational bias, which results in an output that largely reflects the wishes and preferences of those attending and jeopardize the promises of citizen participation.

Thus far, empirical evidence on the actual democratic contribution of citizen participation is ambiguous and seems to depend on many contingent elements (Abels, 2007). This is particularly true for evaluations, in which citizens often serve as an important stakeholder group (Bundi & Pattyn, 2021). For instance, Kim (2008) shows that citizen participation may have improved the realization and outcome of the evaluation using the example of a participatory evaluation in Korea. While citizen participation has not led to more transparent evaluation reports by showing input information nor did it improve the quality of the evaluation, it has nonetheless increased the diffusion of evaluation results among government officials and the general public. Moreover, the participation process was followed by an increased evaluation use in professional associations.

Regardless of the actual added value of citizen participation in evaluation, one can critically ask whether these investments in participatory evaluation make sense if groups of citizens do not support the role of evidence in democracies. As mentioned, there is hardly any research on whether citizens really care about evidence. While decision makers may have strong interest to base policies on empirical evidence, it is not rational per se to expect citizens to support the use of evidence in policymaking, as they often know little about the process leading to this evidence (Baghramian & Croce, 2021) or have little trust in experts

120   *Pirmin Bundi and Valérie Pattyn*

(Bundi & Pattyn, 2022). Hence, what do citizens actually think about the use of scientific evidence in policymaking, and can we discern particular patterns when comparing citizen groups?

Public attitudes toward evidence-informed policymaking

In order to examine public attitudes toward evidence-informed policymaking, we conducted a cross-national survey in six countries—Australia, Belgium, Canada, France, Switzerland, and the United States—between November 2020 and January 2021 (N=8,749). As mentioned, the countries reflect a sample of very diverse cases (Seawright & Gerring, 2008), including countries with stronger and weaker tendencies toward post-truth politics. One can expect that these different political cultures will also influence how citizens perceive the role of evidence in policymaking. The survey was furthermore conducted in the peak of the second wave of the COVID-19 pandemic in fall/winter 2020. Most governments decided to introduce different measures to limit the spread of the virus. Among other things, countries decided to restrict personal liberties (e.g., free movement) or shut down certain sectors (e.g., gastronomy, schools). Even if individuals—and the survey respondents—did not directly contract the virus or knew somebody who did so, they were financially or socially affected by the public measures (Betsch et al., 2020; Clemente-Suárez et al., 2020). In doing so, since the beginning of the current global health crisis, governments' responses have hardly been more under the flagship of evidence-informed policymaking. Governments were (and still are) in active exchange with scientists to cope with the health crisis (Forster & Heinzel, 2021; Stevens, 2020). This makes the COVID-19 setting a particularly interesting context in order to study public attitudes toward evidence-informed policymaking. Table 7.1 provides an overview of the sample.

Table 7.1 Overview of sample

Country	N	Female (%)	Age group (mean)	University degree (%)	COVID-19 handling (mean)	EIPM (mean)
Australia	1,266	58	3.54	42	7.30	7.42
Belgium	1,512	51	3.17	49	4.46	7.23
Canada	1,220	60	3.92	52	6.03	7.39
France	1,220	65	2.97	53	4.22	7.02
Switzerland	2,270	46	3.24	48	5.87	7.29
United States	1,261	55	3.63	52	5.13	7.33
Total	8,749	55	3.39	49	5.53	7.28

Note: The respondents were divided into six age groups: 18–24 (1) to 65+ (6); COVID-19 Affected: I have been personally affected by the pandemic in a negative way; COVID-19 handling: 0 (extremely bad) to 10 (extremely well); Evidence-informed policymaking: 0 (disagree) to 10 (fully agree).

The sample contains at least 1,200 respondents per country, with Switzerland being deliberately oversampled to get sufficient citizens of its three different linguistic groups. While the sample is slightly different in terms of socio-cultural characteristics such as gender, age and education, the table also reveals that respondents from different countries have evaluated their governments COVID-19 crisis management differently. Whereas Australians perceived the crisis handling as very positive, the French, Belgian, and American respondents are much more critical about their political decision-makers. Swiss and Canadians are situated in between these two country groups.

In order to measure public attitudes toward evidence-informed policymaking, we asked the respondents whether they fully disagree (0) or fully agree (10) with the following statement: "*I would like to see policy-makers use scientific evidence more often to make decisions on specific issues.*" Even though the average attitude toward evidence-informed policymaking is quite high with 7.28 and does not vary substantially across countries, Figure 7.1 shows that there is more variance between Australia, the United States, and Canada. The respondents from Belgium, France, and Switzerland are closer to each other. This suggests that external factors are likely related to citizen attitudes about evidence use in politics.

Looking at socio-economic variables, we firstly see that it is very likely that respondents with a university degree are more positive toward scientific evidence, as they can be expected to be more familiar with such evidence in principle, due to their educational training. Secondly, women might have a more positive view

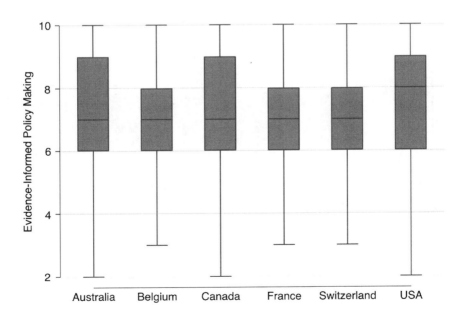

Figure 7.1 Levels of attitudes toward evidence-informed policymaking

toward scientific evidence, consistent with Bundi et al.'s (2021) finding that they more often tend to use evaluation results. Third, elder respondents should show more positive attitudes toward evidence-informed policymaking. Prior studies argued that experience level influences the use of evidence (Bober & Bartlett, 2004; Boyer & Langbein, 1991; Johnson et al., 2009; Marra, 2003). Of these variables, however, only education proves to be positively related to attitudes toward evidence-informed policymaking. Gender and age do not seem to be linked (Figures 7.2–7.4).

In particular in Switzerland and the United States—where fewer citizens graduate from universities—respondents with a university degree have a significant higher level of support for evidence-informed policymaking. This difference is smaller in Australia, Belgium and Canada, even though university graduates from these countries are also more positive toward evidence use. There are hardly any observable differences in France. As to gender differences, women tend to be more positive in Australia, Canada, and the United States. They are generally less fond of evidence in Belgium. No such trend can be observed in France or Switzerland. Finally, the relationship between attitudes toward evidence use and age tends to vary between countries. We only observe increased values for elder respondents in France and Belgium. In Switzerland and the United States (and to some degree Canada), in contrast, we find a rather negative association between age and evidence use. There are no significant differences across age groups however, which suggests that we must focus on other factors to explain attitudes toward evaluation use.

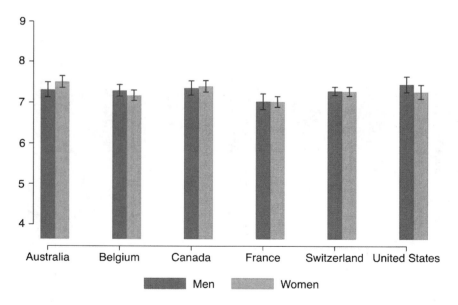

Figure 7.2 Evidence-informed policymaking, gender, education, and age

Do citizens even want to hear the truth? 123

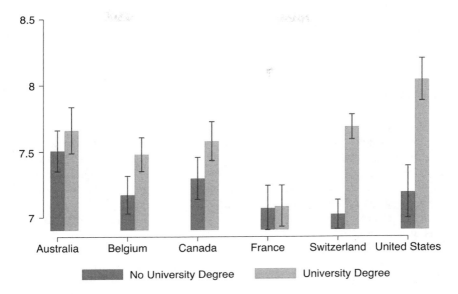

Figure 7.3 Evidence-informed policymaking, gender, education, and age

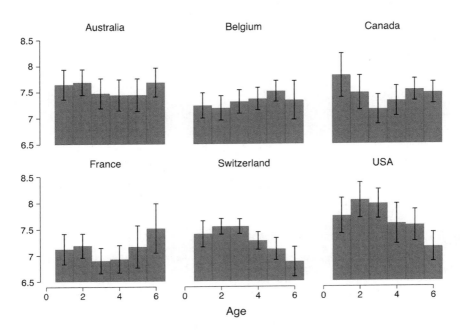

Figure 7.4 Evidence-informed policymaking, gender, education, and age

We therefore turn our attention to political ideologies, which has often been associated with post-truth politics. One should be careful in interpreting the link. Norris et al. (2020) did not find differences across partisan identification, partisan strength, or their affiliation with the losing side in the perception of fair elections for the United States. Instead, they pointed at ideological extremism—independent of party affiliation and partisan strength—as the main factor leading voters to inflate problems with the fairness of the vote count, which draws an important distinction between partisanship and ideology. While it is possible to have a strong attachment to political parties, citizens may not necessarily espouse extreme ideological beliefs that contribute to the "aforementioned paranoid style" of American elections. Despite that, previous studies indicated that citizens who ideologically lean to the political right are in general more skeptical toward scientific evidence due to their aversion about uncertainty and ineffectually that they typically associate with science (Beck et al., 1992; Gauchat, 2015). To test this assumption, we asked the respondents to place themselves on a scale from 0 (left) to 10 (right). Subsequently, we have classified the responses in three political groups: Left (0–3), center (4–6), and right (7–10). Figure 7.5 shows the results for attitudes toward evidence-informed policymaking and left-right ideology.

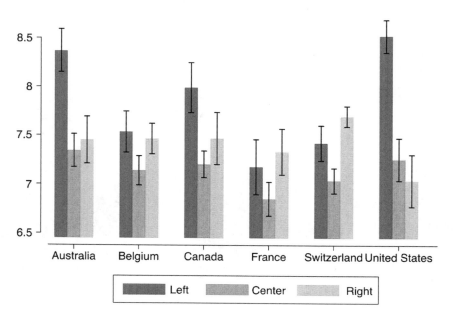

Figure 7.5 Evidence-informed policymaking and left-right ideology

Do citizens even want to hear the truth? 125

The figure shows that there is indeed a tendency that respondents leaning toward the right political spectrum tend to be more skeptical toward evidence-informed policymaking. In particular, in post-truth countries (Australia and United States), there is a strong difference between left and center/right respondents. The same observations—albeit to a lesser degree—can be observed in Canada, while in the European countries the center respondents are less positive toward evidence use. Thus, and in contrast to Norris et al. (2020), we find that center-leaning citizens tend to distrust scientific evidence, which is interesting to highlight.

More nuance can be added when bringing political party dynamics into the picture. Survey respondents were also asked to indicate for which party they usually vote, or which party is generally closest to them. Figure 7.6 illustrates the average mean for attitudes toward evidence-informed policymaking for different party voters. As can be deduced from the figure, it confirms the observations made for political ideology. In our sample's post-truth countries—if we may generalize it this way—we not only have strong differences between left and right parties but also voters for the Australian Green Party and for the democrats are among those with the most positive attitude toward evidence use. Thus, suggesting a polarization within the country. In comparison, Republicans score by far the most negative attitudes toward evidence-informed policymaking. The other countries do not show significant differences across party voters, even

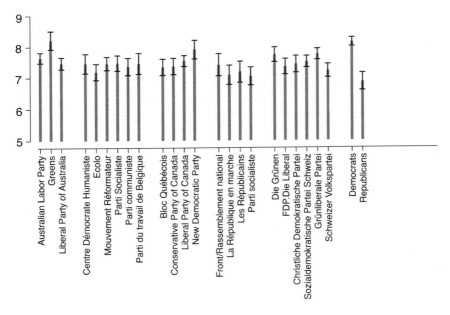

Figure 7.6 Evidence-informed policymaking and parties

though voters for more progressive parties (New Democratic Party in Canada; Die Grünen and Grünliberale Schweiz in Switzerland) also have a significantly more positive attitude toward evidence use. To our knowledge, this finding has not yet been shown in other research.

While adding nuance to existing scholarship, our findings should be treated with care. We signal the following limitations. First, the results are based on survey results, which do not always correspond to the real preferences due to misreporting and self-selection bias (see Bundi et al., 2018; Krawiec & Sliwowski, 2022). We cannot exclude the possibility that respondents do not want to report their real preferences due to a social desirability bias. Similarly, citizens may have difficulties to form their opinion about a complex issue as the use of evidence in policymaking. Second, we aggregated the responses of individuals to the country and the party level for our analysis. Even though we can observe some differences between countries and parties, extreme positions could neutralize themselves. Third, evaluations are usually carried out at the program or organizational level, which are both locally shaped. Hence, public attitudes toward evidence-informed policymaking can provide some insights about the general evaluation culture in a specific country, but this information might be less relevant for single evaluation projects. It may well be the case, for instance, that citizens are open to evidence use at national level, but more restrictive about the use of evaluation findings in the context of specific policy interventions. Complementing our research with a more fine-grained analysis at local, policy field, or project level could help to unpack this in more depth.

Implications for evaluation research and research on evaluation

Having discussed these empirical findings, the important question remains of what they imply for evaluators, being the producers of one important type of scientific evidence, and for scholars investigating evaluation practice. The survey results clearly show that support for the use of scientific evidence in policymaking should not be taken for granted, which is a key element to take into account when thinking about further institutionalizing evaluation in the public sector or developing evaluation or evaluator capacity. In particular, less educated people tend to be more skeptical about science. Political ideology also matters, which can be relevant to consider when designing an evaluation.

Thus, we invite researchers on evaluation to more systematically engage with the topic, and sketch some avenues, related to conceptual and methodological lines of research, that may be worth investigating, but that have received little attention thus far in the evaluation literature. Investigating these becomes even more important in a setting of increased post-truth policymaking, which can be expected to pose major challenges in the upcoming decades. Without citizen support for evidence use in policymaking, government trust can be severely compromised and lead to increasing societal polarization

Do citizens even want to hear the truth? 127

(Fridman et al., 2021). The findings also prompt serious normative reflection. Even within countries, as our study showed, different communities display different attitudes about the inclusion of scientific evidence. Simply ignoring resistance against evidence and evaluation is probably not the right answer. Instead, citizens' fears are best recognized and actively taken on board, as such also to improve the relevance and effectiveness of evaluations themselves. Conceptually, we investigated citizen support for evidence-informed policy-making in general. We cannot rule out, of course, that citizens display various attitudes toward different evaluation types. There are different evaluation models, which involve much variation in terms of potential for citizen involvement themselves (Bundi & Pattyn, 2021). Also stakeholder-oriented models, which have been designed to bring "citizens closer to evaluations," display much variation in this regard. For instance, the empowerment evaluation model has especially been developed to improve programs in a participatory process. Such an evaluation helps program managers, staff, and beneficiaries to carry out their own evaluation together, with external evaluators acting as consultants and service providers (Fettermann, 2001). In this sense, citizens can be conceived as evaluators who assess the object of evaluation themselves. In contrast, the participatory evaluation model is an approach that involves the stakeholders of the evaluated object directly in the evaluation process. They can be involved at any stage of the evaluation process, i.e., from establishing the evaluation design, to data collection, analysis, and reporting (Cousins & Earl, 1992). This may enable citizens to provide new insights as part of the target or beneficiary group. Lastly, cross-cultural evaluation approaches endeavor to be responsive to the cultural context of the evaluation. This model highlights the social relations among stakeholders in evaluation and acknowledges that program evaluators and program participants may have a different cultural background (Chouinard & Cousins, 2009). Citizens with different cultural backgrounds could serve as baseline to adjust evaluation findings.

It may be worth studying how citizens value these various models, and whether citizens who are not in favor of scientific evidence, reject all these models altogether, or nonetheless see potential for policymaking based on particular models. In the same vein, and related to this, our study points out the need for more in-depth knowledge on "why" citizens are skeptical about the use of scientific evidence. Having more insights into the specific causal mechanisms that make citizens more open toward evidence, or which make them rather reluctant can be useful in designing ways to overcome potential obstacles, to the extent possible. Of course, there may be multiple pathways to foster citizen support for evidence, which requires more research about how contextual factors may foster or jeopardize this. Without understanding how broader political and societal pressure is shaping how citizens approach evidence, it will be hard developing evaluation systems that are suited to overcoming such reluctance. Depending on a country's civic epistemology (Jasanoff, 2011) or knowledge regime (Campbell

& Pedersen, 2014), citizens may have developed different preferences about what constitutes legitimate knowledge in a particular setting. In other words, additional cross-country research beyond the OECD countries included in our study would strongly benefit the evaluation field. Different communities likely developed their own language and rationalities as to how scientific evidence and evaluation is perceived (Oliver & Boaz, 2019). Assessing these competing logics more in depth can help developing strategies to bring these different rationalities together.

From a more methodological lens, the study raises the question whether evaluators are sufficiently equipped to deal with communities that are resistant toward evidence, and evaluation in particular. Many evaluations will cut across groups with stakeholders that may have different views on evidence. Evaluators may face hard times positioning themselves in such heterogenous settings. The challenge will probably be most pronounced for evaluations relying on participatory methods, which by nature depend on citizen input and where citizens' diverse opinions will be the most apparent. Ideally, the evaluation toolbox can therefore be expanded with strategies that can help evaluators facilitating and moderating between different citizen communities, or that enable evaluators to combine expert-driven evaluation methods with more participatory methods capable overcoming citizen skepticism about the evaluation enterprise. Similar challenges will exist in evaluation settings that cut across different national boundaries, and potentially different post-truth cultural settings. Multiple research methods, ranging from participatory observations to experimental studies, should be used to analyze and test which evaluation instruments may work. Preferably, evaluators can bring together different examples of situations in which citizens' initial resistance toward evaluation in post-truth settings were overcome, as to draw lessons about what works in which contexts using which methods.

Interestingly, we know from other research fields that the inclusion and participation of citizens—even though they might be skeptical about science in general and evidence use—helps to improve the attitudes toward evidence (see Aarons et al., 2012). The same may apply to evaluations, although we lack robust evidence to make this claim. Nonetheless, a careful well-designed participatory approach toward evaluation may be a useful strategy to consider, also in settings with citizens skeptical of evaluations. And even when more expert-driven evaluation methods are used, a *citizen-friendly approach* is preferably strived for, in line with the "res publica" that evaluations are meant to serve. It is incumbent upon evaluators to think more conceptually how this can look like. In practical terms, this could range from setting up an evaluation communication strategy that uses simple language to setting up citizen panels that discuss evaluation results. While one should not be naïve about the results such citizen-minded approach may bring, it may help making citizens more aware of the value of using evidence in policymaking, and vice versa can it help evaluators to develop a better understanding of "what matters" for citizens in particular settings. For evaluators, developing citizen-friendly evaluation environments is a delicate undertaking, however, as they should be careful not to end up as uncritical propagandists of science in public. Even though evaluations can help assuring that the public receives the same facts, we do not promote blind trust in science or evaluations. An "evaluating society" only merits the label, if it promotes a critical and open attitude toward science and expertise. It is part of the professional duty of evaluators to help developing such critical mindset. We could not put it better than in the words of Schwandt (2008), which are more relevant than ever:

> For an evaluating society to flourish, citizens and professionals have to develop a capacity to be inquisitive, systematic in their inquiry, judicious in their claims, truth seeking, analytical, intellectually humble, sympathetic to opposing points of view, self-critical, and open-minded—not simply open-minded in the sense of being tolerant of other points of view, but open-minded in the sense of recognizing the challenges to one's own way of seeing things that arise from others' ways of making distinctions of worth.

Besides lending support to educating for "intelligent belief in evaluation" (Schwandt, 2008), such society will only flourish if evaluators themselves actively embrace the known unknowns and unknown unknowns in evaluations, and actively communicates about these with citizens. Only under these conditions, we believe that evaluators can secure a sustainable and credible position in an evaluating society challenged by post-truth thinking.

References

Aarons, G. A., Cafri, G., Lugo, L., & Sawitzky, A. (2012). Expanding the domains of attitudes towards evidence-based practice: The evidence based practice attitude scale-50. *Administration and Policy in Mental Health and Mental Health Services Research*, *39*(5), 331–340.

Abels, G. (2007). Citizen involvement in public policy-making: Does it improve democratic legitimacy and accountability? The case of pTA. *Interdisciplinary Information Sciences*, *13*(1), 103–116. https://doi.org/10.4036/iis.2007.103

Bäckstrand, K. (2006). Multi-stakeholder partnerships for sustainable development: Rethinking legitimacy, accountability and effectiveness. *European Environment*, *16*(5), 290–306.

Baghramian, M., & Croce, M. (2021). Experts, public policy, and the question of trust. In *The Routledge handbook of political epistemology*. pp. 446–457 Routledge.

Beck, U., Lash, S., & Wynne, B. (1992). *Risk society: Towards a new modernity* (Vol. 17). Sage.

Bertsou, E. (2022). Bring in the experts? Citizen preferences for independent experts in political decision-making processes. *European Journal of Political Research,61*, 255–267.

Bertsou, E., & Caramani, D. (2022). People haven't had enough of experts: Technocratic attitudes among citizens in nine European democracies. *American Journal of Political Science*, *66*, 5–23.

Betsch, C., Korn, L., Sprengholz, P., Felgendreff, L., Eitze, S., Schmid, P., & Böhm, R. (2020). Social and behavioral consequences of mask policies during the COVID-19 pandemic. *Proceedings of the National Academy of Sciences*, *117*(36), 21851–21853.

Binnema, H., & Michels, A. (2022). Does democratic innovation reduce bias? The G1000 as a new form of local citizen participation. *International Journal of Public Administration*, *45*(6), 475–485.

Bober, C. F., & Bartlett, K. R. (2004). The utilization of training program evaluation in corporate universities. *Human Resource Development Quarterly*, *15*(4), 363–383.

Boyer, J. F., & Langbein, L. I. (1991). Factors influencing the use of health evaluation research in Congress. *Evaluation Review*, *15*(5), 507–532.

Boyle, R., Breul, J. D., & Dahler-Larsen, P. (2008). *Open to the public: Evaluation in the public sector* (Vol. 13). Transaction Publishers.

Bundi, P., Frey, K., & Widmer, T. (2021). Does evaluation quality enhance evaluation use? *Evidence & Policy: A Journal of Research, Debate and Practice*, *17*(4), 661–687. Retrieved Jan 5, 2024, from https://doi.org/10.1332/174426421X16141794148067.

Bundi, P., & Pattyn, V. (2021). Citizens and evaluation: A review of evaluation models. *American Journal of Evaluation*. https://doi.org/10.1177/10982140211047219

Bundi, P., & Pattyn, V. (2022). Trust, but verify? Understanding citizen attitudes towards evidence-informed policy making. *Public Administration*. https://doi.org/10.1111/padm.12852

Bundi, P., Varone, F., Gava, R., & Widmer, T. (2018). Self-selection and misreporting in legislative surveys. *Political Science Research and Methods*, *6*(4), 771–789.

Burton, P. (2009). Conceptual, theoretical and practical issues in measuring the benefits of public participation. *Evaluation*, *15*(3), 263–284.

Cairney, P. (2016). *The politics of evidence-based policy making*. Springer.

Campbell, J. L., & Pedersen, O. K. (2014). *The national origins of policy ideas*. Princeton University Press.

Caputo, D. C. (1973). Evaluating urban public policy: A developmental model and some reservations. *Public Administration Review*, *33*(2), 113–119.

Caramani, D. (2017). Will vs. reason: The populist and technocratic forms of political representation and their critique to party government. *American Political Science Review*, *111*(1), 54–67.

Chouinard, J. A., & Cousins, J. B. (2009). A review and synthesis of current research on cross-cultural evaluation. *American Journal of Evaluation*, *30*(4), 457–494.

Clemente-Suárez, V. J., Dalamitros, A. A., Beltran-Velasco, A. I., Mielgo-Ayuso, J., & Tornero-Aguilera, J. F. (2020). Social and psychophysiological consequences of the COVID-19 pandemic: An extensive literature review. *Frontiers in Psychology*, *11*, 3077.

Cosentino, G. (2020). *Social media and the post-truth world order: The global dynamics of disinformation*. Springer Nature.

Cousins, J. B., & Earl, L. M. (1992). The case for participatory evaluation. *Educational Evaluation and Policy Analysis*, *14*(4), 397–418.

Dommett, K., & Pearce, W. (2019). What do we know about public attitudes towards experts? Reviewing survey data in the United Kingdom and European Union. *Public Understanding of Science*, *28*(6), 669–678.

Do citizens even want to hear the truth? 131

Eberli, D. (2018). Tracing the use of evaluations in legislative processes in Swiss cantonal parliaments. *Evaluation and Program Planning, 69*, 139–147.

Fetterman, D. M. (2001). *Foundations of empowerment evaluation.* Sage.

Fischer, F. (2000). Citizens, experts, and the environment. In *Citizens, experts, and the environment.* Duke University Press. https://www.degruyter.com/document/doi/10.1515/9780822380283/html

Forster, T., & Heinzel, M. (2021). Reacting, fast and slow: How world leaders shaped government responses to the COVID-19 pandemic. *Journal of European Public Policy, 28*(8), 1299–1320.

Frederickson, H. G. (1991). Toward a theory of the public for public administration. *Administration & Society, 22*(4), 395–417.

French, R. D. (2018). Lessons from the evidence on evidence-based policy. *Canadian Public Administration, 61*(3), 425–442.

Frey, K. (2012). *Evidenzbasierte Politikformulierung in der Schweiz*Gesetzesrevisionen im Vergleich. Baden-Baden:Nomos. .

Fridman, A., Gershon, R., & Gneezy, A. (2021). COVID-19 and vaccine hesitancy: A longitudinal study. *PLoS One, 16*(4), e0250123.

Fung, A. (2015). Putting the public back into governance: The challenges of citizen participation and its future. *Public Administration Review, 75*(4), 513–522.

Gauchat, G. (2015). The political context of science in the United States: Public acceptance of evidence-based policy and science funding. *Social Forces, 94*(2), 723–746.

Hanberger, A. (2018). Rethinking democratic evaluation for a polarised and mediatised society. *Evaluation, 24*(4), 382–399.

Head, B. W. (2016). Toward more "evidence-informed" policy making? *Public Administration Review, 76*(3), 472–484. https://doi.org/10.1111/puar.12475

Heldt, E. C., & Herzog, L. (2022). The limits of transparency: Expert knowledge and meaningful accountability in central banking. *Government and Opposition, 57*(2), 217–232.

Hoppe, R. (1999). Policy analysis, science and politics: From 'speaking truth to power' to 'making sense together'. *Science and Public Policy, 26*(3), 201–210.

Jasanoff, S. (2011). Cosmopolitan knowledge: Climate science and global civic epistemology. In John S. Dryzek, Richard B. Norgaard, & David Schlosberg (Eds.), *The Oxford handbook of climate change and society* (pp. 129–143). Oxford University Press. https://doi.org/10.1093/oxfordhb/9780199566600.003.0009

Johnson, K., Greenseid, L. O., Toal, S. A., King, J. A., Lawrenz, F., & Volkov, B. (2009). Research on evaluation use: A review of the empirical literature from 1986 to 2005. *American Journal of Evaluation, 30*(3), 377–410.

Juntti, M., Russel, D., & Turnpenny, J. (2009). Evidence, politics and power in public policy for the environment. *Environmental Science & Policy, 12*(3), 207–215. https://doi.org/10.1016/j.envsci.2008.12.007

Kim, M.-S. (2008). Does citizen participation in the evaluation processes make any difference? With special reference to the evaluation of government policies and programs in the Korean government. In R. Boyle, J. D. Breul, & P. Dahler-Larsen (Eds.), *Open to the public* (pp. 169–185). Routledge.

Marra, M. (2003). *Dynamics of evaluation use as organizational knowledge. The case of the World Bank.* The George Washington University.

132 *Pirmin Bundi and Valérie Pattyn*

Marshall, H., & Drieschova, A. (2018). Post-truth politics in the UK's Brexit referendum. *New Perspectives*, *26*(3), 89–105.

Meyer, R. E., & Hammerschmid, G. (2010). The degree of decentralization and individual decision making in central government human resource management: A European comparative perspective. *Public Administration*, *88*(2), 455–478.

Michels, A., & De Graaf, L. (2017). Examining citizen participation: Local participatory policymaking and democracy revisited. *Local Government Studies*, *43*(6), 875–881.

Mukherjee, I., Coban, M. K., & Bali, A. S. (2021). Policy capacities and effective policy design: A review. *Policy Sciences*, *54*, 243–268.

Norris, N. (2015). Democratic evaluation: The work and ideas of Barry MacDonald. *Evaluation*, *21*(2), 135–142.

Norris, P., Garnett, H. A., & Grömping, M. (2020). The paranoid style of American elections: Explaining perceptions of electoral integrity in an age of populism. *Journal of Elections, Public Opinion and Parties*, *30*(1), 105–125.

Oliver, K., & Boaz, A. (2019). Transforming evidence for policy and practice: Creating space for new conversations. *Palgrave Communications*, *5*(1), 1–10.

Parsons, W. (2002). From muddling through to muddling up-evidence based policy making and the modernisation of British Government. *Public Policy and Administration*, *17*(3), 43–60.

Pastorella, G. (2016). Technocratic governments in Europe: Getting the critique right. *Political Studies*, *64*(4), 948–965.

Perkins, D. D. (1995). Speaking truth to power: Empowerment ideology as social intervention and policy. *American Journal of Community Psychology*, *23*(5), 765–794.

Picciotto, R. (2017). Evaluation: Discursive practice or communicative action? *Evaluation*, *23*(3), 312–322.

Radaelli, C. M. (1995). The role of knowledge in the policy process. *Journal of European Public Policy*, *2*(2), 159–183.

Roberts, N. C. (2015). *The age of direct citizen participation*. Routledge.

Sanderson, I. (2009). Intelligent policy making for a complex world: Pragmatism, evidence and learning. *Political Studies*, *57*(4), 699–719.

Scharpf, F. W. (1999). *Governing in Europe: Effective and democratic?* Oxford University Press.

Schwandt, T. A. (2008). Educating for intelligent belief in evaluation. *American Journal of Evaluation*, *29*(2), 139–150.

Seawright, J., & Gerring, J. (2008). Case selection techniques in case study research: A menu of qualitative and quantitative options. *Political Research Quarterly*, *61*(2), 294–308. https://doi.org/10.1177/1065912907313077

Siaroff, A. (2003). Comparative presidencies: The inadequacy of the presidential, semi-presidential and parliamentary distinction. *European Journal of Political Research*, *42*(3), 287–312.

Smith, S. R., & Ingram, H. M. (2002). Rethinking policy analysis: Citizens, community, and the restructuring of public services. *The Good Society*, *11*(1), 55–60.

Stevens, A. (2020). Governments cannot just 'follow the science' on COVID-19. *Nature Human Behaviour*, *4*(6), 560–560.

Suiter, J. (2016). Post-truth politics. *Political Insight*, *7*(3), 25–27.

Turgeon, L., & Gagnon, A. G. (2013). The politics of representative bureaucracy in multilingual states: A comparison of Belgium, Canada and Switzerland. *Regional & Federal Studies*, *23*(4), 407–425.

Weiss, C. H. (1998). Have we learned anything new about the use of evaluation? *American Journal of Evaluation*, *19*(1), 21–33.

Wildavsky, A. B. (1989). *Speaking truth to power*. Transaction Publishers.

8 Sustaining momentum for evidence-informed policymaking

The case of the US government

Nicholas Hart and Kathryn Newcomer

Over the last six decades around the world there has been a productive shift in attention from how funding is allocated to public services to how service delivery occurs in governments. This focus also meant many governments began measuring programmatic "results" to align and review investments more strategically. This shift occurred in governments at all levels, foundations, funders of international development endeavors— such as the World Bank and the US Agency for International Development (USAID)— think tanks, and academia (Kettl, 2005; Pollitt and Bouckaert, 2000; Dubnick and Frederickson, 2011; Moynihan, 2008, 2009, 2011; Hatry, 2008; Newcomer, 1997). Since the beginning of the 21st century, the idea of "evidence-informed policy" increasingly gained widespread attention as a goal for the use of data and evaluation by governments.

The United States has a unique story in this regard that situates lessons learned for the evidence ecosystem and specifically the evaluation field in a global context. Importantly, the US experience also leads to observations about cautions and even potential risks for how the momentum evolves in the contemporaneous constraints of modern evaluation and measurement practice, in a dynamic, value-laden, and politicized decision-making environment. While the story is imperfect, it demonstrates a broad goal of improvement, capacity enhancements, intentional process and structural features, and also the critical features necessary to sustain initiatives over time in a shifting political and cultural landscape. This chapter first outlines the key moments in moving the US government forward in embracing evidence-based policymaking. Second, we describe a two-year governmental commission established by the US government to study and accelerate this work in the US national government, and a new national law created from that effort. Finally, we illuminate some challenges and opportunities as we look to the years ahead.

Key moments in the US national government embracing evidence-based policymaking

Since the 1960s the dialogue—literally reflected in the terminology—in the US and other Western democracies about the criteria to judge governments' performance changed from a focus on "effectiveness" to "outcomes," and then

DOI: 10.4324/9781032719979-9

Sustaining momentum for evidence-informed 135

"results" to "evidence" (Newcomer and Hart, 2022). Efforts to begin promoting the use of evidence in the early 21st century initiated with resources focused on the dissemination and translation of research and practices. The establishment of the Campbell Collaboration, the Coalition for Evidence-Based Policy, and later the Results First Initiative in the US were all examples of the goal to translate and disseminate evidence-based practice to usable evidence. Similar efforts for foreign assistance occurred with funding in the establishment of the publicly-funded Millennium Challenge Corporation in 2004.

More formally, the White House's Office of Management and Budget (OMB) began directing government agencies to assess "evidence of program effectiveness" in 2000 during the George W. Bush and Barack Obama Administrations. The Bush Administration directives were among the earliest steps to align program performance information with budget information, that is, demonstrating performance information along with requests for resources then building additional evaluation requirements and program assessment tools (known as the Program Assessment Rating Tool) (GAO, 2008; Heinrich, 2012). At the time, some conversations about evaluation in the US government narrowly focused on particular methods and approaches, and randomized evaluations were preferred as the sole methodological approach for demonstrating program impacts. This narrow perspective met with strong reactions from the evaluation community and professional associations as too narrow to be used in practice (Bernholz et al., 2006).

One feature intended to rapidly promote the use of evidence was the publication of studies and practices through clearinghouses. In the United States, multiple such clearinghouses now exist such as the Department of Education's What Works Clearinghouse and the Substance Abuse and Mental Health Services Administration launched the National Registry of Evidence-Based Programs and Practices. There are now more than 40 English language websites that present evidence-based interventions or models, many modeled off the What Works Clearinghouse which emphasized experimental methods and quantitative data (Wadhwa et al., 2022; Zheng et al., 2022). Yet, many of these sites and resources have documented low useability, suggesting a potential misalignment in how results are communicated and translated to the user community for policy and practice. More recent efforts to align what are described as "core components" are beginning to develop a new translational model for aligning information from the clearinghouses with potential users (see Data Foundation-White House, 2022).

Beginning in 2008, during the Obama Administration, calls for evidence became more frequent in government through directives to agencies from the White House, signaling alignment between performance measurement and evaluation to produce "evidence on what works" (OMB, 2010, 2013, 2014a, 2014b; CRS, 2011). A critical piece of guidance from OMB in 2015 updated the definitions used by the US government, stating that "evidence is the available

136 Nicholas Hart and Kathryn Newcomer

body of facts or information indicating whether a belief or proposition is true or valid. Evidence can be quantitative or qualitative and may come from a variety of sources, including performance measurement, evaluations, statistical series, retrospective reviews and other data analytics and research. Evidence has varying degrees of credibility, and the strongest evidence generally comes from a portfolio of high-quality evidence rather than a single study" (OMB, 2015). This entire approach was intended to then be applied in a broad framework that used high-level goal-setting, called cross-agency goals, and then ultimately applied evidence through tiers, though the framework was ultimately only applied in a more limited setting through some selected grant programs.

In the 2010s, the US government also invested in expanding evaluation capacity in some human services and workforce agencies. In addition to creating yet new websites to disclose evaluation results (DOL, 2014b; NIJ, 2014) and establishing evaluation principles (HHS, 2014) in agencies to encourage transparency, the Obama Administration spearheaded an effort to establish a "common evidence framework" to facilitate public dissemination of results (OMB, 2013), with standards agreed to by bureaus within HHS (HHS, 2013), Labor (DOL, 2014a), and Education (IES, 2014). The White House encouraged agencies to consider options, such as chief evaluation officers, in order to empower agency officials to produce evaluations (OMB et al., 2013), and a few agencies, including the Labor Department and the Centers for Disease Control, created new chief evaluation officer positions. These early-stage efforts would set the stage for some of the more broad-based efforts to come in the years that followed, demonstrated the possibilities and building strong cases and examples of what was possible with people, resources, and processes established with strong evaluation, data, and evidence capacity (Haskins and Margolis, 2015).

The US commission on evidence-based policymaking

During the same period in which the Obama administration was discussing ways to increase the use of evidence within agencies, two elected officials of the US Congress—Paul Ryan and Patty Murray—led to the creation of the US Commission on Evidence-Based Policymaking. Spurred by frustrations that the system of data sharing and use was moving too slowly, too unintegrated, and producing evidence that was not integrated for policymaking needs. The very creation of the Evidence Commission was a clear signal not only about the growing prominence of the evidence movement in the US but also the need for more organizing and clarity about the next steps to support government-wide implementation.

The Evidence Commission's work from 2016 to 2017 itself was an example of how the demand for evidence directly relates to the supply of evidence, leading to use. The Evidence Commission collected data, analyzed the information, made decisions, then presented in 2017 to Congress and the President in *The*

Promise of Evidence-Based Policymaking (CEP, 2017). The expansive fact-finding process involved (1) a survey of US government agencies; (2) qualitative information gathered from public hearings, meetings with expert testimony, and solicitation of written public comments; and (3) additional agency, commissioner, and staff research (CEP, 2017). The recommendations from the Evidence Commission were, in fact, based on evidence. The Evidence Commission focused on strategies to improve access to data, to strengthen privacy protections, and to enhance government's capacity for evidence-based policymaking. Altogether the effort culminated in a set of 22 expert recommendations constructed from a highly participatory process that the US Congress viewed as valid and credible, then transformed into a new law in 2019 known as the Foundations for Evidence-Based Policymaking Act, or Evidence Act.

One detail of this process that is often surprising to those unfamiliar with the discussion and process in the discourse about evidence-informed policymaking is that the recommendations from the Evidence Commission were transmitted to a Republican Congress and Republican President Donald Trump. Indeed, half the members of the Evidence Commission had been appointed by the Republican Party in the United States—the entire process had been set-up to ensure not only expertise from a substantive perspective but also broad political buy-in to substantiate the eventual recommendations and future action on those recommendations. This was a commission established from the outset to spur action, to solve problems in the evidence ecosystem, and all-the-while intended to maintain both public trust and the trust of the policy actors through which future actions would be sought. (For further detail about the decision-making of the Commission's deliberations see Hart, 2019).

The Commission's recommendations stressed enabling the production of valid and reliable evidence, promoting a new statistical agency to securely and temporarily link data, changing laws to enable certain types of data uses, and building mechanisms to ensure confidentiality of data when data files or results are made public. One recommendation included developing a chief evaluation officer position to provide a senior leader to promote production and use of evaluations, as well as the creation of learning agendas in agencies to provide signals to senior leaders and researchers about what knowledge gaps are most critical to address in future decisions. The Commission also recommended the establishment of senior leadership positions to focus on data policy, a role that would later be called chief data officers.

Creating the evidence act

The Commission only had the legal authority to make recommendations. It could not change laws or policies, just make suggestions to Congress and the president. Thus, any resulting change to laws or regulations would require action from Congress or the Executive Branch agencies. When the recommendations were publicly announced in 2017, the two legislative champions of the initiative also announced they would propose legislation to advance the proposals from the Evidence Commission. In October 2017, Paul Ryan and Patty Murray jointly filed the Foundations for Evidence-Based Policymaking, which would advance through the US legislative process over the course of less than 18-months to become law. In addition to establishing new leadership positions to encourage evaluation activities and the use of data, the Evidence Act—now a law in the US—directs agencies to make their data open by default. This means that the expectation is that, to the extent possible, agencies create publicly accessible datasets. Agencies also must document what data they collect and manage, improve privacy protections by better managing risks, and take steps to protect public trust in data and statistics. One particularly valuable provision of the law enables improved access to administrative, operational data for generating statistics in privacy-protective ways. The law also directs agencies to establish many of the core features of basic program evaluation capacity, including written policies and a supporting workforce for conducting evaluations of programs and policies.

The process of advancing the Evidence Act through the legislative process provides some illumination on the value of evidence in policymaking, even for activities aimed at improving evidence-based policymaking themselves. Even though the legislation was about evidence and the use of data, advancing the effort very much required the use of trusted intermediaries and knowledge brokers, credibility, and a robust body of knowledge and evidence. For example, expertise and advice on the legislation emerged in various forms. Publicly, a series of editorials in newspapers were placed to keep attention on the importance and bipartisan nature of the proposed legislation (Abraham and Haskins, 2018; Feldman and Hart, 2018; Hart and Shea, 2018; McCann and Hart, 2018). The former leaders of federal statistical agencies also lent additional credibility to the commission's recommendations and report, particularly with regard to confidentiality protections (Bipartisan Policy Center, 2018a). Non-profit intermediaries also offered informal assistance to countless other stakeholders in educating constituencies about the commission's report and the legislation through briefings, statements, and events (Bipartisan Policy Center, 2018b). The effects of some of these discussions could also be seen publicly, as some lines of inquiry resulted in the production of public technical papers to explain core concepts and how they applied in certain circumstances. For example, experts published varies white papers to respond to congressional inquiries on topics related to executive performance management activities, the relationship between evaluation officers and data officers, modern confidentiality protections related to data sharing, and a detailed understanding of data-sharing barriers (Hart, 2017; Hart and Carmody, 2018; Hart and Wallman, 2018; Hart and Newcomer, 2018). Behind the scenes, BPC's evidence team offered extensive technical assistance related to the sponsors' goal

Sustaining momentum for evidence-informed 139

of fidelity to the commission recommendations. Countless other organizations played a role in either advocating for the Commission recommendations or advancing the legislation. The American Evaluation Association and Results for America, for example, encouraged attention on program evaluation (Title 1), the Data Coalition (now part of the Data Foundation) championed the OPEN Government Data Act (Title 2), the American Statistical Association encouraged passage of the Confidential Information Protection and Statistical Efficiency Act (Title 3).

In parallel with Senate consideration of the Evidence Act, the Trump Administration announced various activities to advance some of the Commission's recommendations without waiting for congressional or legislative action. The president's reorganization proposal from 2018 announced an intent to have agencies create evaluation officers and develop learning agendas (Hart, 2018a). The President's Management Agenda also announced the creation of a new Federal Data Strategy to incorporate other Evidence Commission recommendations (Hart, 2018b). Both proposals referenced the Commission's work and report, and were intended to administratively build capacity and take steps to address core gaps identified by the Evidence Commission in the broader evidence ecosystem. Ultimately when Congress passed the Evidence Act, it was President Trump who signed the legislation into law then, in the months following enactment, the Trump Administration continued to promote effective implementation of the new law in its budget proposal to Congress (Hart, 2019). Importantly, implementation of the law has not taken on a partisan or political nature. The Biden Administration demonstrated strong support for implementation, first, by issuing a "Memorandum on Restoring Trust in Government Through Scientific Integrity and Evidence-Based Policymaking," that called for government actions to base based on evidence (Biden, 2021b). In June 2021, the Biden Administration then issued guidance to agencies directing new emphasis on evaluation planning and capacity, with a goal of encouraging the eventual use (OMB, 2021):

> OMB expects agencies to use evidence whenever possible to further both mission and operations, and to commit to build evidence where it is lacking. A culture of evidence is not a new idea, and there are already leading examples of this culture throughout government. Nonetheless, we cannot achieve our nation's great promise unless these pockets of excellence are expanded to become the core of how the Federal Government operates. This Memorandum affirms the Federal Government's commitment to the Evidence Act and to building and nurturing a culture of evidence and the infrastructure needed to support it. This includes strengthening the Federal workforce to ensure that staff with the right skills and capabilities are positioned across the Federal Government.
>
> (OMB, 2021, p.2)

140 *Nicholas Hart and Kathryn Newcomer*

There were other specific and important messages in same guidance to agencies that signaled clear support for processes and infrastructure for evidence-based policymaking, including:

- Recognizes evaluation as a central, "mission-critical" function within agencies;
- Articulates an expectation that evaluation will be a whole-of-government activity, building a culture of learning within agencies;
- Affirms commitment to implement the Evidence Act and to social equity in evaluation work;
- Provides additional guidance on learning agendas and evaluation plans, stressing the need for broad stakeholder engagement;
- Builds on past guidance to recognize and support a range of methods and evaluation approaches to building a "portfolio" of useful evidence;
- Calls for investments in evaluation within all agencies and establishment of Evaluation Officers—beyond the 24 largest agencies that are actually covered by the Evidence Act.

Thus, Congress has expressed support for the use of evidence through the Evidence Act, as well as inserted pieces into many other laws, and the Biden administration signaled clear support for the use of evidence to inform policymaking and for investing in evidence building capacity.

Challenges and opportunities as implementation of the evidence act proceeds

The Evidence Commission and implementation of the Evidence Act collectively establish a broad legal and policy framework for renewed momentum in the United States that brings together many aspects of the capacity—though not all—believed to be critical success factors for enabling evidence-based policymaking practice. Yet, there are challenges that will slow the impressive momentum toward embracing evidence-based decision-making in the US government. These challenges include: How are disconnected data generators and producers in government aligned? How transferable is evidence across domains and applications? Where is evidence to inform priority and timely actions, such as inequities and racial disparities? How adequate is the capacity to generate demand for evidence in government, and how can this capacity be rapidly addressed where there are gaps?

Challenge #1: Evidence and data producers are unintentionally disconnected, despite the benefits of co-production and collaboration

Within the US government there are a large number of potential users and providers of evidence, but there is typically a lack of connectivity across

Sustaining momentum for evidence-informed   141

organizations or sometimes even the components within organizations that make producing evidence difficult (CEP, 2017). There are many offices that produce data, but there is incredibly little collaboration and synergies among the different potential providers of evidence. This includes across national statistical programs, administrative data collections, performance reporting information, evaluation production, social sciences and behavioral research, and spending information in the US context (Newcomer and Brass, 2016). While the Evidence Commission's recommendations solve for some of these issues, there is not a panacea for data sharing and evidence sharing envisioned in the near-term.

There are also major differences in terms of what potential users view as rigorous evidence. These differing standards and criteria for evidence are accepted by different professions (e.g., lawyers, accountants, engineers, and economists) which may be a matter of professional training, but also reflect perspectives about methodological preferences. Disagreements about which methodologies are "more rigorous" within professional groups persist and have been reflected within the past decade in how evidence is presented to decision-makers. For example, the idea that experimental methods are a "gold standard" for actionable evidence (see summary in GAO, 2009), and that clearinghouses historically applying "standards of evidence" differ in their ratings (Wadhwa et al., 2022).

Collectively addressing the number of users on the one hand and the varying perspectives about what is reliable evidence on the other, suggests challenges for the field and movement in navigating actionable, usable evidence. At the same time decision-makers are not homogenous, decision-making processes are not linear, and evidence-based policymaking is rarely a script—which offers promise that how this body of evidence *informs* future actions and a range of users is worth further discussion, and effort (Hart and Yohannes, 2019).

Challenge #2: Evidence transferability across potential uses and users is challenged by dynamic contexts

Despite the efforts to create a vast supply of evidence and data systems to address a host of potential questions in the policymaking community, the range of users is vast and the speed at which decisions are made across those ever-shifting users is rapid. Differences exist among potential users regarding how easily evidence of success from one context can be transferred to other contexts (e.g., Cartwright, 2013). Change is the one constant in the nature of the problems and the characteristics of the targeted beneficiaries of government programs and policies. Frequently we do not know all the causal mechanisms needed to produce intended impact, nor do we appreciate and document the support factors needed to ensure that a set of causal mechanisms will be able to succeed in new and different contexts. Clearinghouses that provide "evidence-based interventions" that they vet for methodological quality typically do not pay attention to the extent to which contextual factors (supportive or not) affect the performance of interventions (Gough and White, 2018).

The emerging field of "living evidence" offers some guidance about how to build a body of evidence in this dynamic range, recognizing the shifts in knowledge and benefits of pooled methodologies for addressing the diverse questions that arise in real-world decision-making (Elliott et al., 2021). Still yet further, is the work to establish what are known as "core components," or the central features in identifying program attributes and characteristics that influence success and impacts when implemented effectively, which are often demonstrated in the living evidence approaches and also can be more emergent in dynamic, real-world decision-making as levers and action points (Data Foundation-White House, 2022).

Challenge #3: Evidence can inform priority issues like inequities and racial disparities, but is currently too limiting

The Biden Administration issued an Executive Order on the president's first day in office that requires the US government to examine racial and economic inequities that can be addressed by national agencies (Biden, 2021a). During 2021 and 2022, agencies in the US government—including through their Evaluation Officers established by the Evidence Act—undertook efforts to examine policies and programs that "serve as barriers to equal opportunity." Yet, agencies quickly realized and observed that frequently data collection did not permit stratification of data by key characteristics like race, ethnicity, gender, and age, at least without data linkages. Published studies funded through government investments, including in government clearinghouses of evidence were too often sparse on key characteristics useful for determining how to address inequities among affected populations.

The dearth of existing evidence suggested that yet further evidence was needed to address key issues. In 2022, national agencies began collecting new data to study the disparities in administrative data collections. In some ways, this frustration was years in the making, a recognition that had materialized in the US during then-president Obama's 2016 hallmark initiative called My Brother's Keeper, which launched an effort in partnership with the federal statistical system to stratify new race, gender, and age datasets for the first time with public use information. But the mere fact that basic descriptive information on key descriptive characteristics about the population and key indicators about the country's well-being are not available across core subgroups is an indicator of the challenge ahead. When considering how this affects the research and evaluations that are produced:

- In 2020, out of 1,065 studies listed in the Labor Department's clearinghouse in the https://clear.dol.gov database, two studies focused on equity, both of which examined gender equity. No studies reviewed focused on racial equity.

- Out of nearly 200 studies listed by the Campbell Collaboration in the https:// campbellcollaboration.org/ database, three studies focused on broad equity considerations. Two of those studies have an international focus and the other is a systematic review.
- Out of 10,700 studies in the What Works Clearinghouse at https://ies.ed.gov/ ncee/wwc/FWW only 23 studies focused on educational equity.

With a focus on encouraging equitable outcomes, more effort is needed to collect relevant data and ensure the evidence is available to draw upon for the policy-making community.

Challenge #4: Knowledge brokers and intermediaries are essential for the growth of evidence-based policymaking; they are too few and under-resourced

Ensuring the users of evidence have access at the right time, in the relevant way, and that the translation to the process, form, and function of the decision at hand is possible is not just something to be left to chance—often intermediaries or the growing profession of knowledge brokers fill this void. These roles negotiate among users and providers, allocating time and resources to understand and strengthen the linkage between the producers of evaluative data and the many potential users of that information. Brokering of evidence to generate demand and interest among potential users requires attention and resources (Olejniczak et al., 2016).

Other proponents of evidence-based policymaking propose that performance data and relevant analytical information should be used by managers and administrators at all levels of government. Yet there is still an emerging body of research to inform how decision-makers best understand and process insights from evidence. Research in cognitive psychology, behavioral economics, and organizational behavior provide relevant insights to help understand when and how executives and managers take into account evidence when making decisions (see Kahneman, 2011; Heath and Heath, 2010; Sunstein and Hastie, 2015; World Bank Group, 2015; Langer and Gough, 2012). But there are no easy answers or strategies for addressing these challenges, ensuring credibility, aligning with relevant processes, values, and methods preferences. These decisions are further affected by the fact that managers and administrators making decisions are embedded within organizations, affected by the very cultures they are also seeking to change with the decisions they make.

Opportunities moving forward

Despite the recent advances for evidence-based policymaking in the US, there are currently many challenges to using evidence to inform decision-making within government. But there are also many successes, in fact, a growing array ranging from applications in mental health services and public health outreach. Moving forward, there are at least three key areas for how evidence might be used more frequently to inform and improve government.

First, cultivating an agency culture receptive to learning from evaluation and evidence requires consistent attention from leadership who exert the efforts needed to shape a learning culture. There is a need for visible and continuous leadership commitment to the use of evaluation and learning from data. Leadership needs to assess and address factors that may be perpetuating a compliance mentality among potential users of data who may be too accustomed to reporting data, but not using the data themselves.

The extent to which agency leaders promote the use of evidence is a critical element for the use of evidence, and this can include with meaningful incentives (Nussle and Orszag, 2014; Hart and Yohannes, 2019). The extent to which an organizational culture within an agency is developmental and open to learning is key to increasing the likelihood that any data, or evidence, will be used to inform decision-making.

Evaluation capacity is clearly necessary as well. Accessible technical support and training for evaluation among managers—not just technical staff who are not involved in operations—especially to interpret data and study findings to inform decisions is needed. Capacity is needed to support both the demand for and supply of relevant evidence to inform decision-making (GAO, 2021). To promote organizational learning, government needs trained evaluation staff. With technical skills and training on the appropriateness of different methods for different evaluation questions and purposes, these staff-level analysts may help push learning forward. But organizations also need managers and executives, as well as budget and financial staff, who possess basic evaluation competencies and who use an evaluation mindset in their work.

Second, knowledgeable and respected knowledge brokers are also needed within government agencies to cultivate the demand for relevant evidence among government executives and managers, and then ensure that the demand is met in a timely and convincing manner (Olejniczak et al., 2016). Knowledge brokers who bring the requisite evaluation skills can identify who might use the information they are provided and how and when they may use it. Importantly, brokers can help executives and managers frame the questions they should address to inform their decisions.

Excellent examples of knowledge brokers exist within the US federal government, and the role of Evaluation Officer required by the Evidence Act drew upon these models. Prior to being required by law, a Chief Evaluation Officer (CEO) was established within the US Department of Labor who coordinated the collection of and use of evidence effectively for agency decision-making. An Evaluation Officer was also established in the Centers for Disease Control (CDC) at the Department of Health and Human Services in 2013 to bridge evaluation and measurement units, among other agencies.

Sustaining momentum for evidence-informed 145

Finally, knowledge brokers assess decision-makers' information processing needs to ensure they receive and value the evidence provided. One of the most promising tools that the Chief Evaluation Officer at the US Department of Labor established was to co-create a "learning agenda" with each of the executives who run units across the agency. The Evaluation Officer worked closely with executives to establish a list of questions which they wanted to address about the programs they managed, then worked collaboratively to collect or generate relevant evidence to address the information needs.

Conclusion

Evidence-based policymaking is officially the law of the land in the United States, but much remains to realize the vision and goals of that law. There will be long-term challenges to build capacity and to realize the uses intended, yet the field continues to itself learn and adapt in the broader evidence ecosystem as implementation of the new framework is ongoing. One critical limitation has been ensuring that adequate resources are available for the people, processes, and data capabilities to address the supply, demand, and translation needed for success of the framework. These sustained—and increased—investments from government funders are needed to enhance competencies for executives and managers alike in supporting the capabilities of the entire system. Investments in knowledge brokers and intermediaries will also help support this capacity for use in coming years.

As with most of life, expectations matter. Expectations that government executives and managers carefully weigh evidence when they make decisions may be overly ambitious in some arenas, but not all. Evidence is generated and valued in many cases. However, within government many values are in play, and both partisan politics and bureaucratic politics inject many—sometimes competing-priorities. And fiscal austerity and reluctance to fund non-mission or service-oriented activities may constrain the support needed to generate evidence in some contexts. A bottom line is that if mission achievement and the production and the use of evidence to inform decision-making are desired within government, these goals will more likely be attained if they are adequately and strategically funded.

References

Abraham, K. G. and R. Haskins. (2018). "Time for Action to Improve Government Data Analysis." *The Hill*, September 4, 2018. Available at: https://thehill.com/opinion/finance/404928-time-for-action-to-improve-government-data-analysis.

Bernholz, E., A. Ginsburg, M. Habibion, J. Heffelfinger, D. Introcasco, C. Oros, N. J. Scheers, S. Shipman, L. Stinson, and B. Valde. (2006). *Evaluation Dialogue Between OMB Staff and Federal Evaluators*. Washington, DC: Federal Evaluators.

146 Nicholas Hart and Kathryn Newcomer

Biden, J. (2021a). *Advancing Racial Equity and Support for Underserved Communities through the Federal Government.* Washington, DC: White House. Available at: https://www.whitehouse.gov/briefing-room/presidential-actions/2021/01/20/executive-order-advancing-racial-equity-and-support-for-underserved-communities-through-the-federal-government/.

Biden, J. (2021b). *Memorandum on Restoring Trust in Government Through Scientific Integrity and Evidence Based Policymaking.* Washington, DC: White House. Available at: https://www.whitehouse.gov/briefing-room/presidential-actions/2021/01/27/memorandum-on-restoring-trust-in-government-through-scientific-integrity-and-evidence-based-policymaking/.

BPC. (2018a). "Former Government Statistical Agency Heads Call for Better Use of Data in Policymaking." January 24, 2018. Available at: https://bipartisanpolicy.org/press-release/former-government-statistical-agency-heads-call-for-better-use-of-data-in-policymaking/.

BPC. (2018b). *Evidence: A Year of Progress on Evidence-Based Policymaking.* Evidence-Based Policymaking Initiative, September 2018. Washington, DC.

Cartwright, N. (2013). "Knowing What We Are Talking about: Why Evidence Doesn't Always Travel." *Evidence & Policy: A Journal of Research, Debate and Practice,* 9(1), 97–112.

Congressional Research Service (CRS). (2011). *Obama Administration Agenda for Government Performance: Evolution and Related Issues for Congress.* Memorandum: World Wide Web. Available at: http://www.scribd.com/doc/48106516/CRS-Memo-on-Obama-Performance-Agenda-1-19-11.html.

Data Foundation-White House. (2022). *Evidence 2.0: Exploring New Approaches for Applying Evidence in Active, Real-Time Decision-Making Environments.* Washington, DC. Available at: https://www.datafoundation.org/events-list/evidence-20-exploring-new-approaches-for-applying-evidence-in-active-real-time-decision-making-environments/2022.

DOL. (2014b). *Clearinghouse for Labor Evaluation and Research.* Washington DC: DOL.

Dubnick, M. J. and H. G. Frederickson. (2011). *Accountable Governance: Problems and Promises.* New York: ME Sharpe.

Elliott, J., R. Lawrence, J. C. Minx, O. T. Oladapo, P. Ravaud, B. T. Jeppesen, J. Thomas, T. Turner, P. O. Vandvik, and J. M. Grimshaw. (2021). "Decision Makers Need Constantly Updated Evidence Synthesis." *Nature,* 600, 383–385.

Feldman, A. and N. Hart. (2018). "OMB Wants to Strengthen a Learning Culture in Government." *Government Executive,* May 21, 2018. Available at: https://www.govexec.com/excellence/promising-practices/2018/05/omb-wants-strengthen-learning-culture-government/148350/?oref=river.

GAO. (2008). *Lesson Learned for the Next Administration on Using Performance Information to Improve Results.* GAO Testimony, July 24, 2008.

GAO. (2021). *Evidence-Based Policymaking: Survey Data Identify Opportunities to Strengthen Capacity across Federal Agencies.* GAO-21–536. Government Accountability Office, Washington, DC.

Gough, D. and H. White. (2018). *Evidence Standards and Evidence Claims in Web-Based Research Portals.* London: Centre for Homelessness Impact. Available at: www.homelessnessimpact.org.

Government Accountability Office, U.S. (GAO). (2009). *Program Evaluation: A Variety of Rigorous Methods Can Help Identify Effective Interventions.* GAO-10–30. Available at: http://www.gao.gov.

Hart, N. (2017). *Improved Data Coordination and Use Required for Evidence-Based Policymaking.* Bipartisan Policy Center. Available at: https://bipartisanpolicy.org/blog/improved-data-coordination-and-use-required-for-evidence-based-policymaking/.

Hart, N. (2018a). *President's Government Reform Plan Includes Evidence Proposals.* Bipartisan Policy Center, June 21, 2018. Available at: https://bipartisanpolicy.org/press-release/presidents-government-reform-plan-includes-evidence-proposals/.

Hart, N. (2018b). *Trump's Management Agenda Proposes Data as a Strategic Asset.* Bipartisan Policy Center, March 26, 2018. Available at: https://bipartisanpolicy.org/blog/fact-sheet-trumps-management-agenda-proposes-data-as-a-strategic-asset/.

Hart, N. (2019). "Entering the Evidence Promised Land: Making the Evidence Act a Reality." In *Evidence Works*, edited by N. Hart and M. Yohannes, 192–203. Washington, DC: Bipartisan Policy Center.

Hart, N. and K. Carmody. (2018). *Barriers to Using Government Data: Extended Analysis of the Commission on Evidence-Based Policymaking's Survey of Federal Agencies and Offices.* Bipartisan Policy Center, October 2018. Available at: https://bipartisanpolicy.org/library/barriers-to-using-government-data-extended-analysis-of-the-u-s-commission-on-evidence-based-policymakings-survey-of-federal-agencies-and-offices/.

Hart, N. and K. Newcomer. (2018). *Presidential Evidence Initiatives: Lessons from the Bush and Obama Administrations' Efforts to Improve Government Performance.* Bipartisan Policy Center, February 2018. Available at: https://bipartisanpolicy.org/wp-content/uploads/2018/03/Presidential-Evidence-Initiatives.pdf.

Hart, N. and K. Wallman. (2018). *Transparency, Accountability and Consent in Evidence Building: How Government Ethically and Legally Uses Administrative Data for Statistical Activities.* Bipartisan Policy Center. Available at: https://bipartisanpolicy.org/wp-content/uploads/2018/07/Transparency_accountablility_and_consent_in_evidence_building.pdf.

Hart, N. and M. Yohannes (editors). (2019). *Evidence Works: Cases Where Evidence Meaningfully Informed Policy.* Washington, DC: Bipartisan Policy Center.

Hart, N. and R. Shea. (2018). "Opinion: Is there Room for Science and Evidence in Trump's Budget?" *Roll Call*, February 5, 2018. Available at: https://www.rollcall.com/news/opinion/opinion-room-science-evidence-trumps-budget.

Haskins, R. and G. Margolis. (2015). *Show Me the Evidence: Obama's Fight for Rigor and Results in Social Policy.* Washington, DC: Brookings Institution.

Hatry, H. (2008). "Emerging Developments in Performance Measurement: An International Perspective." In *The International Handbook of Practice-Based Performance Management*, edited by P. De Lancer Julnes, F. Stokes Berry, M. Aristigueta, and K. Yang, 3–23. Thousand Oaks, CA: Sage Publications, Inc.

Health and Human Services, Assistant Secretary for Planning and Evaluation (HHS-ASPE). (2020). *Core Components Approaches to Building Evidence of Program Effectiveness.* Washington, DC. Available at: https://aspe.hhs.gov/reports/core-components-approaches-building-evidence-program-effectiveness.

Heath, C. and D. Heath. (2010). *Switch: How to Change Things When Change is Hard.* New York: Broadway Books.

Heinrich, C. (2012). "How Credible is the Evidence, and Does it Matter? An Analysis of the Program Assessment Rating Tool." *Public Administration Review*, 72(1), 123–134.

HHS. (2013). *Common Evidence Framework (draft)*. Washington, DC.

HHS. (2014). Evaluation Policy. *Federal Register*. Washington DC: GPO.

Kahneman, D. (2011). *Thinking, Fast and Slow*. Farrar: Straus and Giroux Publishers.

Kettl, D. F. (2005). *The Global Public Management Revolution*. Washington, DC: Brookings Institution Press.

Langer, L., J. Tripney, and D. Gough. (2012). *The Science of Using Science: Researching the Use of Research Evidence in Decision-Making*. EPPI-Centre Social Science Research Unit UCL Institute of Education University College London Technical Report, April 2016. Available at: https://eppi.ioe.ac.uk/cms/Portals/0/PDF%20reviews%20and%20summaries/Science%20Technical%20report%202016%20Langer.pdf?ver=2016-04-18-142648-770.

McCann, T. and N. Hart. (2018). "'Evidence' is the Word of the Year. Neither Party Owns It." *Roll Call*, October 1, 2018. Available at: https://www.rollcall.com/news/opinion/evidence-word-year-neither-party-owns.

Moynihan, D. (2008). *The Dynamics of Performance Management: Constructing Information and Reform*. Washington, DC: Georgetown University Press.

Moynihan, D. (2009). "How Do Public Organizations Learn? Bridging Cultural and Structural Perspectives." *Public Administration Review*, 69(6), 1097–1105.

Moynihan, D. (2011). "The Big Question for Performance Management: Why Do Managers Use Performance Information?" *Journal of Public Administration Research and Theory*, 20, 849–866.

National Institute of Justice (NIJ). (2014). *CrimeSolutions.gov*. Washington DC: Department of Justice.

Newcomer, K. (editor). (1997). *Using Performance Measurement to Improve Public and Nonprofit Programs*. New Directions in Program Evaluation. No 75. San Francisco, CA: Jossey-Bass Publishers.

Newcomer, K. and C. Brass. (2016). "Forging a Strategic and Comprehensive Approach to Evaluation within Public and Nonprofit Organizations: Integrating Measurement and Analytics within Evaluation." *American Journal of Evaluation*, 37(1), 80–99.

Newcomer, K. and N. Hart. (2022). *Evidence-Building and Evaluation in Government*. Los Angeles, CA: Sage.

Nussle, J. and P. Orszag (editors). (2014). *Moneyball for Government*. New York: Disruption Books.

Office of Management and Budget (OMB). (2009). *Increased Emphasis on Program Evaluations*. Memorandum M-10–01. Washington, DC: Office of Management and Budget.

Olejniczak, K., E. Raimondo, and T. Kupiec. (2016). "Evaluation Units as Knowledge Brokers: Testing and Calibrating an Innovative Framework." *Evaluation*, 22(2), 168–189.

OMB. (2010). *FY 2011 Budget of the United States Government, Analytical Perspectives*. Washington, DC: Office of Management and Budget.

OMB. (2013). *Next Steps in the Evidence and Innovation Agenda*. Memorandum M-13–17. Washington, DC: Office of Management and Budget.

Sustaining momentum for evidence-informed 149

OMB. (2014a). *FY 2015 Budget of the United States Government, Analytical Perspectives.* Washington, DC: Office of Management and Budget.

OMB. (2014b). *Guidance for Providing and Using Administrative Data for Statistical Purposes.* Memorandum M-14–06. Washington, DC: Office of Management and Budget.

OMB. (2015). Circular A.11. Washington, DC: Office of Management and Budget.

OMB. (2021). *Evidence-Based Policymaking: Learning Agendas and Annual Evaluation Plans.* Memorandum M-21-27. Washington, DC: Office of Management and Budget. Available at: https://www.whitehouse.gov/wp-content/uploads/2021/06/M-21-27.pdf.

OMB, OSTP, DPC, and CEA. (2013). *Next Steps in the Evidence and Innovation Agenda (M-13-17).* Washington, DC: The White House.

Pollitt, C. and G. Bouckaert. (2000). *Public Management Reform: A Comparative Analysis.* New York: Oxford University Press.

Sunstein, C. and R. Hastie. (2015). *Wiser: Getting Beyond Groupthink to Make Groups Smarter.* Boston, MA: Harvard Business Review Press.

U.S. Commission on Evidence-Based Policymaking (CEP). (2017). *The Promise of Evidence-Based Policymaking: Report of the Commission on Evidence-Based Policymaking.* Washington, DC: GPO.

Wadhwa, M., J. Zheng, and T. D. Cook. (2022). "How Consistent Are Meanings of 'Evidence-Based'?: A Comparative Review of 12 Clearinghouses that Rate the Effectiveness of Educational Programs." Working paper. How Consistent are Meanings of "Evidence-Based"? A Comparative Review of 12 Clearinghouses that Rate the Effectiveness of Educational Programs. The Trachtenberg School of Public Policy and Public Administration, George Washington University, Unpublished Manuscript.

World Bank Group. (2015). *Mind, Society and Behavior*, Washington, DC.

Zheng, J., M. Wadhwa, and T. D. Cook. (2022). "How Consistently Do 13 Clearinghouses Identify Social and Behavioral Development Programs as 'Evidence-Based'?." *Prevention Science*, 23(8), 1–16.

9 Participatory budgeting, evaluation, and the post-truth world

Where are we, and where do we go from here?

Yaerin Park

Introduction

Today's policymaking involves various actors and social, political, and institutional elements to design and implement policies and programs to solve complex challenges and meet the needs of the beneficiaries. Policymaking was considered to be an area to be dealt with solely by the government, and control or "steer" decision-making in relation with other actors such as citizens (Denhardt and Denhardt, 2000). Now with a high level of complexity and uncertainty in the policymaking environment and the changing nature of policy issues, the government has been equipped with different mindsets in making policy decisions in a way that "serves" its citizens (Denhardt and Denhardt, 2007) and collaborates with them in solving policy challenges in various policy fronts.

In this context, many democratic and participatory policy platforms and governance practices have emerged. One of the notable democratic governance practices is Participatory Budgeting (PB). By directly engaging citizens in the budgetary decision-making process, PB aims to promote transparency and accountability in the budget allocation and use, public deliberation and civic participation, empowerment of citizens through including voices from various walks of life.

With PB expanding and diffusing throughout the world, PB is a promising practice to examine the implications of evaluative inquiries in the post-truth era. In this chapter, I will explore PB and its significance, particularly in the context of program evaluation, and will provide implications for evaluation in the post-truth world. Particularly, throughout this chapter I aim to address the following key research questions: (1) What are the key lessons from PB and its evaluation practice; (2) To what extent does PB facilitate smarter and more inclusive decisions; (3) How can the lessons from PB be integrated with processes of evaluation that are fit for the post-truth challenges? In particular, I will explore the lessons from PB and program evaluation based on evaluation theories including Alkin (2012)'s Evaluation Tree framework and Lemire et al. (2020)'s review of mechanism in the realist evaluation framework.

DOI: 10.4324/9781032719979-10

Participatory budgeting as a notable democratic governance platform

What is participatory budgeting?

Participatory Budgeting (PB hereinafter) is a budgetary decision-making process that directly involves citizens to make decisions on how to spend a portion of public money. PB has emerged as one of the notable democratic governance processes in the context of the New Public Service (NPS), which places citizens at the center of the policymaking process, and the public service should be responsive to the citizens' needs and preferences (Alkadry, 2003; Meier et al., 2006; Denhardt and Denhardt, 2007). PB is a policy decision-making platform that elicits citizens' budget and policy preferences, provides a forum for citizens to deliberate on policy issues, and mutually share knowledge and learn from each other. It also has key objectives of empowering citizens through public deliberation and participation, and enhancing public-sector transparency and accountability by providing citizens opportunities to witness how their tax money is spent and policy decisions are made (Park, 2020).

PB started in 1989 in Porto Alegre, Brazil, as democratic reform and social justice initiative adopted by the Workers' Party (PT). It quickly diffused throughout the different regions and continents. Until today, PB is being implemented in over 7,000 localities around the world.[1]

PB is run mostly at the local (citywide or district) level. There are PB processes operated at the national or federal level, such as in Portugal. PB models may change or evolve over time. For instance, New York City has been implementing a district-level PB program since 2011, but the City voters approved the PB process to become a citywide process in the 2018 election and established the Civic Engagement Commission (CEC) to run a citywide PB program.[2] At times, PB at different levels coexist. Portugal has had city-level PB from the early 2000s, but has launched a nationwide PB process in 2017 that is recognized as the first of its kind globally.[3] Korea's Ministry of Economy and Finance has launched an experimental national PB pilot program called "My Budget" alongside the PB processes that are being operated at the municipality level.[4]

Although there may be variations, the PB process is usually comprised of common stages of rule-setting or design, brainstorming, proposal development, voting and implementing projects, as seen in Figure 9.1. In the design stage, stakeholders and participants set rules and guidelines for participation, item development, and voting for the specific cycle. In the brainstorming stage, participants and community members gather ideas together for budget proposals based on the community priorities through forums such as neighborhood assemblies, community meetings, and online communication channels. In the development stage, usually the Budget Delegates develop budget ideas into proposals to place them on the ballot. In the voting stage, community members cast their ballot on budget proposals. Voting takes place either online or offline. The selected

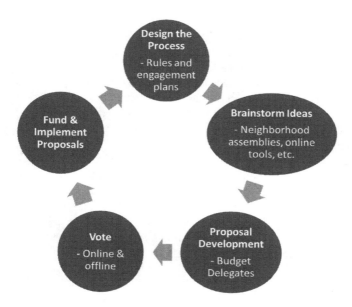

Figure 9.1 Typical PB procedure by stage.

Source: Constructed based on Participatory Budgeting Project (https://www.participatorybudgeting.org/what-is-pb/)

budget proposals through voting proceed to be funded by the local government and executed as projects.

PB and its impacts

Impact on public service delivery and quality of life

Through empirical examination, it has been recognized that PB has had a positive impact on the improvement of public service delivery and promoting citizens' quality of life and well-being in various areas such as health and sanitation, education, public infrastructure, and water. For instance, Goncalves (2014) examines the patterns of public expenditures in municipalities in Brazil, and finds that the municipalities that have adopted PB have allocated budgets according to residents' preferences and invested in public health and sanitation areas. This eventually has led to a decrease in infant mortality rates in the PB-implementing municipalities. Through an empirical assessment, Touchton and Wampler (2020) also find that municipalities in Brazil that have adopted PB and social programs (such as Bolsa Familia or other cash transfer and social welfare programs to assist low-income families in health and education) have made significant improvements in public health, in particular, reducing infant mortality rates. Through an empirical review of public expenditure and budget allocation pattern of more than 20,000 PB projects in 20 cities around the world, Cabannes (2015) finds that PB is associated with a significant improvement in delivery and management of basic services including water and sanitation, public transportation, and solid waste management. Likewise, having a direct channel for citizens to influence budgetary decision-making through PB draws people's budget preferences and helps channel necessary funds according to their preferences in basic public services, and thus, improves people's quality of life and well-being.

Local governance

PB has been examined in the context of its impact on local governance, particularly on municipal revenue administration. For example, Touchton et al. (2020) see the association between the existence of participatory institutions and the tax revenue collection in Brazilian municipalities. Through parametric estimation, they find that the municipalities that have participatory institutions, such as voluntarily adopted policy management councils and PB processes, have collected more tax revenues compared with those municipalities without participatory mechanisms. Particularly, municipalities with PB have collected 16 percent more tax revenues than those without PB (Touchton et al., 2020, p. 14). Beuermann and Amelina (2014) examine an experimental evaluation of PB in the context of decentralization in Russia and find that PB promotes increased public participation in the budgetary process and hence, increases tax revenue collection at the municipality level. Among 20 cities examined, having a PB is associated with increased tax revenue collection in three cities by encouraging the taxpayers to see how their money is spent and having them expect the execution of the projects they have voted for (Cabannes, 2015, p. 272). Cabannes (2015) also finds that implementing PB has restructured and promoted organizational reform to design and implement PB in several municipalities that conduct PB. Likewise, PB increases interaction between civil servants or PB administrators with citizens, and therefore, increases trust and confidence of citizens toward government. Also, with increased trust in government and public-sector transparency and accountability due to more openness and participation, PB is found to be positively associated with taxpayers' tax compliance and eventually on the municipality's capacity in tax revenue collection and administration.

Increased civic participation

PB is a participatory vehicle that has emerged in the context of transition from representative democracy to redistributive, deliberative, and participatory democracy (de Sousa Santos, 1998; Cabannes, 2004). In this process, citizens have become an essential part of public policymaking and administration by formulating policy issues and agenda, forming opinions and exercising an influence on policy implementation and assessment, and collaborating in public services and goods delivery.

There has been a continuous discourse on the importance of citizen's budget deliberation and participation (Ebdon and Franklin, 2006). PB is an approach that moves beyond the frame of public deliberation by providing a platform where citizens can directly cast a ballot on the budget proposals based on their preferences. Primarily, there are mechanisms and tools for citizens to jointly establish guidelines and rules, brainstorm budget proposal ideas, and formulate budget proposals for ballots. There are variations among municipalities that implement PB, but there are PB councils, citizen and community PB bodies to ensure that PB rules and guidelines, and operational strategies and plans are in place. Normally, citizens and community members get to work with their elected officials, city council members, and administrators to facilitate the implementation of PB projects in their district or locality. Tools like neighborhood assemblies and community meetings are crucial to collect ideas based on communities' immediate and long-term policy demands and priorities. Based on these procedures, Budget Delegates, who are usually representatives or members from the community, commit their time to conduct research and investigation on the proposed areas for budget distribution and reform and incorporate these processes in the Budget Delegate meetings that are set up to fully develop budget proposals to be placed as ballot measures for voting (Park, 2020). When the budget proposals on the ballot are ready, there can be an additional stage of demonstrating and pitching to the entire community or citizens (this stage is called "Budget Expos").

As explained previously, the voting process is a unique element to PB compared with other citizen participatory mechanisms. This voting element has become a leverage point for PB to become a widespread and well-received citizen participation channel. For instance, approximately 106,000 voters in New York City cast their ballots in Cycle 6 of the PBNYC (2016–2017), which was approximately a 45 percent increase compared with the previous cycle, in which the voter turnout was around 68,000.[5] There may have been disruptions against active participation and voter turnouts in PB due to the ongoing global pandemic (Covid-19), but this participation trend is projected to grow as PB expands in existence and scale.

Another notable impact of PB on civic participation is that it has invigorated the growth of civil society in places where PB has been implemented. With the emergence of PB, civil society and government relation has shifted from a subordinate and hierarchical one to more open, innovative and transparent (Novy and Leubolt, 2005; Baiocchi et al., 2011; Wampler, 2012). Also, evidence from places that has a long history of implementing PB such as Brazil, indicates that PB has promoted the growth of civil society, such as numbers and presence of civil society toward advocating the importance of PB (Sintomer et al., 2008; Touchton and Wampler, 2014). Likewise, PB has had a positive impact on the enlargement of public participation and the growth of civil society through its notable tools and vehicles for deliberation and participation.

Empowerment of citizens

One of the critical objectives of PB is to include and empower citizens who have not had access or opportunities in the conventional policymaking process. This refers to the marginalized populations including low-income groups, ethnic and racial minority groups, women and youth, immigrant communities, people with disabilities, LGBTQ communities, and indigenous communities. PB has tools to ensure the participation of these communities in the PB process and incorporate their voices in the budgetary decision-making process. For instance, PB councils set guidelines, rules, and toolkits to make sure that inclusion of marginalized communities by quota, equity in participation, and diversity of participants actually get realized (Cabannes, 2015). Places in North America and Glasgow have developed a toolkit to ensure the participation of people of color and low-income groups.[6] In this context, PB has enfranchised the conventionally marginalized communities in participating in the policymaking process to a certain degree (Su, 2017). As one of the examples, in cities in the US and Canada that have adopted PB, youth population as young as the age of 11 can cast their ballots in the PB voting stage. Also, a number of PB administrative bodies have eliminated ID verification to encourage marginalized communities—such as undocumented people—to vote in the PB process (Park, 2020).

Why PB has passed the test of time

Since its inception at Porto Alegre, Brazil, PB has evolved and spread to different parts of the world through a variety of forms depending on the contexts of each jurisdiction where it has been implemented (Bartocci et al., 2022). According to Bartocci et al. (2022), one of the primary reasons why the PB has passed the test of time is the increasing attention paid to the importance of the concepts such as civic engagement, democratic governance, and co-production (p. 2). Especially, civic engagement is considered as a core element to promote the quality of public service delivery and to address social and economic challenges (Michels (2011) in Bartocci et al., 2022). Along with the civic engagement as a conceptual backbone, technological advancements and widened availability of communication tools utilized for PB processes have contributed to expanding PB worldwide.

PB and the post-truth world

Post-truth phenomenon: Where are we?

In the policymaking context, the term "post-truth" refers to the state where policy formulation and implementation are more affected by people's personal beliefs or emotions, rather than facts, human rational reasoning, or scientific evidence.[7] It is also defined in the Oxford Dictionary as the state "in which objective facts are less influential in shaping public opinion than appeals to emotion and personal belief."[8] The term is not an entirely new concept, as renowned scholars like Hannah Arendt

156   *Yaerin Park*

recognized and mentioned that "political lies" are big in their existence in the modern world in that they rearrange factual structure and texture (in Bufacchi, 2021, p. 350). The "post-truth" term regained the spotlight in the recent politically unanticipated turn of events of the victory of Donald Trump in the 2016 US Presidential Election, and the Brexit. Most recently, the circumstances surrounding the ongoing public health crisis of the novel coronavirus (Covid-19) pandemic can be added to the above list, where the "post-truth" challenges have emerged due to the issues related to disinformation, disbelief, and polarization.

Based on the literature and observations, the "post-truth" world can be characterized as follows: (1) A high level of distrust against the powerful, the elites, and the experts; (2) distrust and low confidence against conventional institutions, political system, and the mainstream media; (3) clash of viewpoints, the prevalence of conflict and polarization among different groups of people; (4) increased use of social media and technology tools.

In a world like this, we pose this next big question: What is the significance of PB and how does it align with addressing the post-truth challenges? In the next section, I will explore answers to the big question on the key elements of PB that can be aligned with the policy challenges in the post-truth world, and what we can learn from PB.

How does PB align with addressing the post-truth challenges?

PB is a policy practice and platform that has multidisciplinary implications for practitioners and researchers alike. The term "Participatory Budgeting" gives clear ideas in this regard. On the budgeting aspect, PB is a novel budgeting tool that utilizes citizens' inputs and votes, and allocates program (e.g., after-school programs) and capital expenses (e.g., local infrastructure such as schools, libraries, parks, and neighborhood facilities) based on the citizen preferences. On the participation side, PB involves various public policymaking, administration, and management dimensions including collaborative governance, public deliberation, and participation. The complexity and multidimensionality of PB practice will enable us to explore PB in the context of addressing challenges in the post-truth world. I will explore notable characteristics of PB practice and present how they align with the core traits of the post-truth world as seen in the previous section.

Reliance on the use of social media and online mechanisms

Social media and the internet are inseparable in our lives today. According to the Pew Research Center survey (as quoted by Gooch (2017)), about 62 percent of US residents responded that they rely on social media as their main news source. Social media is an indispensable platform in human lives today where people post opinions, share news and information, buy and sell items and learn things.

Social media and the internet play a crucial role in public policy and administration, and it is no exception to PB. Social media is a critical tool to share information about how PB will be administered and executed. Administrators share any guidelines and rules, public announcements for any community meetings or neighborhood assemblies, information about budget ideas and proposals, voting information (on which budget items are on the ballot, voting venues and time), and selected projects and how they will be implemented through social media platforms such as Twitter, Facebook, and YouTube.

Social media has brought two key positive aspects in running and participating in PB: (1) It enables interactive communication between stakeholders involved in the PB process; (2) it enhances accessibility to information regarding policymaking opportunities of PB. Primarily, elected officials, PB administrators, civil society organizations, and citizens utilize social media channels to freely exchange viewpoints and ideas on how to implement PB. For instance, Korean municipalities encourage the use of YouTube to submit ideas for budget proposals. Submitters can create a short video through YouTube on the purpose, goals, and expected outcomes of the proposed budget ideas. Participants can take part in neighborhood and community PB meetings which are livestreamed through social media platforms. This process promotes creativity in the policymaking process. This trend has become prevalent with the disruptions of in-person meetings and communications due to the global Covid-19 pandemic. Also, social media has enhanced accessibility of knowledge and information regarding PB implementation to the larger base of citizens. In this regard, PB administrators and participants work together to share information in more user-friendly ways through social media, such as avoiding the use of policy jargon. For example, the policy messaging strategy in the major cities in the US to mobilize higher participation in the PB process was to come up with easier and straightforward message that can appeal to as many participants as possible. Hence, the administrators used the term "participatory budgeting" as little as possible, but instead used the message "Your Money, Your Voice," "Real Money, Real Power," or "Our City, Our Voice" to make PB more accessible to the potential participants.

For instance, according to a study conducted by the IBM Center for the Business of Government (quoted by Gorden (2014)), in the cities that implemented PB such as Boston, Chicago, and St. Louis, the use of social media platforms encouraged residents to look into PB programs and participate. However, based on the interviews and surveys with the participants, the study suggests that the stakeholders involved in PB should have institutional social medial policies in place in order to drive forward rational decisions. Also, the use of social media platforms should complement other communication channels, promote mutual communications between public officials and citizens, and look out for who are "being left behind" with regards to using social media platforms.[9]

The increased use of online and social media tools in the PB process has changed the game in public deliberation and participation, and brought positive impacts including the increased number of voters and increased number and scale of proposed budget projects. In the post-truth era where social media and online channels thrive as people's primary source of news, knowledge, and information, and main communication medium, the case of PB well demonstrates how policy can be launched, implemented, and assessed through utilizing online and social media tools, connect relevant actors in the process, and facilitate the inclusion of non-conventional actors (citizens) into the policymaking arena.

Trust enhancing policy mechanism in the age of distrust

PB is an open and transparent platform where citizens get to witness how their tax money is spent. It is also designed as a mechanism to enhance citizens' trust and confidence in policymaking and among stakeholders in the policymaking process to watch what the government actually does (Lerner, 2011; Kim, 2014; Swaner, 2017).

Today's "post-truth" era, as mentioned earlier, can be characterized as a world of distrust and a low level of confidence. This has held particularly valid against the traditional political system, state institutions, and the mainstream media. This phenomenon is not only occurring in authoritarian regimes or dictatorships, but also in liberal democracies as well. According to Pew Research Center (2020), only around 20 percent of the US adults have responded that the government is "doing the right job," meaning that they have a lower level of confidence and trust in government and its decision-making.[10]

There have been theoretical and empirical observations that institutional arrangements which encourage more public participation and has a high level of openness and transparency, are associated with a higher level of trust and confidence in government and policymaking process and thus leads to a higher level of tax morale and compliance (Torgler, 2005; Sjoberg et al., 2019). PB which has an exemplary forum for citizens (taxpayers) to raise their voice and exercise their influence in the budgetary decision-making process, is intended as a process to enhance transparency and accountability and raise mutual trust and confidence among government and citizens. PytlikZillig et al. (2012) conducted an empirical survey study with participants in PB discussions in the city of Lincoln, Nebraska. According to their study, participants favor having opportunities for deliberation and provision of inputs in policymaking both in-person and online. Also, participants tend to have a higher level of confidence and trust in government due to their ability to select policy options and their satisfaction with government performance. High level of trust and confidence in institutions may serve as key factor to curb disinformation, information bubbles, and tribalism.[11]

As noted in the previous section, one of the notable characteristics of the post-truth phenomenon is that there are high levels of distrust against traditional institutions and expert/elite groups. Against this backdrop, PB has significance in two dimensions: (1) PB is a vehicle that encourages citizens to take initiatives and ownership in formulation and allocation of budgets to their policy priority areas, rather than being dependent on expert or specialist opinions or analyses on the citizens' budget preferences; (2) beyond the conventional tools and mechanisms of public budget participation such as community and townhall meetings and surveys, PB equips participants with a powerful tool, which is voting, to directly engage in policymaking and play a role as a leading actor in the process. Thanks to these participatory aspects of PB, citizens have come to the forefront of the policymaking arena, and have transitioned from merely as "clients" or "customers," but to "equal partners and collaborators" of the policymaking process (Denhardt and Denhardt, 2007). As PB expands and diffuses in scale globally, it would be meaningful to observe the development of this discourse and the empowerment of citizens in the policymaking process in the context of the post-truth era.

Ideal vs. reality—values of democracy and inclusion vs. divide

One of the downsides of the post-truth world, is that it is observed with deep and frequent divides and conflicts of opinions among different groups of people. There have been apparent divides between the elites and those who are not, those who are well-educated and those who are not, the rich and the poor, and so forth. There are apparent conflicts and clashes of viewpoints surrounding the factors such as political affiliation, race and ethnicity, wealth, and sexual orientation. This phenomenon of the divide is projected to deepen with the confluence of factors that we have examined previously, such as the increased use of social media. Social media has enabled the independence and liberation of individuals creating news and information distinctively from the traditional media, and it has facilitated the consumption of news and information tailored to one's belief or viewpoints (Gooch, 2017). An individual's opinion or point of view may become a critical news source for other people who share similar views. This phenomenon of social media use and the prevalence of misinformation, distrust and divide thereof, are interlinked in the age of post-truth and has become a great challenge to the policymakers.

Against this background, PB has gained ground as a policy tool to bring people together from various backgrounds. Especially, one of the primary goals of the PB is to empower the citizens and particularly, the traditionally marginalized groups or communities (Baiocchi and Ganuza, 2014; Su, 2017) and promote inclusive democracy. Baiocchi and Ganuza (2014) suggest four core criteria to assess the empowerment dimension of PB: the primacy of the forums, the scope and importance of budgets, the extent of actual participatory power over

160 *Yaerin Park*

budgets, and the self-regulating aspect of participation (Baiocchi and Ganuza, 2014, p. 39). As an example, through observation of participatory governance tools including PB that involve women in the process in Medellin, Colombia, it is found that local level participatory democracy leads to women's empowerment with regards to addressing the issues of violence against women and women's exclusion in decision-making (Hajdarowicz, 2018). Youth groups, especially those who do not yet have voting rights in regular political elections, can get empowered through participation in PB by obtaining competence about the democratic process and encouraging fellow youths in the process (Augsberger et al., 2019). In fact, in countries like France, the US, and Canada, PB is implemented in schools and school districts, encouraging participation of students, teachers, and parents to promote innovative spending of school budgets and provide civic educational opportunities.[12] In Portugal, the national budget law stipulates the implementation of Youth Participatory Budgeting.[13] Likewise, PB provides "voice" to the conventionally marginalized and excluded people in policymaking, and promotes diversity and inclusion of participation of various groups and communities in budgetary decision-making.

PB is a relevant platform designed to bridge the gap between various groups of people, include participants and incorporate viewpoints from various backgrounds, and empower them with outlets to raise their voices and opinions. It will be worthwhile to continue examining the progress of diversity, inclusion, and empowerment dimensions of PB as it expands in scale within the context of post-truth policy challenges.

Making process understandable and accessible for non-experts

Although there still is room for improvement, PB to a certain degree has made the process understandable and accessible for non-experts. For instance, Kota Kita, a Malaysian NGO has developed the "Mini Atlas," which is an interactive mapping tool to track the progress of PB projects by compiling communication database between residents and community members through SMS tools. It began as a pilot project in a city called Solo, but now expanded to other cities in Indonesia like Makassar and Panang, and the Atlas now has attracted even international users. Similarly, NYC has developed an interactive map where communities can track and see the progress of the voted projects through PB. Likewise, stakeholders involved in PB processes jointly work together to disseminate results and make information accessible to the public through intuitive, interactive, and user-friendly methods. Although these efforts are still in the inception stage and there may be challenges related to inclusion of people who lack access to digital technology, municipalities that adopted PB are collaborating with various actors to make PB data and information understandable and accessible to community members and non-experts (Figure 9.2).

Participatory budgeting and evaluation 161

Figure 9.2 Interactive Map of PB Projects in NYC.
Source: New York City Council Participatory Budgeting (Retrieved from http://ideas.pbnyc.org/page/about)

162   *Yaerin Park*

I have examined PB and its purpose and traits in alignment with the character-istics of the post-truth world. PB is intended to be responsive to citizens' needs, transparent, inclusive, and empowering policy platform, but how have they been effective in real life? What are the implications for the post-truth world?

Has PB promoted making smarter and more inclusive decisions?

PB making smarter decisions?

In this section, we will look at how PB has contributed to making "smarter" policy decisions in alignment with bounded rationality of the decision-makers. In the world of bounded rationality, rationality is bounded by human cogni-tive limits and complex circumstantial factors. In Simon (1947)'s words, the "administrative man" adopts the "satisficing" approach due to bounded rational-ity, rather than the "maximizing" approach based on classical and rational inter-est-maximizing "economic man."

PB process involves an expanded boundary and scope of institution com-pared with Simon (1947)'s administrative behavior within the organization perspective since it involves citizens and people as participants. In borrowing the perspective on bounded rationality (Simon, 1947), PB has contributed to making smarter decisions in given circumstances in several ways: (i) Public administrators and citizens adopt procedurals devices and mechanisms to adopt smarter approaches (satisficing devices as H. Simon notes them), such as estab-lishing the guidelines and rules of practice, building communication channels, and providing training and information sessions; (ii) decision-making through PB tends to be choosing the "most satisfying" alternatives through gathering knowledge by group thinking and voting for the most optimal choice of budgets. As seen earlier, public servants, civil society, and citizens jointly establish the procedural rules and guidelines, and standards on how to run the PB process in that given cycle, utilize both formal and informal communication channels, and adopt knowledge-sharing devices such as training and workshops, informa-tion sessions, and community meetings. For the second point, citizens' budget idea formulation and proposal development complement public administrators' decision-making on how to optimize the allocation of public budget tailored to the public budget preferences. Community participants can bring in ideas based on their actual living experience and observation of the community needs and priorities, which can be difficult to be seen by administrators or other actors. Voting is also a powerful tool for citizens to decide how to make the most sat-isfying budget choices and decisions, as it documents the participants' will on budget spending (Park, 2020).

However, PB also has demerits with regards to the most satisfying and smart-est decision-making. It still is largely a process affected by political factors. As Waldo (1948) puts it, the politics-administration dichotomy is not feasible in reality, and politics and political theories are underpinnings of administrative decision-making and leadership. PB is no exception to this case. For example, in Porto Alegre, Brazil, which is the birthplace of PB, PB has been suspended recently due to the fall of PT in power who had PB in their core political reform agenda, and the rise of centrist or right-wing political leaders.[14] Strong political support and commitment of the leadership to implement PB can mean opportunity, but the reverse situation can mean a threat to PB's sustainability and institutionalization. Also, there may be variations among places where PB is being implemented, but limited financial and administrative resources can hinder smart decision-making by PB. For instance, tight PB budget constraints and limits to fiscal and financial resources may be obstacles to increased PB participation and sustainable implementation for the long term. Inefficient organization or shortage of administrative capacity in running PB can also be a problem in the long run.

PB and more inclusive decisions?

Another key purpose of the PB as noted earlier is to promote empowerment of citizens through ensuring diversity and inclusion of participants and drawing conventionally marginalized populations into the policymaking process. PB serves as an opportunity for these marginalized communities to raise their voices in the budgetary process and have their budget preferences reflected in the process through budget idea and proposal formulation and voting. To achieve this goal, the stakeholders collaboratively establish rules and guidelines to ensure a certain quota of participation based on gender or racial equity.

The question then is, is PB really achieving its goal to make more inclusive decisions? The answers can be mixed. As we examined earlier, PB has contributed to a certain degree to promoting the empowerment of youth, women, lower-income communities, and communities of color. However, as in the dimension of PB making smarter decisions, it also has had demerits with regards to promoting inclusion in the decision-making process. Primarily, while PB intends to enhance equal participation of citizens, it is not entirely immune from bargaining or interest group politics. Citizens' joining interest groups is not always negative to influence public officials, as PB encourages various modes of participation (Miller et al., 2019). However, when interest group politics play out particularly within the limited PB budget constraints, there may be possible tension or conflicts among the interest groups, or between interest groups and ordinary citizens. This becomes especially critical when limited resources are not directed toward the needs of marginalized communities due to interest group politics.

Furthermore, while PB intends to bridge the gap between citizens by making sure the diversity and inclusion of participation, PB cannot be a panacea of closing the divide between different groups of people. This has been prevalent

164 *Yaerin Park*

with the increased use of social media and digital communication mechanisms in the PB process. The utilization of social media and digital tools has contributed to expanding PB in scale with regards to launch and implement PB in different municipalities and the increase in the number of PB participants and voters. Also, it increased the efficiency of the process by making sharing information and knowledge of PB easier among the stakeholders of PB. However, there still exists a digital divide between those who possess digital mechanisms and those who do not, and this brings stark division among citizens and citizens from marginalized communities. In fact, in many PB cases, public administrators spread PB information through word-of-mouth or through direct and physical interaction with community members such as through community centers, flyers and posters, and so forth, in communities that have limited access or knowledge to digital and virtual tools and social media (Park, 2020). As the use of social media and digital mechanisms intensifies in the PB process, there would be a continuous demand for a stratified approach to target different participant groups, especially the marginalized communities.

In summary, PB is designed to improve and enhance smarter and inclusive decisions by incorporating inputs from citizens as equal collaborators in the process. However, in reality, PB has both strengths and weaknesses in these dimensions. Can PB make improvements to make smarter and inclusive decisions? In the next section, I will integrate the lessons examined about PB and how this PB process and evaluation practices can make synergetic fit to address policy challenges in the post-truth world.

Integrating lessons from PB into evaluation practices fit for post-truth challenges

In this section, I examine the lessons from PB and the implications to evaluation practices fit to address policy challenges in the post-truth world. As discussed, PB operates in various contexts, and does not offer one-fits-all and generalizable solutions. Rather, some features and inspirations that are fit for post-truth world and policymaking environment could be carefully adapted to specific evaluation situations. As examined in the previous sections, PB is a multifaceted policy vehicle that serves as a "participatory" decision-making platform and as a "budgeting" tool to allocate local or national budgets according to participants' budget preferences. In this regard, PB and program evaluation practices can mutually provide synergies. Primarily, evaluations can be good guidelines and resources for evaluators, researchers, policymakers, and program participants (community members and citizens) to assess whether a PB program is actually achieving its intended goals and purposes. Assessing PB programs can greatly benefit from utilizing tools and metrics widely used in program evaluation of other policy interventions.[15] Conducting an effective evaluation of a PB program can help decide whether PB can be institutionalized as a formal and sustainable

Participatory budgeting and evaluation 165

decision-making process or expanded and diffused into different levels of government or other locations. Reciprocally, evaluators or relevant stakeholders in evaluation can greatly benefit from PB by having real-life experience, implications, and applications of evaluation theories. For instance, evaluators are readily aware that participative approaches are critical in conducting evaluations. Participation dynamics observed through existing PB practices in many parts of the world, and the unique traits of PB practices such as the enfranchisement for youth population or the variety of languages used during PB processes in many cases, may contribute to generating knowledge with regards to each procedural step in evaluation. Evaluation community may obtain living life lessons from establishing evaluation questions based on contextual factors, creating a more represented sample to delivering evaluation results in user-friendly ways.

As PB continues to gain momentum as exemplary public-sector reform and participatory approach within the context of complexity and uncertainty in the post-truth world, lessons from PB can feed into program evaluation practices which can lead to PB's long-term effectiveness as a sustainable democratic governance practice. I will explore how PB implications can create synergies with evaluation practices using Alkin (2012)'s evaluation theory tree framework, which looks at evaluation in the dimensions (branches) of method, use, and value. Additionally, I also examine how PB can deliver implications for evaluation in the post-truth world within Lemire et al. (2020)'s review of mechanisms in realist evaluations.

Alkin (2012)'s evaluation tree

method

In the post-truth era, people have disbelief and distrust against science and evidence-based policymaking. Also, PB operates in different settings and within various political, social, and cultural contexts. However, the lessons from PB on the method branch of evaluation imply that while evaluation methods may focus on contextual factors and supporting mechanisms (Cartwright, 2013) which help to understand why and how a certain intervention (PB) works, at the same time there is still a need to identify and understand the observed association between PB and the outputs that can be delivered in transferable or generalizable, and replicable ways. To achieve this, it is suggested that for the predictable and explainable PB evaluation, the evaluation community needs to (i) gather and create reliable data and information to look at different dimensions of PB and explore its effectiveness in more objective ways; (ii) set clear objectives of the use of methods through logic and theoretical base. Given Organisation for Economic Co-operation and Development (OECD) (Gooch, 2017)'s experience in dealing with Brexit issue amid the age of disinformation and distrust, it is recommended that the evaluation community discuss methods and approaches used and how they are attributable to the power of findings and outcomes with clarity and humility.

166   *Yaerin Park*

Use

Identify and involve stakeholders in the evaluation process

As mentioned earlier, PB is an extensive collaborative governance platform that is specifically designed to incorporate citizens' inputs in the budgetary decision-making process. It is designed with purposes to incorporate voices from various backgrounds, and to provide decision-making opportunities for especially those who have been conventionally marginalized. Although PB has made significant progress in the involvement of marginalized communities in the budgetary decision-making process, there are still obstacles against the broader participation of citizens due to digital and information divide. At times, due to the lack of outreach, politics, bureaucratic constraints, and resource/budget constraints, the budgets do not get allocated to the most needed places or groups. These lessons can provide implications to a better evaluation of PB on the user or utilization-focused evaluation. Particularly, as Patton (2008) mentions, PB implies that evaluators should clearly identify the primary intended uses and users in the beginning of the evaluation process and ensure that the primary intended users are engaged in the entire evaluation process. To achieve this objective, the evaluators should clearly establish evaluation goals and evaluation/research questions that delineate the primary intended users and the intended use of evaluation. Also, the evaluators should set program logic and theory of change accordingly that focus on the primary intended users and the utilization of evaluation. Additionally, evaluators should design and implement methods that engage a broad scope of stakeholders and increase the possibility for the evaluation findings to be used by the intended users (Patton, 2008). In the face of post-truth challenges characterized by distrust against existing systems, opening up about the evaluation process by engaging and informing stakeholders into the evaluation process will be especially critical.

Utilization of evaluation findings by the decision-makers

To restore trust and confidence between citizens and government, the shared data, information, and knowledge throughout the evaluation process should be effectively delivered to the decision-makers. This is key given that informing the decision-makers will lead to an improvement of the practice of PB and sustainable implementation of the practice in the long term. To achieve this goal of enabling decision-makers to improve and institutionalize the program, appropriate methods and channels of reporting and monitoring of the evaluation process to the decision-makers should be adopted. Also, unlike the traditional viewpoint on evaluation that evaluators should be completely independent and objective from the evaluation process, the evaluator participates in and facilitates in the decision-making process and lead the discourse on evaluation results in the use branch of evaluation (Patton, 2010). For instance, if the evaluation of PB has

Participatory budgeting and evaluation 167

shed light on the participants' call for an improved tracking system of how the budget proposals voted are being implemented or more inclusive participation rules and opportunities, these messages should be delivered to the decision-makers in concise, clear, and effective ways. For PB to continually gain momentum in the future as promising civic participation and budgetary tool even within the post-truth context, knowledge sharing through communications and reporting tools among stakeholders and to ultimately decision-makers, is important in addressing the trust-deficit issues (Gooch, 2017) and promoting accountability and openness of the decision-making process.

Valuing

The last dimension of Alkin's evaluation tree is the valuing aspect. PB is a practice that values count—such as equity, diversity, inclusion, empowerment, transparency, and accountability. Evaluation scholars from the valuing branch see that valuing distinguishes evaluation from pure research, and evaluators have a role in placing values and writing value statements on evaluation results.[16] PB implementation and assessment imply that achieving the intended goals and enhancing the values of a certain policy or governance practice is important, and it relates to the valuing aspect of program evaluation.

Evaluation should enhance social justice

The most critical purpose of PB is that it is designed to enhance social change and justice by bridging the gap between policy decision-makers and marginalized people and incorporating their voices into the process. In this regard, PB evaluation can be a crucial mechanism to promote social justice (Mertens, 2008). Marginalized communities such as lower-income groups, women, and people of color, have gained opportunities to formulate budget and policy ideas and express their will through voting in the PB process. However, there is still room for progress on the empowerment dimension of PB, and evaluation can be an essential tool for promoting empowerment and social justice. To design and implement an evaluation process that promotes social justice, evaluators should reflect social justice goals throughout every stage of the evaluation process, including establishing evaluation objectives, evaluation questions, participant recruitment, data collection and analysis, and results reporting. Evaluators must identify and recruit appropriate participants and continuously communicate with them throughout the evaluation process. Particularly, in the data collection and analysis procedure, evaluators may use diversified and combined approaches and methods from different strands to figure out patterns from numerical data as well as to capture various viewpoints and voices and write out narratives accordingly. Evaluators should be able to report evaluation findings in ways to promote social change and justice to various stakeholders including decision-makers and help these stakeholders to make appropriate decisions. Particularly,

168 *Yaerin Park*

in the post-truth era where people's values, perceptions, and opinions matter, evaluators should adopt and execute evaluation design and methods that can accurately depict the phenomenon surrounding social justice issues and incorporate these factors into carrying out evaluation aimed to promote social justice and change.

Converging values from different perspectives

In the value branch of program evaluation, evaluators should be able to make value statements (Scriven, 2007), and be able to mediate different values from a range of value perspectives stemmed from the evaluation process and results. PB provides implications in that it is a policy platform where participants with different viewpoints, backgrounds, and preferences meet, and the evaluator should have the capacity to mediate different or conflicting perspectives and converge into adequate value statements about the evaluation results. For example, if there is a policy debate on whether more funds should be allocated to the marginalized community, there will be various stakeholders involved, including elected officials, PB administrators and decision-makers, and community representatives and members raising different voices. At times, different organizations or groups (including interest groups) may have different or conflicting perspectives on the types and allocation methods of PB funding. These various viewpoints construct multiple or intersectional realities (Zaveri, 2020). The most important skill of an evaluator in the evaluation process is to listen and gather perspectives from a broad range of stakeholders and mediate and converge the value judgment and statement accordingly.[17] The evaluator's value judgment capacity would be especially important in the context of post-truth challenges amid the flow of information and prevalent divide, conflict, and disinformation, to prevent and block fake news or disinformation and make fair and appropriate value judgments.

Lemire et al. (2020)'s review of "Mechanisms" in realist evaluation

Lemire et al. (2020) have reviewed the definition of "mechanisms" within the realist evaluation framework. According to the authors, the standard formula of the realist evaluation is formulated as "Context-Mechanism-Outcome" (CMO) relationship. The authors refer to mostly Pawson and Tilley (2005)'s realist evaluation framework to define each component. The "context" refers to the individual capacities of administrators and program participants, the interpersonal relationships among the stakeholders involved, the institutional settings of the program, and infrastructure and welfare system surrounding the program (p. 75). "Mechanisms" can be referred to as program components that introduce ideas, resources, activities, and opportunities, participants' reaction and responses to a program, and an explanatory and underlying account such as behavior and interrelationship of the processes (p. 76).

Participatory budgeting and evaluation   169

If we apply the case of PB in the post-truth world, the "context" would be the circumstance surrounding the program (PB) that can be defined by the characteristics of the post-truth policymaking world: distrust between the citizens and governments, information bubbles and disinformation, policymaking by appealing to human beliefs, opinions, and emotions, and the emergence of alternatives to conventional media such as social media. The PB process can deliver implications for "mechanisms" dimension discussed in the realist evaluation as follow.

Program Components Evaluators should take into account opportunities, activities, ideas, and resources that PB brings. For example, there are unique activities and opportunities of PB that tell it apart from other citizen participation forums, such as voting and broadened participation base through providing opportunities for marginalized population in conventional political platforms. Increased use of online communication tools and social media channels in every stage of PB alongside with offline and in-person communications, may open wide doors for evaluators to delve into new ways to collect and analyze data, and interact with participants.

Participants' Reactions Evaluation community may pay attention to the dynamics of how participants, stakeholders, and beneficiaries of PB react or interpret the program. That is, the case of PB can provide implications on the key factors for evaluation that drive public participation in the context of the post-truth world. Key factors may include how PB deals with minimizing information bubbles and disinformation, how social media and technological tools promote rational decisions, how PB contributes to making rational decisions amid belief or emotion-driven decision-making, and how PB disseminates information and knowledge for various users/stakeholders, and user-friendly ways throughout every stage of evaluation.

Explanatory Account PB's explanatory account element may deliver implications to evaluation on how a program works "beneath the surface" (Lemire et al., 2020, p. 78) in the post-truth world. The intended goals of PB, such as empowerment of citizens, promoting transparency and accountability, and enhancing inclusion and social justice goals, can be foundational guidelines of the direction of evaluation and key to identifying how a change or reform can be achieved through the program. PB practice can guide evaluators' thinking through establishing evaluation goals, relevant evaluation questions, and whom to engage in evaluation, to identify how a policy intervention/program like PB can operate and thrive as a democratic policymaking platform in the post-truth environment.

Conclusion

With the development of social media and digitalization and the emergence of various groups and actors, policymaking in the post-truth age is influenced by people's beliefs, opinions, and perceptions, more than facts, rational reasoning, or scientific evidence. There is an increasing inclination of people's distrust against the traditional political and administrative systems, and media, and flux of disinformation or fake news. Likewise, the post-truth phenomenon can pose potential threats to policymaking and evaluation, as well as some opportunities.

PB has been adopted as an innovative citizen participation platform in budgeting in Brazil in the late 1980s, and has been expanding in scale and numbers ever since. PB is projected to gain momentum in the future as a promising participatory governance practice, albeit policy challenges in the post-truth era. PB has contributed to the improvement of people's quality of life, governance indicators and public-sector transparency and accountability, empowerment of citizens and civil society. PB has helped adopt "smarter and most satisfying" decisions by implementing information sharing and learning mechanisms and inviting and collaborating with citizens and other stakeholders to adequately identify budget needs and preferences. Also, PB has provided a forum for marginalized populations who had been conventionally excluded in political processes, to deliberate and participate in budgetary decision-making. However, PB still has limitations to making more smarter and inclusive decisions given that PB still is largely influenced by politics, and there is still a divide caused by the possession of digital and social media tools and mobilization power (interest groups) which hinder full empowerment of citizens regardless of their backgrounds.

To address such threats and to promote PB's effectiveness as an institutionalized and sustainable vehicle for citizen participation in the post-truth era, the PB lessons can be incorporated into processes of evaluation practice to make it fitter for the post-truth challenge. PB evaluation methods can be diversified to capture both patterns and voices/narratives to fully depict the PB landscape and the use of methods should be communicated to the stakeholders of the evaluation. The users of PB evaluation should be identified and encouraged to participate throughout the evaluation process, and the results should be clearly communicated with and delivered to various stakeholders and decision-makers. Moreover, the PB evaluation should put more focus on enhancing social change and justice and make negotiable value judgments and statements based on various perspectives of stakeholders. Particularly, evaluators' skills and capacity are crucial in selecting and sharing correct and appropriate information, data, and knowledge and bridging divides between stakeholders involved in the process in response to post-truth policy challenges.

PB has made progress in various dimensions of public deliberation and participation, policymaking, and public administration. However, it has had both merits and demerits. Policy and decision-makers, program participants, and evaluation community should understand and recognize the social, political, and institutional contexts of PB within the post-truth world, and establish efficient and positive feedback loops between PB and evaluation to institutionalize the process in the long run and contribute to the thriving of the process to serve as many citizens as possible and make smarter policy decisions in the future.

Notes

1 What is PB?. The Participatory Budgeting Project. Retrieved from https://www.par ticipatorybudgeting.org/what-is-pb/.
2 NYC Civic Engagement Commission. About Civic Engagement Commission. Retrieved from https://www1.nyc.gov/site/civicengagement/about/about.page.
3 Kuenkel, L. (March 22, 2018). Participatory budgeting—Portuguese style. Centre for Public Impact. Retrieved from https://www.centreforpublicimpact.org/insights/participatory-budgeting-portuguese-style.
4 The International Observatory on Participatory Democracy (OIDP). "My Budget," a National Participatory Budgeting experiment in South Korea. Retrieved from https://oidp.net/en/practice.php?id=1236.
5 New York City Council. Participatory Budgeting. Retrieved from https://council.nyc .gov/pb/results/cycle-6-results/.
6 Please see 15 Key Metrics for Evaluating PB (retrieved from https://www.partici patorybudgeting.org/15-key-metrics-for-evaluating-pb/) and Glasgow's Participatory Budgeting Evaluation Toolkit (retrieved from http://whatworksscotland.ac.uk/publications/glasgows-participatory-budgeting-evaluation-toolkit/).
7 Gooch, A. (2017). Bridging Divides in a Post-Truth World. Organisation for Economic Co-operation and Development. Retrieved from https://www.oecd.org/digital/bridging-divides-in-a-post-truth-world.htm.
8 Glasser, S. B. (December 2, 2016). Covering Politics in a "Post-Truth" America. The Brookings Institution. Retrieved from https://www.brookings.edu/essay/covering -politics-in-a-post-truth-america/.
9 Gorden, V. (December 16, 2014). Social Media and Participatory Budgeting. PA Times. American Society for Public Administration. Available at: https://patimes.org /social-media-platforms-participatory-budgeting/.
10 Pew Research Center. (September 14, 2020). Americans' Views of Government: Low Trust, but Some Positive Performance Ratings. Retrieved from https://www.pewresearch.org/politics/2020/09/14/americans-views-of-government-low-trust-but-some -positive-performance-ratings/.
11 Rainie, L., Keeter, S. & Perrin, A. (July 22, 2019). Trust and Distrust in America. Pew Research Center. Retrieved from https://www.pewresearch.org/politics/2019/07/22/ trust-and-distrust-in-america/.
12 Participatory Budgeting Project. Participatory Budgeting in Schools and School Districts. Retrieved from https://www.participatorybudgeting.org/wp-content/ uploads/2016/04/PB-in-Schools-Info-Sheet.pdf.
13 Paz, C. Youth Participatory Budgeting—Portugal. PBAtlas. Retrieved from https:// www.pbatlas.net/uploads/7/0/6/1/70619115/portugal_3.pdf.
14 De Renzio, P., Spada, P. & Wampler, B. (November 25, 2019). Paradise Lost? The crisis of participatory budgeting in its own birthplace. International Budget Partnership. Retrieved from https://www.internationalbudget.org/2019/11/paradise-lost-the-crisis -of-participatory-budgeting-is-its-own-birthplace/.
15 Participatory Budgeting Project (February 7, 2018). How to make evaluations awesome and meaningful. Retrieved from https://www.participatorybudgeting.org/evaluations-surveys-pb/.
16 The Power to Persuade. (April 10, 2015). The evaluation theory tree. (Retrieved from http://www.powertopersuade.org.au/blog/ihs226p8pv4xnt4vc56zw64zggxliq/15/3 /2016).
17 Ibid.

172   *Yaerin Park*

References

Alkadry, M. G. (2003). Deliberative discourse between citizens and administrators: If citizens talk, will administrators listen? *Administration & Society, 35*(2), 184–209.

Alkin, M. C. (Ed.). (2012). *Evaluation roots: A wider perspective of theorists' views and influences.* Sage Publications.

Augsberger, A., Gecker, W., & Collins, M. E. (2019). "We make a direct impact on people's lives": Youth empowerment in the context of a youth-led participatory budgeting project. *Journal of Community Psychology, 47*(3), 462–476.

Baiocchi, G., & Ganuza, E. (2014). Participatory budgeting as if emancipation mattered. *Politics & Society, 42*(1), 29–50.

Baiocchi, G., Heller, P., & Silva, M. (2011). *Bootstrapping democracy: Experiments in urban governance in Brazil,* Stanford: Stanford University Press.

Bartocci, L., Grossi, G., Mauro, S. G., & Ebdon, C. (2022). The journey of participatory budgeting: A systematic literature review and future research directions. *International Review of Administrative Sciences.* https://doi.org/10.1177/00208523221078938.

Beuermann, D. W., & Amelina, M. (2014). *Does participatory budgeting improve decentralized public service delivery?* (No. IDB-WP-547). IDB Working Paper Series. Inter-American Development Bank.

Bufacchi, V. (2021). Truth, lies and tweets: A consensus theory of post-truth. *Philosophy & Social Criticism, 47*(3), 347–361.

Cabannes, Y. (2004). Participatory budgeting: A significant contribution to participatory democracy. *Environment and Urbanization, 16*(1), 27–46.

Cabannes, Y. (2015). The impact of participatory budgeting on basic services: Municipal practices and evidence from the field. *Environment and Urbanization, 27*(1), 257–284.

Cartwright, N. (2013). Knowing what we are talking about: Why evidence doesn't always travel. *Evidence & Policy: A Journal of Research, Debate and Practice, 9*(1), 97–112.

De Renzio, P., Spada, P. & Wampler, B. (2019, November 25). Paradise lost? The crisis of participatory budgeting in its own birthplace. Retrieved from https://www.internationalbudget.org/2019/11/paradise-lost-the-crisis-of-participatory-budgeting-is-its-own-birthplace/.

Denhardt, J. V. (2007). *The new public service, expanded edition: Serving, not steering.* ME Sharpe.

Denhardt, R. B., & Denhardt, J. V. (2000). The new public service: Serving rather than steering. *Public Administration Review, 60*(6), 549–559.

Ebdon, C., & Franklin, A. L. (2006). Citizen participation in budgeting theory. *Public Administration Review, 66*(3), 437–447.

Glasgow City Council, Glasgow Community Planning Partnership. What works Scotland. Glasgow's participatory budgeting evaluation toolkit. Retrieved from http://whatworksscotland.ac.uk/publications/glasgows-participatory-budgeting-evaluation-toolkit/.

Glasser, S. B. (2016, December 2). Covering politics in a "Post-truth" America. Retrieved from https://www.brookings.edu/essay/covering-politics-in-a-post-truth-america/.

Gonçalves, S. (2014). The effects of participatory budgeting on municipal expenditures and infant mortality in Brazil. *World Development, 53,* 94–110.

Gorden, V. (2014, December 16). Social media and participatory budgeting. *PA Times.* American Society for Public Administration. https://patimes.org/social-media-platforms-participatory-budgeting/.

Participatory budgeting and evaluation 173

Gooch, A. (2017). *Bridging divides in a post-truth world.* Organisation for Economic Co-operation and Development. Retrieved from https://www.oecd.org/digital/bridging-divides-in-a-post-truth-world.htm.

Hajdarowicz, I. (2022). Does participation empower? The example of women involved in participatory budgeting in Medellin. *Journal of Urban Affairs, 44*(1), 22–37.

International Observatory on Participatory Democracy (OIDP). "My budget", a national participatory budgeting experiment in South Korea. Retrieved from https://oidp.net/en/practice.php?id=1236.

Kim, S. (2014). *Citizen participation, transparency, and public trust in Government: Participatory budgeting in local governments of Korea* (No. 2014-03). KDI Research Monograph, Korea Development Institute (KDI), Sejong,https://doi.org/10.22740/kdi.rm.e.2014.03 .

Kuenkel, L. (2018). Participatory budgeting – Portuguese style. Retrieved from https://www.centreforpublicimpact.org/insights/participatory-budgeting-portuguese-style.

Lemire, S., Kwako, A., Nielsen, S. B., Christie, C. A., Donaldson, S. I., & Leeuw, F. L. (2020). What is this thing called a mechanism? Findings from a review of realist evaluations. *New Directions for Evaluation, 2020*(167), 73–86.

Lerner, J. (2011). Participatory budgeting: Building community agreement around tough budget decisions. *National Civic Review, 100*(2), 30–35.

Meier, K. J., O'Toole Jr, L. J., & O'Toole, L. J. (2006). *Bureaucracy in a democratic state: A governance perspective.* JHU Press.

Mertens, D. M. (2008). *Transformative research and evaluation.* Guilford Press.

Michels, A. (2011). Innovations in democratic governance: How does citizen participation contribute to a better democracy?. *International Review of Administrative Sciences, 77*(2), 275–293.

Miller, S. A., Hildreth, R. W., & Stewart, L. M. (2019). The modes of participation: A revised frame for identifying and analyzing participatory budgeting practices. *Administration & Society, 51*(8), 1254–1281.

New York City Council. Participatory budgeting. Retrieved from https://council.nyc.gov/pb/results/cycle-6-results/.

Novy, A., & Leubolt, B. (2005). Participatory budgeting in Porto Alegre: Social innovation and the dialectical relationship of state and civil society. *Urban Studies, 42*(11), 2023–2036.

NYC Civic Engagement Commission. About civic engagement commission. Retrieved from https://www1.nyc.gov/site/civicengagement/about/about.page.

Park, Y. (2020). *Participatory budgeting and willingness to pay taxes: Evidence from an exploratory sequential mixed methods study* (Doctoral dissertation, The George Washington University).

Participatory Budgeting Project. 15 key metrics for evaluating PB. Retrieved from https://www.participatorybudgeting.org/15-key-metrics-for-evaluating-pb/.

Participatory Budgeting Project. Participatory budgeting in schools and school districts. Retrieved from https://www.participatorybudgeting.org/wp-content/uploads/2016/04/PB-in-Schools-Info-Sheet.pdf.

Participatory Budgeting Project. What is PB? Retrieved from https://www.participatorybudgeting.org/what-is-pb/.

Participatory Budgeting Project. (2018, February 7). How to make evaluations awesome and meaningful. Retrieved from https://www.participatorybudgeting.org/evaluations-surveys-pb/.

174 *Yaerin Park*

Patton, M. Q. (2008). *Utilization-focused evaluation.* Sage Publications.

Patton, M. Q. (2010). *Developmental evaluation: Applying complexity concepts to enhance innovation and use.* Guilford Press.

Pawson, R., & Tilley, N. (2005). Realist evaluation. In S. Mathison (Ed.), *Encyclopedia of evaluation* (pp. 362–367). Thousand Oaks, CA: Sage.

Paz, C. Youth participatory budgeting – Portugal. Retrieved from https://www.pbatlas.net/uploads/7/0/6/1/70619115/portugal_3.pdf.

Pew Research Center. (2020, September 14). Americans' views of government: Low trust, but some positive performance ratings. Retrieved from https://www.pewresearch.org/politics/2020/09/14/americans-views-of-government-low-trust-but-some-positive-performance-ratings/.

PytlikZillig, L. M., Tomkins, A. J., Herian, M. N., Hamm, J. A., & Abdel-Monem, T. (2012). Public input methods impacting confidence in government. *Transforming Government: People, Process and Policy, 6*(1), 92–111.

Rainie, L., Keeter, S., & Perrin, A. (2019, July 22). Trust and distrust in America. Pew Research Center. Retrieved from https://www.pewresearch.org/politics/2019/07/22/trust-and-distrust-in-america/.

Scriven, M. (2007). *The logic of evaluation.*https://philpapers.org/rec/SCRTLO-5

Simon, H. A. (1947). Administrative behavior: A study of decision. *Making Processes in Administrative Organization.* New York: Macmillan

Sintomer, Y., Herzberg, C., & Röcke, A. (2008). Participatory budgeting in Europe: Potentials and challenges. *International Journal of Urban and Regional Research, 32*(1), 164–178.

Sjoberg, F. M., Mellon, J., Peixoto, T. C., Hemker, J. Z., & Tsai, L. L. (2019). *Voice and punishment: A global survey experiment on tax morale.* World Bank Policy Research Working Paper 8855.World Bank, Washington, DC.http://hdl.handle.net/10986/31713.

de Sousa Santos, B. (1998). Participatory budgeting in Porto Alegre: Toward a redistributive democracy. *Politics & Society, 26*(4), 461–510.

Su, C. (2017). From Porto Alegre to New York City: Participatory budgeting and democracy. *New Political Science, 39*(1), 67–75.

Swaner, R. (2017). Trust matters: Enhancing government legitimacy through participatory budgeting. *New Political Science, 39*(1), 95–108.

The Power to Persuade. (2015, April 10). The evaluation theory tree. Retrieved from http://www.powertopersuade.org.au/blog/ihs226p8pv4xnt4vc56zw64zggxliq/15/3/2016.

Torgler, B. (2005). Tax morale and direct democracy. *European Journal of Political Economy, 21*(2), 525–531.

Torgler, B., & Schneider, F. (2007). *Shadow economy, tax morale, governance and institutional quality: A panel analysis.* IZA Discussion Paper No. 2563. The Institute for the Study of Labor.

Touchton, M., & Wampler, B. (2014). Improving social well-being through new democratic institutions. *Comparative Political Studies, 47*(10), 1442–1469.

Touchton, M., & Wampler, B. (2020). Public engagement for public health: Participatory budgeting, targeted social programmes, and infant mortality in Brazil. *Development in Practice, 30*(5), 681–686.

Touchton, M., Wampler, B., & Peixoto, T. (2020). Of democratic governance and revenue: Participatory institutions and tax generation in Brazil. *Governance, 34,* 1193–1212.

Waldo, D. (1948). The administrative state: A study of the political theory of American. *Public Administration.*New York: The Ronald Press Company.

Wampler, B. (2012). Participatory budgeting: Core principles and key impacts. *Journal of Public Deliberation, 8*(2), 1–13.

Zaveri, S. (2020). Making evaluation matter: Capturing multiple realities and voices for sustainable development. *World Development, 127*, 104827.

10 Evidence use in a post-truth world

A unique opportunity for evaluators?

Steffen Bohni Nielsen and Sebastian Lemire

The Post-truth paradoxes of evidence use in the political and public domains

We live in ambiguous times. In a world of increasing globalization, interconnectedness, and complexity, rational thought prescribes that evidence from studies and streams of evaluative knowledge must form the bedrock of sound decision-making (Stame, 2006). After all, implications of decisions will become increasingly difficult to foresee, let alone what future conditions will affect policy development in, and across, interconnected domains.

In the section that follows, we will consider how these post-truth conditions lead us toward interconnected paradoxes on evidence use in both the political and public domains. Informed by these considerations, we will then discuss the implications of these paradoxes for the practice and profession of evaluation.

The post-truth paradox of evidence use in the political domain. On the one hand, we live in a post-truth world where a growing number of political actors and parties intentionally question, or willfully ignore, evidence and use social media to spread false news to attain political ends and serve partisan interests. The uncurated, direct and real-time, communication through social media—such as X or Facebook—is more amenable to clickbait and quick political points than to long reads delving into the complexities of evidence on substantive issues. Political actors can communicate directly to their electoral base, cherry-picking facts and research to suit their own political agenda (Völker, 2019). In this post-truth world, political and public debates reach beyond competing interpretations of a shared set of facts. There are no shared facts.

On the other hand, many national governments and transnational organizations have also institutionalized policies that support evidence-based policymaking (Marra, Olejniczak, Paulson, this issue). As just one example, the United States federal government instituted the Foundations for Evidence-Based Policymaking Act of 2018 ("Evidence Act"), which has since be reaffirmed by different executives orders (US White House, n.d.). Similar pieces of policy, at either central or departmental levels can be found in numerous countries around the world. Indeed, globally these efforts have been bolstered by the establishment of a growing number of (domain specific) evidence clearinghouse

DOI: 10.4324/9781032719979-11

Evidence use in a post-truth world 177

functions. These clearinghouses are often fully, or in part, funded by national or local governments (Hansen & Rieper, 2011; Oliver, Lorenc, & Innvær, 2014).

These two competing trends leave us with an apparent paradox in the policy domain of evidence use: While we live in an era where a growing number of political actors are weaponizing evidence for political gains, governments continue to institutionalize the production, synthesis, and use of evidence across public domains. We shall posit here that the former is perhaps more prevailing in the executive branch with politicians and political appointees as messengers seeking to persuade their opponents and electoral base. The unprecedented commitment to partisanship and volatility of political processes is conducive to applying all means necessary. Meanwhile, the implementation of evidence-based policies has permeated public organizations for decades (Cairney & Oliver, 2017; Lemire, Peck, & Porowski, 2020). This institutionalization, perhaps, becomes more apparent at the bureaucratic, administrative tiers of government.

The post-truth paradox of evidence use in the public domain. Reaching beyond the policy domain, there are also competing trends in the public domain of evidence use.

On the one hand, and perhaps at least in part because of the trends discussed in the preceding pages, public trust in and respect for expertise and research is dwindling (Marra, Olejniczak, & Paulson, this issue; Nichols, 2017). This development is of course lamented by researchers and research organizations within and outside of the academia, as a large part of their cultural and social capital stems from their very expertise called into question. As a side note, one is left to wonder, whether some members of academia must also look themselves in the mirror. Arguably, certain constructivist and highly politicized research approaches can also serve to blur the distinction between (research) knowledge and political action. After all, it can be hard to argue that research is inherently political, why researchers must engage politically, yet claim that research knowledge is superior to political statements. The lines easily get blurred. These lines are further blurred by researchers and even research organizations committed to advancing certain political agendas. The libertarian Cato Institute comes to mind. However, these research organizations span the left-right political divide.

On the other hand, and to make matters more complicated, the democratization of previously privileged knowledge appears to gain momentum. Sustained calls for open data in government and in academia, and the drive toward open access publications in academic books and journals, only furthers the accessibility of knowledge (Cope & Kalantzis, 2014). According to a recent White House directive, academic journals will now have to provide immediate access to publicly-funded research papers, effectively ending a policy that had allowed publishers to keep publications behind a paywall for up to a year. To be sure, the Internet provides an abundance of research. The challenge is to critically sort through and assess credible sources to facts. This democratization of data, of research, also encourages that the public at large question expertise. A pertinent

178 *Steffen Bohni Nielsen and Sebastian Lemire*

example is that of patients asking for second opinions, googling evidence to support or refute a particular diagnosis or medical treatment. They may cite systematic reviews from clearinghouses, or from curated online platforms, that support a particular treatment.

This is perhaps not too surprising. As French philosopher, Paul Ricoeur, remind us, in the written language the said and the intention of the subject ceases to overlap. The text ceases to refer to the world of the writer in the direct sense of the dialogue but starts to signify the world of the reader. In this process the communicative act of the written language frees itself from the narrowness of the dialogical situation (Ricoeur, 1979). The reader will use the text in his, or her, own interpretation and to their own ends. This is true for research and evidence, too. In short, one must expect interpretations by the public, once the texts leave the researchers. In a political context, such interpretations are, not surprisingly, politicized. Researchers must expect that stakeholders are ready to contest evidence and findings that are not aligned with their political agenda. They are using research. The research is making a societal impact, albeit not necessarily as intended.

Considered collectively, these competing trends lead us to an apparent paradox on evidence use in the public domain: While the democratization of access to evidence may advance the role and influence of evidence, the very access to evidence may also be used to call into question and further erode public trust in expertise and research organization.

Implications for the practice and profession of research. As a researcher or evaluation practitioner, these emerging paradoxes—reaching across the political and public domains—may be leave us in an uncomfortable position, institutionally and individually. Therefore, it is all the more important that research producers (universities, research institutions, independent think tanks) and publishers (academic journals, book etc.) are judicious about how they position themselves as credible, independent sources of information. Moreover, researchers and research organizations must also expect and prepare for increased levels of antagonism from both public and political actors that dislike their findings. In the post-truth era, this is the price to be paid for societal impact of research.

Evaluation—as a form of applied research—is in many ways positioned well to take on these trends. Evaluation is effectively born and bred into the political domain as it is intended to assess the merit and worth of public policies and programs (Vedung, 2004). Therefore, considerable research on evaluation has also focused on the non- or misuse of evaluation. Building on the work of the great Carol Weiss, Evert Vedung (2004, 2021) has observed that evaluation use may be intentional, sometimes unintentional, legitimate or illegitimate and there are many kinds of process, and product, uses. The implication is that evaluators as part of their practice have learned to anticipate and manage stakeholders in politically charged climates. Therein, lies a learning potential for the research community at large.

Evidence use in a post-truth world 179

The potential role of evaluation in the post-truth era

With the post-truth paradoxes of evidence use as a backdrop, we will in the following section describe how some of the characteristics and complexities of evaluation provides unique opportunities for evaluators in the current political climate. These include the professionalization of evaluation, the transdisciplinary nature of evaluation, as well as the marketplace and commission-driven context for evaluation. In extension, we will describe some of the tools that evaluators have used to anticipate and manage stakeholders and that seem relevant and valuable for researchers navigating the post-truth landscape.

Some characteristics and complexities of evaluation

In recent decades, there has been worldwide and significant attention devoted to the professionalization of evaluation (Lemire, Peck, & Porowski, 2020, Picciotto, 2011; Schwandt, 2017). This professionalization is reflected in the establishment of professional associations and journals dedicated to evaluation (Nielsen & Winther, 2014), evaluation standards and guidelines (Stevahn et al., 2005), definition of core evaluator competencies, as well as formal degree programs in evaluation and even credentialing of evaluators (Schwandt, 2017). While this development has, arguably, been driven to carve out a distinctive space in the professional distribution of labor (Abbott, 1988), it has also been met with criticism by some for having focus on the institutional and instrumental features of professionalizing evaluation rather than reflexivity of the profession (ethics, valuing, judging), which Thomas Schwandt refers to as reflective practice (2017).

Despite these central efforts to professionalize the practice and profession of evaluation, significant debate still revolves around whether evaluation constitutes a scientific discipline in its own right or whether it is better viewed as a transdiscipline—a discipline that draws liberally from theories and methodologies from disciplines such as anthropology, economics, political science, psychology, public health, sociology, among others (Scriven, 2003).

Another lens through which to view evaluation is that of the evaluation marketplace. Lemire, Nielsen, and Christie (2018) observe that evaluation practice is fragmented into regional- and domain-specific markets where different actors, designs, theories, interests, and methodologies prevail. The authors also point out that most evaluation practice never finds its way into peer-reviewed journals and is largely carried out under market conditions (Nielsen, Lemire, & Christie, 2018a, 2018b). Important contributions to our knowledge of the marketplace of evaluation have been provided for in the United States (Hwalek & Straub, 2018; Kinarsky, 2018; Lemire et al., 2018; Peck, 2018), Canada (Lahey, Elliott, & Heath, 2018), the United Kingdom (Davies, Morris, & Fox, 2018), Denmark (Nielsen, Lemire, & Christie, 2018c), and Norway (Askim, Bøving, & Johnsen, 2021). Lemire, Nielsen, and Christie (2018) conclude, that the evaluation market is dependent on "buyer power" as commissioners set out the terms of services rendered.

180 *Steffen Bohni Nielsen and Sebastian Lemire*

A further distinctive feature of evaluation is that it is always demanded by somebody (a commissioning body), whether internal or external. Mark, Greene, and Shaw (2006) note that evaluations are commissioned and, by logical extension, always defined by the interplay between a demand for evaluation (from commissioners of evaluation) and a supply of evaluation (from producers of evaluations). As noted above, this implies that evaluation, at its outset, is both contracted and negotiated. This is on the one hand the nature of evaluation practice, wherein there are negotiated trade-offs and methodological compromises in the relation between commissioners, who sets out the overarching conditions (monetary, timing, scope) of the evaluation and the evaluator. Academic purists may discount evaluative knowledge as less rigorous for this very reason. In contrast, evaluation has since its infancy positioned itself as applied research. Consequently, evaluation has originally modeled itself against social scientific ideals such as independence, objectivity, and value-free knowledge production. (Nielsen, Lemire, & Christie, 2018a). This is the predicament of evaluation. In some ways its commercial aspects are incompatible, or at least in potential conflict, with the scientific ideals.

The fact that evaluations are, more often than not, commissioned and subject to contractual agreement has several implications. In practice, commissioners set out a terms of reference wherein the main evaluation questions are specified. In market terms, the buyer (commissioner) of evaluation holds the cards in so far as they decide when, what, and how the evaluation should be conducted. This often implies that evaluations are carried out under less-than-ideal conditions, wherein design, data collection, and analytical options are restricted. However, in our view, it is exactly these imperfect conditions that have prepared evaluators to navigate the post-truth era.

Commissioned evaluations are surrounded by stakeholders with diverse, sometimes opposing, interests and stakes. The fact that evaluation, as opposed to foundational research, is an applied form of social science implies that it focuses on real-world problems and interventions designed to address these problems. Interventions, such as policies, programs or projects, all have stakeholders such as decision-makers, commissioning body, service provider organizations, professionals delivering the services, their professional associations, service recipients, interest groups, and citizens at large. These stakeholders all hold stakes in the evaluation findings and have vested interests in affecting the use of the evaluation. Different kinds of stakes are involved such as political, financial, reputational, discretionary stakes. Evaluators must be acutely cognizant of these because evaluation findings are more often than not scrutinized and contested because of these vested stakes.[1]

These factors all contribute to the complexities of evaluation as a practice field. It makes evaluation inherently complex. In practice, the evaluator must comply with contractual requirements, ensure timely deliverables, get necessary permissions from institutional or governmental review boards, design and

Evidence use in a post-truth world 181

implement the evaluation, oversee and quality assure data, ensure data are stored and collected in compliance with data protection regulation, analyze data, report accurately, draft appropriate conclusions and recommendations, quality assure the report, manage the team, manage the client, and manage stakeholders.

In this context of the "post-truth era" managing stakeholders is particularly important, that is informing, consulting, and responding to stakeholder pressures and treating all legitimate stakeholders fairly. It is a difficult task. *We would argue that it is exactly this practice, that positions evaluation as superior to operate as a knowledge producer in the current post-truth era.*

The task of skillfully analyzing the social and organizational context, stakeholder needs, and display situational awareness is crucial. It is therefore also recognized in the core competencies for evaluators published by a number of different professional bodies, such as the American Evaluation Association, the Canadian Evaluation Society, the European Evaluation Society, the German Evaluation Society, and the United Kingdom Evaluation Society. All professional bodies recognize and list the ability to manage stakeholder relations as a core competency (American Evaluation Association, 2018; Canadian Evaluation Society, 2018; European Evaluation Society, n.d.; German Evaluation Society, n.d; United Kingdom Evaluation Society, 2012). In many ways, evaluators are better equipped to operate in the contested realms of post-truth society. Therefore, an examination of some of the tools from the evaluators' toolbox is topical.

Evaluation tools to manage stakeholders

From our perspective, the transdisciplinary depth and breadth of evaluation provides for multiple perspectives and practices and enable multi-, cross-, and interdisciplinary cross-pollination (Lemire, Peck, & Porowski, 2020). It provides a deeper and broader toolbox. It is up to the evaluation provider to design methodology, process and combine competency profiles in an evaluation team that fits the narrow and greater purpose of the evaluation. It is here paramount to acknowledge that different evaluation purposes (accountability, learning, establish causation, summative/formative) may imply the application of very different evaluation models, wherein some tools are appropriate, and others are not.

Bearing this disclaimer in mind, let us exemplify how evaluators at an operational level may apply different processes and tools to remediate stakeholder concerns and influence stakeholders' decisions. When doing so, it is beneficial to structure these after the major phases in an evaluation process: (i) structuring and planning the evaluation, (ii) collecting data, (iii) analyzing data, (iv) developing evaluative judgments and reporting, and (v) promoting utilization (Nielsen & Ejler, 2008). Table 10.1 below provides an overview.

Structuring and planning the evaluation. This phase is arguably the most important in the evaluation process. In the current post-truth era evaluators'

Table 10.1 Evaluation tools to manage stakeholders throughout the evaluation

Phase	Purpose	Activity	Evaluation Tools
Structuring and planning	1. Identify key stakeholders, stakes and anticipate potential responses to findings 2. Contractual basis for process and deliverables is explicit 3. Involve legitimate stakeholders, anticipate responses 4. Clarify legitimate roles, responsibilities, and actions 5. Ensure alignment among stakeholders on scope of evaluation 6. Contractual basis for process and deliverables is explicit 7. Contractual basis for deliverables is explicit	1. Conduct a stakeholder analysis 2. Be explicit about exemptions to ToR 3. Create advisory or steering groups 4. Clarify roles 5. Ascertain importance and meanings of evaluation questions 6. Consolidate in methodology note 7. Ensure sign off on major deliverables	1. Power wheel (Fenn, 1979), Stakeholder map 2. N/A 3. See Skolits, Morrow, & Burr, 2009, King & Stevahn, 2002 4. Matrix for selecting and ranking evaluation questions (Morra Imas & Rist, 2009) 5. Design matrix template (Morra Imas & Rist, 2009) 6. N/A 7. N/A
Collecting data	1. Ensure fair and validated representation of data 2. Ensure fair and validated representation of data 3. Lock-in client on stakeholders on major decisions	1. Ensure agreement on data 2. Validate interview documentation 3. Brief client and stakeholders on deviation and progress	1. Evaluation matrix (Morra Imas & Rist, 2009) 2. N/A 3. N/A
Analyzing data	1. Lock-in client on stakeholders on major decisions	1. Brief client and stakeholders on deviation and progress	1. N/A

(Continued)

Table 10.1 (Continued)

Phase	Purpose	Activity	Evaluation Tools
Developing evaluative judgment and reporting	1. Ensure fair and transparent basis for judgment in accordance with evaluation questions 2. Ensure transparent basis for judgment of quality of evaluation 3. Assess feasibility and prewire stakeholders 4. Ensure transparent basis for judgment of quality of evaluation	1. Explicit judgment—evaluation criteria, evaluation norms, and judgment 2. Explicit methodology—design data, triangulation, analytical strategy 3. Consult on recommendations 4. Transparency in reporting	1. Scriven (1994), European Commission (n.d.) 2. N/A 3. N/A 4. N/A
Promoting utilization	1. Anticipate different needs and uses 2. Tailor reporting output to different audiences 3. Tailor reporting output to different audiences	1. Revisit stakeholder analysis 2. Evaluation report as only one output 3. Executive summaries	1. Power wheel, Stakeholder map 2. N/A 3. N/A

184 *Steffen Bohni Nielsen and Sebastian Lemire*

ability to accurately anticipate stakeholder concerns and likely responses is crucial. An accurate analysis should have implications on how the evaluation is designed and carried out. It is here important steps to manage stakeholders are planned for.

In typical evaluation practice, this phase stretches across the several stages; the Request for proposal (bidding) stage wherein the evaluator submits a proposal, the won/loss stage, and detailed structuring and planning stage if the projects have been won. This may be more or less formalized depending on the commissioner and procurement regulations. In internal evaluation, the process is somewhat more fluid. Therefore, the tools below are somewhat generic.

1. *Conduct a stakeholder analysis.* A crucial initial step is to understand the context of the evaluation. Here subject-matter expertise is crucial. The evaluator must identify all (key) stakeholders, identify their stakes (political, economic, reputational, discretionary), and anticipate how they are likely to respond to particular findings (i.e., the intervention is ineffective). The stakeholder analysis can take the form of a power wheel (Fenn, 1979), which is a tool to map actors, relations, and power centers on particular issues. Such identification of stakeholders' relations and interests helps to identify create natural alliances. It should be updated throughout the evaluation process. The analysis will help evaluators better understand and anticipate stakeholders' responses to the evaluation process and findings.

2. *Be explicit about exemptions to the Terms of Reference.* One can view the commissioner's terms of reference as a *this-is-what-we-think-we-want* outline. These terms may be unrealistic due to timing of the evaluation, budget constraints, data availability, among other constraints. The evaluator must make clear why exemptions to the ToR are necessary and how the predicament should be solved (*this-is-what-you-get*). One way to do is to emphasize the value added by outlining the constraints and the actionable potential of the knowledge that will be generated from the proposed evaluation approach. For example, if evaluators are to evaluate a novel intervention in highly contested political climate, they may emphasize the advantages of adaptive approaches with rapid and iterative improvement cycles, such as developmental evaluation (Patton, 2011).

3. *Create advisory or steering groups.* Often a way to ensure fair treatment of stakeholders is to create a representative steering or advisory groups. This also ensures that stakeholders are briefed about findings prior to publication of the report, which allows evaluators to anticipate their response. We have several examples of the involvement by key stakeholders that enabled evaluators to phrase evaluation questions more accurately, identify relevant judgment criteria and norms, provide insights to accuracy of data, and test recommendations etc. More often than not stakeholders are accustomed to deal with research findings that does not support their agenda. Involvement

Evidence use in a post-truth world   185

gives them time to prepare and anticipate their responses. It is more difficult to refute findings when you have been involved all along. These processes are more often than not a delicate balancing act between multiple demands.

4. *Clarify roles.* Skolits, Morrow, and Burr (2009) argue that evaluators take on a multiplicity of roles throughout the evaluation process. Different evaluation purposes, model, and designs render different roles and require different kinds of stakeholder involvement (King & Stevahn, 2002). Simply consider the roles of the evaluator in formative versus summative evaluations, a participatory evaluation or a randomized controlled trial. In general, evaluators' engage more directly in and involve stakeholders in participatory models, whereas their role is more observational in experimental studies. The implications of an evaluation's purpose and corresponding roles should be clear to commissioner and stakeholders alike.

5. *Ascertain importance and meanings of evaluation questions.* Morra Imas and Rist (2009) have written at length about the importance of clarifying and deciding on evaluation questions (descriptive, normative, causal). Often prioritization is needed. Consulting with stakeholders may be crucial in this process.

6. *Consolidate in a methodology note.* In procurement processes there is often a need to negotiate the Terms of Reference (*what we think we want*) and the proposal (*this-is-what-you-can-get*). This may be based on clarifying the (importance of) evaluation question, data availability, analytical strategy, among other key parameters of the evaluation. A useful means to transparently document these decisions is to write up a methodology note (*what-we-actually-plan-to-do*), which in turn can be communicated to relevant stakeholders.

7. *Sign off on major deliverables.* In some high stakes, evaluations may be particularly pertinent to ensure that stakeholders have accepted the methodology before proceeding. This may involve the formulation of evaluation questions, evaluation criteria, and judgment references. If stakeholder have accepted the methodology, they are locked-in by approving the evaluation scope and methodology. It is harder to discredit findings if one has formally accepted the methodology used to produce the very same findings.

Collecting data. In this phase stakeholder involvement is limited, yet there are still some issues that need to be managed if they are not to backfire at later stages.

1. *Ensure agreement on data.* Particularly in Europe, there is an increased regulatory attention to individual rights and data privacy (the General Data Protection Regulation). From both a regulatory (legal) and stakeholder (ethical) point of view, consent is important.

2. *Validate interview documentation.* Often, in qualitative and mixed-methods studies, the evaluator will collect interview data from stakeholders. It is therefore important that interviewees validate interview data (transcripts,

186 *Steffen Bohni Nielsen and Sebastian Lemire*

summaries). This is important to avoid retraction that may question validity of the overall findings.

3. *Brief client and stakeholders on deviation and progress.* Here the concept of *pre-wiring* is important (MacDonald, 2014). It simply means briefing stakeholders prior to deliverables and meetings. If the evaluation model and purposes permits, there are several advantages to keeping commissioner and stakeholders in the loop on work progress and findings. Sometimes data collection does not fare as planned (i.e., low response rate in surveys, poor data quality in administrative registries, etc.).

Analyzing data. As in the previous phase, stakeholder involvement is limited, yet there are still some issues that need to be managed.

1. *Brief client and stakeholders on deviation and progress.* As in the previous phase, pre-wiring is important. This is especially the case when deviations from the intended analytical strategy is needed.

Developing evaluative judgment and reporting. In this phase, the anticipation of stakeholder responses is critical. In practice, there exists a balancing act between "speaking truth to power" and selecting words or statements that unnecessarily "over-state" or "understate" certain findings. Different stakeholders have different sensitivities. Evaluators must choose their battles with care. The tools below may aid the process of judicious selection of these battles.

1. *Explicit judgment—evaluation criteria and judgment reference.* The process of valuing is central to evaluative thinking (Vo & Archibald, 2018). More often than desired, evaluation reports are not explicit on the evaluation criteria on the basis of which the evaluators assess the merit and worth of an intervention. Being explicit about these criteria is crucial if stakeholders are to be managed well. Ideally, these have already been discussed and decided on with stakeholders, as well as included in the methodology note in the initial phase of the evaluation.
2. *Explicit methodology—design data, triangulation, analytical strategy.* No design is perfect. Stakeholders will always look at criticizing the methodology if they dislike the findings. Evaluators need to be explicit about the strength and limitations of the evaluation methodology.
3. *Consult on recommendations.* The genre of evaluation reporting contains recommendations. Recommendations are fraught with potential conflict. Often it is pertinent to consult intended recommendations to assess their feasibility and implications. Such consultations also prewires and involves stakeholders. While stakeholders may not agree with all the recommendations, they should feel consulted.

Evidence use in a post-truth world 187

4. *Transparency in reporting.* The evaluation report is the text which will form the basis for subsequent debate of the evaluation findings. Particular attention to the quality of the report is essential. Many evaluators have instituted rigorous quality assurance processes to ascertain its quality. Some poignant points of attention concerning stakeholder responses: be explicit about the evaluation mandate, process, and evaluation questions; describe the strength and limitation of the methodology; be explicit about evaluation criteria and judgment; pay particular attention to the chain of logic from data to findings to conclusions leading to recommendations; reflect on to what extent evaluation findings resonate with existing evidence for similar interventions; ensure recommendations are relevant and feasible.

Promoting utilization. Considerations of (legitimate) use of the evaluation should be paramount throughout the evaluation process. Evert Vedung has written incisively about the different forms of process and product use (2021). These tools below refer to the preceding phase of reporting and aims at securing intended use by intended users following Michael Quinn Patton's adage.

1. *Revisit stakeholder analysis.* Once the evaluation findings are clear, evaluators should revisit their stakeholder analysis. Their anticipation of stakeholder responses is likely more detailed. On this basis, they must draft a detailed communication plan.
2. *Evaluation report as only one output.* Different audiences require different formats. In example, decision-makers have very little time to prepare for each issue they deal with. Research literacy of the general public (and some stakeholders) is likely to be limited. And on it goes. If evaluation findings are to be communicated to intended users, the format must adapt accordingly. Examples of such *written formats* are one page executive summary (see below), slide decks, personas (user-driven examples of how the program affected lives), short reports (no more than 20 pages) with appended documentation and methodology, *visual formats* such as infographics, customer journey maps, or *oral formats* such as podcasts, oral presentations (in long and short formats).
3. *Executive summaries.* One pertinent example is the executive summary. This may require tailoring the summary to different audiences, using infographics and other visuals to support the narrative. For evaluators it is a way to control the narrative meeting intended users. If a summary of the evidence is left to stakeholder, it is more likely, that it will be summarized to fit their ends.

In this section, we have exemplified some of the activities and tools amenable to managing stakeholders and thereby their responses to evaluation findings. In the subsequent section, we discuss these observations in a broader context of evaluation in the post-truth era.

Discussion

In this chapter, we have discussed the role of research in the post-truth era. We are in paradoxical times. The contention of expert knowledge, and the experts co-exists with calls for evidence-based policymaking and practice. The former implies that (the refutation of) research is contested in the political realm by stakeholders. It is an uncomfortable position for many academics. The latter—the promise of evidence-based policy, has hitherto shown to be just that; a promise. In the real world, policymaking is much more complex and competing considerations, interests, and forms of knowledge all blend into policy decision-making.

Cairney and Oliver (2017), while reflecting on the ambition of evidence-based policymaking, observe that the research community needs a better understanding of how policies get made, get implemented, and responded to and must be able to engage with policymakers throughout the policy process. As they go on to explain:

> Rather, scientists compete with many influential actors to present evidence to secure a policymaker audience at many levels of government. Support for evidence-based solutions varies according to which organisation takes the lead and how its rules encourage policymakers to understand the problem. Some networks are close-knit and difficult to access because bureaucracies have operating procedures that favour some sources of evidence and participants over others. There is a language in institutions and networks that takes time to learn.
>
> (p.5)

The ability to navigate such institutional and personal relationships is both difficult and uncomfortable for many in the research community. There is an inherent risk that such engagement may be perceived of as positioned and partisan. It may call into question the role of experts. This complexity may be lamented by some actors. It implies that researchers must jog for positioning their research as a particularly credible form of knowledge that should inform decision-making in the realms of the private, not-for-profit, and public sector.

However, it also provides tremendous opportunity to evaluators. As we have argued, evaluation practice is inextricably linked to such institutional processes, and thus better equipped to tailor to stakeholders' needs from a large and varied toolbox. Evaluation is born in the complexity of varied stakeholder demands and interests. At the very core, this complexity has supplied evaluators with approaches and tools that are perhaps more relevant than ever and from which academia at large must and should learn from. These are advantages, if applied sensibly and with rigor, that may enable evaluators to design processes and provide best available evidence to decision-makers in the post-truth era. As with any tool, these will never be better than the skill set and purpose of those who apply them. This calls for a situational expertise well recognized in the core competencies of the evaluation community. Nevertheless, in the climate of the

Evidence use in a post-truth world 189

post-truth era, the ability calls for skills honed by evaluators to engage with and manage stakeholders' engagement in, reception, and use of research findings.

The position we hold is that evaluation is situated in a liminal position between craftsmanship and science. It is inherently applied, negotiated, and contested. While these predicaments have often been used against the field of evaluation (Nielsen, Lemire, & Christie, 2018a), we argue that they can serve as an advantage in the post-truth world as evaluators are accustomed to and have developed ways to cope with competing interests of stakeholders. As such, evaluators are uniquely equipped to manage stakeholders and their contesting claims to truth.

Note

1 We refer to Matthews' highly illustrative flowchart of "go to" responses to research findings (Matthews, 2013).

References

Abbott, A. (1988). *The system of professions. An essay on the division of expert labor.* Chicago, IL: University of Chicago Press.

American Evaluation Association. (2018). Evaluator competencies. Retrieved from (July 2022): https://www.eval.org/Portals/0/Docs/AEA%20Evaluator%20Competencies.pdf

Askim, J., Døving, E., & Johnsen, Å. (2021). Evaluation in Norway: A 25-year assessment. *Scandinavian Journal of Public Administration, 25*(3/4), 109–131.

Cairney, P., & Oliver, K. (2017). Evidence-based policymaking is not like evidence-based medicine, so how far should you go to bridge the divide between evidence and policy? *Health Research Policy and Systems, 15*(35), n.p.

Canadian Evaluation Society. (2018). Competencies for Canadian evaluation practice (2018). Retrieved from (July 2022): https://evaluationcanada.ca/competencies -canadian-evaluators

Cope, B., & Kalantzis, M. (2014). Changing knowledge ecologies and the transformation of the scholarly journal. In B. Cope & A. Phillips (Eds.), *The future of the academic journal* (pp. 9–83). Oxford: Chandos Publishing.

Davies, P., Morris, S., & Fox, C. (2018). The evaluation market and its industry in England. *New directions for evaluation* (Vol. 160, pp. 29–43).

European Commission, DEVCO. (n.d.). Evaluation judgment. Retrieved from (August 2022): https://europa.eu/capacity4dev/evaluation_guidelines/wiki/judgement-references-0

European Evaluation Society. (n.d.). Evaluation capabilities framework. Retrieved from (July 2022): https://europeanevaluation.org/wp-content/uploads/2020/03/EES -EVALUATION-CAPABILITIES-FRAMEWORK.pdf

Fenn, D. H. (1979). Finding where the power lies in government. *Harvard Business Review, 57*(5), 144–153.

German Evaluation Society (DeGEval). (n.d.). Recommendations on education and training in evaluation. Retrieved from (July 2022): https://www.degeval.org/fileadmin /Publikationen/Publikationen_Homepage/Recom_Education_Training.pdf

Hansen, H. F., & Rieper, O. (2011). Institutionalization of second-order evidence-producing organizations. In O. Rieper, F. L. Leeuw, & T. Ling (Eds.), *The evidence book. Concepts, generation and use of evidence* (pp. 27–49). New York, NY: Routledge.

Hwalek, M. A., & Straub, V. L. (2018). The small sellers of program evaluation services in the United States. *New directions for evaluation* (Vol. 160, pp. 125–143).

Kinarsky, A. R. (2018). The evaluation landscape: U.S. Foundation spending on evaluation. *New directions for evaluation* (Vol. 160, pp. 81–96).

King, J. A., & Stevahn, L. (2002). Three frameworks for considering evaluator role. In K. E. Ryan & T. A. Schwandt (Eds.), *Exploring evaluator role and identity* (pp. 1–16). Greenwich, CT: Information Age Publishing.

Lahey, R., Elliott, C., & Heath, S. (2018). The evolving market for systematic evaluation in Canada. *New directions for evaluation* (Vol. 160, pp. 45–62).

Lemire, S., Fierro, L. A., Kinarsky, A. R., Fujita-Conrads, E., & Christie, C. A. (2018). The U.S. federal evaluation market. *New directions for evaluation* (Vol. 160, pp. 63–80).

Lemire, S., Nielsen, S. B., & Christie, C. A. (2018). Toward understanding the evaluation market and its industry— Advancing a research agenda. *New directions for evaluation* (Vol. 160, pp. 145–163).

Lemire, S., Peck, L. R., & Porowski, A. (2020). The growth of the evaluation tree in the policy analysis forest: Recent developments in evaluation. *Policy Studies Journal, 48*, 47–70.

MacDonald, D. (2014). *The firm: The story of McKinsey and its secret influence on American business.* New York, NY: Simon & Shuster.

Mark, M. M., Greene, J. C., & Shaw, I. F. (2006). The evaluation of policies, programs, and practices. In I. Shaw, J. Greene, & M. Mark (Eds.), *The SAGE handbook of evaluation.* Thousand Oaks, CA: SAGE Publications.

Matthews, D. (2013). How people argue with research they don't like. *The Washington Post.* Retrieved from (July 2022): https://www.washingtonpost.com/news/wonk/wp/2013/09/12/how-to-argue-with-research-you-dont-like/?wprss=rss_national

Morra Imas, L. G., & Rist, R. C. (2009). *The road to results. Designing and conducting effective development evaluations.* Washington, DC: The World Bank.

Nichols, T. M. (2017). *The death of expertise: The campaign against established knowledge and why it matters.* New York, NY: Oxford University Press.

Nielsen, S. B., & Ejler, N. (2008). Improving performance?: Exploring the complementarities between evaluation and performance management. *Evaluation, 14*(2), 171–192.

Nielsen, S. B., Lemire, S., & Christie, C. A. (Eds.). (2018a). Editors' note. *New directions for evaluation* (Vol. 160, pp. 7–11).

Nielsen, S. B., Lemire, S., & Christie, C. A. (2018b). The evaluation marketplace and its industry. *New directions for evaluation* (Vol. 160, pp. 13–28).

Nielsen, S. B., Lemire, S., & Christie, C. A. (2018c). The commercial side of evaluation. Evaluation as an industry and as a professional service. In J. E. Furubo & N. Stame (Eds.), *The evaluation enterprise. A critical view* (pp. 243–265). New York, NY: Routledge.

Nielsen, S. B., & Winther, D. M. (2014). A Nordic evaluation tradition? A look at the peer-reviewed evaluation literature. *Evaluation, 20*(3), 311–331.

Oliver, K., Lorenc, T., & Innvær, S (2014). New directions in evidence-based policy research: A critical analysis of the literature. *Health Research Policy and System, 12*(34). https://health-policy-systems.biomedcentral.com/articles/10.1186/1478-4505-12-34#citeas

Patton, M. Q. (2011). *Developmental evaluation. Applying complexity concepts to enhance innovation and use.* New York, NY: Guildford Press.

Peck, L. R. (2018). The big evaluation enterprises in the United States. *New directions for evaluation* (Vol. 160, pp. 97–124).

Picciotto, R. (2011). The logic of evaluation professionalism. *Evaluation, 17*(2), 165–180.

Ricoeur, P. (1979). The model of the text: Meaningful action considered as text. In P. Rabinow & W. M. Sullivan (Eds.), *Interpretive social science: A reader* (pp. 73–102). Berkeley, CA: University of California Press.

Schwandt, T. A. (2017). Professionalization, ethics, and fidelity to an evaluation ethos. *American Journal of Evaluation, 38*(4), 546–553.

Scriven, M. (1994). The final synthesis. *Evaluation Practice, 15*(3), 367–382.

Scriven, M. (2003). Evaluation in the new millennium: The transdisciplinary vision. In S. I. Donaldson & M. Scriven (Eds.), *Evaluating social programs and problems: Visions for the millennium* (pp. 19–42). Wahwah, NJ: Lawrence Erlbaum Associates.

Skolits, G. J., Morrow, J. A., & Burr, E. M. (2009). Reconceptualizing evaluator roles. *American Journal of Evaluation, 30*(3), 275–295.

Stame, N. (2006). Introduction. Streams of evaluative knowledge. In R. C. Rist & N. Stame (Eds.), *From studies to streams: Managing evaluative systems* (pp. vii–xxi). London: Transaction Publishers.

Stevahn, L., King J. A., Ghere, G., & Minnema, J. (2005). Establishing essential competencies for program evaluators. *American Journal of Evaluation, 26*(1), 43–59.

United Kingdom Evaluation Society. (2012). Framework of evaluation capabilities. Retrieved from (July 2022): https://www.evaluation.org.uk/app/uploads/2019/04/UK-Evaluation-Society-Framework-of-Evaluation-Capabilities.pdf

United States White House. (n.d.). Evidence and evaluation. Retrieved from (July 2022): https://www.whitehouse.gov/omb/information-for-agencies/evidence-and-evaluation/

Vedung, E. (2004). *Public policy and program evaluation.* New York, NY: Routledge.

Vedung, E. (2021). The twelve-part typology of evaluation uses. *Zeitschrift für Evaluation, 20*(1), 101–130.

Vo, A. T., & Archibald, T. (2018). New directions for evaluative thinking. *New directions for evaluation* (Vol. 158, pp. 139–147).

Völker, T. (2019). Deliberative democracy in the age of social media. *Revista Publicum, 5*(2), 73–105.

Conclusions

Some suggestions for evaluators' daily work in a post-truth world

Karol Olejniczak, Mita Marra, and Arne Paulson

The evaluation aims to improve public interventions (policies and programs) and ultimately contribute to social betterment and justice (Chelimsky, 2006; Henry & Mark, 2003). Daily practice typically involves evaluators assisting policy-makers and policy-takers in finding a better match between policy problems and available policy solutions. Previous volumes of The Comparative Policy Evaluation series have comprehensively discussed the challenges associated with the evaluation mission and its practices (see, for instance: Leeuw et al., 1994; Rieper et al., 2012; Palenberg & Paulson, 2020). However, post-truth, which in short denies evidence and facts, provides a new context in which evaluators work, making the evaluation mission even more challenging.

In our concluding remarks, we offer two things. First, we distill the novel characteristics and ramifications of this contemporary post-truth milieu for the work of evaluators, as elaborated upon in various chapters of this volume. Second, we propose a framework that builds on the insights presented in the book's individual chapters and brings together various evaluative strategies offered by the contributors to this volume. Our aspiration is that this consolidated effort will help the evaluation community navigate the complexities of the post-truth landscape and conduct productive and impactful work.

Summary of key characteristics of contemporary evaluation

Five key issues emerged as new characteristics of contemporary evaluation in post-truth era. First, the introduction and the chapters across this book show that post-truth is a complex, multilayered problem, deeply rooted in our human cognitive mechanisms and bounded rationality but substantially exacerbated by latest changes in information infrastructure, modes of social communication, and social dynamics of hyper-polarization.

Second, evaluators become involved in a much broader spectrum of decisions (also called: action situations) than we used to be in traditional program evaluation. These conversations now focus on framing the policy problems and co-designing pilot interventions. The examples are discussed in the first three chapters of this book: Chapter 1 by Marra, Chapter 2 by Guerrero, and Chapter 3 by Boyle and Redmond.

DOI: 10.4324/9781032719979-12

This chapter has been made available under a CC-BY-NC-ND 4.0 license.

Conclusions 193

Third, the extended spectrum of decision situations involves different types of actors that use different types of heuristics and evidence hierarchies and are exposed to different biases. This issue is analyzed in detail by Krawiec and Śliwowski in Chapter 5. Furthermore, as discussed in Chapter 7 by Bundi and Pattyn, policy-takers' attitude toward evidence and expertise also differs in specific national contexts.

Fourth, there is a substantial difference in the degree of (ir)rationality among decision situations, and the exposure to post-truth challenges. The chapters in this book illustrate the broad spectrum of decision situations. On the one hand, Jacob and Milot-Poulin in the Chapter 4 discuss political dynamics with many shades of truth and lie, and even degrees of deception. On the other hand, book reports on the continuous efforts for development of evidence-driven practices. In particular, Chapter 8 by Hart and Newcomer presents institutional development of architecture for evidence-informed system at national level, while Chapter 3 by Boyle and Redmond and Chapter 9 by Park bring insights on the smaller in scale but also pragmatic content of co-design processes.

Fifth, a clear practice emerges across chapters of this book to involve various stakeholders in the evaluation process, especially to co-produce and co-create with citizens and final users of policies (so-called policy takers). Turning evaluation practice into "multilogue," that is, the dialog of various actors would bring new perspectives, a more in-depth understanding of policy issues, and potential better buy-in for solutions.[1] However, this participation could make the evaluation process more challenging since new groups will bring to the table not only their ideas but also their biases. The conceptual details and practical examples of these co-creation efforts are discussed in numerous chapters in this book. The specific insights are brought by Chapter 1 by Marra, Chapter 3 by Boyle and Redmond, Chapter 9 by Park, and Chapter 10 by Nielsen and Lemire.

Framework for evaluators' work in the post-truth era

The diverse and dynamics circumstances of post-truth milieu requires from evaluation practitioners to recognize the differences in contextual situations and adapt our roles and tactics to specific contexts and degrees of challenges. The idea of such an agile approach emerged in two chapters of this book— Chapter 6 (Olejniczak and Jacoby) and Chapter 10 (Nielsen and Lemire). In our Conclusions, we follow this idea and propose a framework to flexibly organize evaluators' actions, roles, and choices.

We recognize that addressing the challenge of post-truth in democratic societies is an effort much bigger than the evaluation practice and requires systemic responses and adaptations at the level of our institutions, rules, and processes. Selected chapters in this book touch upon this issue and provide the big picture suggestions: Jacob and Milot-Poulin, in Chapter 4, present mechanisms to restore trust in democracy and political process; Bundi and Pattyn, in Chapter

194   *Karol Olejniczak, Mita Marra, and Arne Paulson*

7, point out the importance of engaging the general public, while Hart and Newcomer in Chapter 8 focus on a regulatory framework for evidence-informed policymaking.

Most of the professional evaluation practice, however, takes place in the context of projects and programs, with limited influence on changing the grand institutional and regulatory settings of whole public policy systems. Therefore, in our Conclusions, we propose a bottom-up approach, focusing our attention on improvements that evaluators could implement in their daily work with policy-makers and policy-takers, becoming change agents on a small scale. The choice of this human-centered approach is also justified by the fact that the underlying mechanisms of post-truth are rooted in human reasoning and biases.

We propose considering various decision/action situations in which evaluators engage during the policy process. Each type of situation has its specific function from the policy decision-making perspective, specific actors/participants, dynamics, and degree of (ir)rationality. Depending on the situation, evaluators would play specific roles, working with different stakeholders and using different strategies to minimize the risk of policy failure.

The decision/action situation perspective is well recognized in social-science literature on collective decision-making (Ostrom, 2005). Also, specific adaptations have been proposed to characterize government decision-making (Baumgartner & Jones, 2005; Hallsworth et al., 2018).

Introduction to the framework

Our framework is built on the Theory of Disproportionate Information-Processing (Baumgartner & Jones, 2005). This theory explains how the government processes information in producing public policies. The whole policy process is portrayed as a collective problem-solving effort. Attention allocation and biases in decision-making are crucial factors explaining the outcomes of this process. We have adopted this perspective to evaluation needs.

Building on the earlier literature (Baumgartner & Jones, 2005; Dörner, 1990; Hallsworth et al., 2018), we have identified four main types of action situations that evaluators can encounter in public policy. These are: (1) noticing policy issue, (2) defining policy problem, (3) choosing a solution, and (4) executing policy solution.

The following paragraphs discuss the four types of action situations in detail. Each situation is described in terms of its function in collective problem-solving, the spectrum of actors it engages in, and potential post-truth limitations it brings to the participants. For each situation, we propose roles that evaluators could take and assistance that evaluators could provide to the participants of the decision situation. Those concise descriptions are linked back to the detailed discussions in the specific chapters of this book.

Conclusions 195

Noticing policy issue

This action situation is concerned with making public and policymakers' aware of a particular policy issue. The main participants involved in these decision situations are politicians, various sectoral stakeholders, interest groups, and general public opinion, usually through mass media discourse. Actors noticing policy issues usually could face several biases and challenges. Two major are attention deficit and salience effect, when the most salient issues draw attention regardless of whether they are the most urgent or important, while slow-developing problems often go unnoticed. Another potential bias is availability heuristics, a tendency to rely on immediate examples, more recent information, salient anecdotes, and previous events that are easy to recall. Framing could also kick in at this stage. In this situation, it means that the presentation of an issue determines whether it is noticed and how it is interpreted, and at the same time, policy actors often passively accept the formulation of problems as given. Other challenges at this stage could include confirmation bias (seeking and interpreting evidence that aligns with one's pre-existing views and beliefs) and simple information noise.

We are convinced that in this type of action situation, evaluators could assist participants by monitoring trends and situations and scanning the horizon for emerging policy issues. Also, evaluators can help notice the problem by changing the main narrative or providing new theory lenses to see policy issues from a different perspective. Finally, evaluators could, supported with data, prioritize the attention of the policymakers and public opinion. The specific solutions available for evaluators were discussed in Chapter 2 by Guerrero, Chapter 8 by Hart and Newcomer (systemic settings and institutional perspective), and Chapter 6 by Olejniczak and Jacoby (individual, evaluator-decision-maker perspective).

Defining policy problem

The second type of action situation focuses the energy of policy actors on making sense of the policy problem. That means framing the policy issues in specific terms (for example, economic, societal, ecological, or technological problems), understanding the system's structure affected by the problem, and tracing the roots of malfunctioning.

Defining policy problems engages a slightly different group of actors than in previous action situation. These are high-level decision-makers, stakeholders of the specific policy issues in question, policy designers responsible for developing concrete programs and projects as a response to a policy problem, and citizens—however, not a broad public but rather specific groups that are directly affected by policy issue and its solutions (so-called policy-takers or policy users).

As in the previous stage, those actors can face challenges of availability heuristics (explaining problem using already familiar facts or previous situations), salience effect (focusing on first most visible or media-present aspect of the

196   *Karol Olejniczak, Mita Marra, and Arne Paulson*

problem), and confirmation bias. Additionally, they can experience an illusion of similarity, assuming that others have similar views, determination, and understanding of the policy issue. Other challenges at this stage include insufficient goal elaboration (Dörner, 1990 calls it the "repair-shop principle" when an initially diagnosed problem is quickly matched with a solution already available in the system) and falling into myopia by neglecting the side effects and long-term implications of specific policy problems (Smith, 1995).

At this stage, evaluators could support policy actors in articulating the main assumptions on how the system works and the causes of the problem. The basics of evaluators work starts here with simple fact-checking. Evaluators can also bring new voices to the conversation, including varied voices and perspectives of different stakeholders group, especially those excluded or marginalized. Critical questioning of the mainstream frames and theories used in problem analysis can also be a valuable contribution from an evaluation practice. Evaluators can also find ways to communicate and engage citizens with evidence—create a laymen-friendly (non-expert) merit discourse on the roots and perspectives of the policy problem. Specific chapters in our book (Chapter 2 by Guerrero, Chapter 3 by Boyle and Redmond, and Chapter 7 by Bundi and Pattyn) show how all those efforts can help deepen the understanding of the policy problem and see new aspects of the discussed policy issue.

Choosing a solution

The third type of action situation covers several specific activities leading to the final choice of policy intervention. That includes formulating options for policy solutions, generating policy alternatives, debating options, and finally, making collective choices.

Participants involved in those decisions include senior decision-makers in public institutions, stakeholders, policy designers, and representatives of target groups. At this stage, policy options are focused on technical aspects (e.g., choice between a set of programs or regulations) but the political dynamics can often turn that conversation into a broad discussion on the logic of intervention (or non-intervention) and the role of the state. That in turn, can draw the attention and involvement of the broad public and high-level politicians.

Biases that can emerge among those participants during this decision situation include status quo bias (sticking to the current state of affairs and perceiving any change from the baseline as less advantageous) and loss aversion (weighing possible losses larger than possible gains). When discussion on policy options returns to the broader public arena, it often triggers the Dunning-Kruger effect—the less policy actors know, the more confident they are about simplistic solutions (Motta et al., 2018). Also, the myopia of neglecting the side and long-term effects can kick in when choosing a solution. An illusion of similarity can also emerge, but it plays slightly differently—the more policy actors favor a policy,

Conclusions   197

the more they assume that others have similar views (Straßheim, 2020). Usual time pressure at this stage can also exacerbate confirmation bias—with too much information and too little time, policy actors can focus on the information supporting their preferred proposals.

Finally, during the choice of solution, several challenges can emerge related to group dynamics, such as the bandwagon effect (a tendency to adopt the positions or solutions because decision-maker perceives that everyone else is doing it, e.g., other public agencies or countries), group reinforcement (self-censoring and conforming to the group-majority view, not challenging arguments and views within a group) often combined with inter-group opposition (rejecting arguments of other groups, even if they are good ones).

Chapters in this book and core evaluation literature indicate that evaluators are well-prepared to help articulate and choose priority criteria for assessing policy options (effectiveness, efficiency, utility, equity, etc.). That is because the logic of assessment and the aspects of valuing has a long tradition in evaluation practice. The unique added value of evaluators is in helping policy designers articulate alternative theories of change—that is, a set of assumptions about what policy tools could trigger what type of change and why. Thus, evaluators are well prepared to assist participants in clarifying policy options, providing inspiration on similar problem-policy solutions, and animating merit-based discussion on options among various, often conflicting groups of stakeholders. Numerous chapters in this book provide practical insights and examples on evaluators' activities related to facilitating policy choices (see: Chapter 6: Olejniczak and Jacoby, Chapter 9 by Park, and Chapter 10 by Nielsen and Lemire).

Executing policy solution

The final action situation focuses on establishing the implementation details, delivering the solution, and tweaking the cogs and wheels of change mechanisms that drive policy intervention.

This situation is the primary interest of policy designers, street-level bureaucrats, specific stakeholders, and policy takers/users of the specific policy intervention. Here the logic of policy dominates, but if a major implementation failure occurs, the dynamic could be turned into political accountability.

The participants engaged in these decisions usually overestimate the quality of their plans, the abilities of the institutions to implement policy options, the likelihood of successful policy delivery (optimism bias and overconfidence), and their ability to control outcomes, often downplaying uncertainties and challenges (the illusion of control). The latter bias is related to linear thinking (that is, ignoring mechanisms and complex system dynamics). As Hallsworth et al. point out (2018) policy often deals with complex systems where the link between cause and effect is not direct. Addressing a problem in one area can create unintended consequences in another part of the system and push policy actors to keep trying to intervene with new actions without realizing that the system is not responding as they intend. Finally, in our complex world of organizations and implementation systems, policy actors can face such challenges as competing solutions implemented simultaneously, and measure fixation (focus on reporting performance indicators of progress rather than the success of underlying objective).

The action situation of executing policy solution is a traditional realm of program evaluation activities. Thus, the evaluators have extensive possibilities in assisting policy participants. We want to point out four things in particular. First, evaluators can help unpack the black box of mechanisms, articulating theories of change and underlying assumptions that drive specific policy interventions. Second, evaluation practitioners can keep bringing the user perspective to the table, showing actual user experiences as specific programs unfold. Third, evaluators can help coordinate different policy measures, seeing synergies or conflicts among them (in public policy literature, this is discussed under the term of policy mixes (Howlett, 2023). Last but not least, evaluation can help balance operational vs. strategic perspective and indicators since the daily implementation routines often create measure fixation on short-term products at the expense of long-term, more difficult-to-measure effects. The dynamics of this decision type are discussed in particular by Chapters 1 (Marra), 3 (Boyle and Redmond), and 10 (Nielsen and Lemire).

The above-discussed perspective of thinking in terms of policy actors, decisions they face, and biases they experience has recently emerged in public policy literature (Dudley & Xie, 2019; Gofen et al., 2021; Hallsworth et al., 2018). Our approach follows these developments but focuses on evaluation. We recognize that, in reality, the evaluation practices can and should be present in all identified action situations, and we indicate possible roles that evaluators could undertake.

Looking more broadly, as has often been said, the only constant in this world is change, and indeed the world has changed and will continue to change in the future. Theocracies have been replaced by the divine right of kings, which was replaced by feudalism, which evolved into democracy, and some democracies have failed, devolving into autocratic regimes and even, in some cases, to a resurgence of pseudo theocracy. The chapters of this book have examined various ways in which our world has been molded politically, socially, and intellectually by the "Post-Truth" phenomenon, but it is worth noting that there is nothing new about this phenomenon—it just seems that way, because we happen to be here now. Evaluation can help us understand our situation, and help guide change, if we let it. Evaluation offers the opportunity to develop shared intelligence, involve more stakeholders, take account of opposing views to co-produce democratically solutions to complex problems. Of course, excessive information can turn public attention off; and the need is for evaluation to separate the grain from the chaff. This is part of the permanent tension between the public good and private ambition, and that is why evaluation matters.

Conclusions 199

Note

1 We borrow the term "multilogue" from Richard Duke—a classic author of serious gaming literature and practice, who promoted games as collective sensemaking, that improves communication among competing stakeholders (Duke, 2011).

References

Baumgartner, F. R., & Jones, B. D. (2005). *The Politics of Attention: How Government Prioritizes Problems*. Chicago, IL: The University of Chicago Press.

Chelimsky, E. (2006). The Purposes of Evaluation in a Democratic Society. In I. Shaw, J. C. Greene, & M. M. Mark (Eds.), *Handbook of Evaluation. Policies, Programs and Practices* (pp. 33–55). London, Thousand Oaks and New Delhi: SAGE Publications.

Dörner, D. (1990). The Logic of Failure. *Philosophical Transactions of the Royal Society of London. Series B, Biological Sciences, 327*(1241), 463–473.

Dudley, S. E., & Xie, Z. (2019). Designing a Choice Architecture for Regulators. *Public Administration Review, 80*(1), 151–156. http://doi.org/10.1111/puar.13112

Duke, R. (2011). Origin and Evolution of Policy Simulation: A Personal Journey. *Simulation & Gaming, 42*(3), 342–358. http://doi.org/10.1177/1046878110367570

Gofen, A., Moseley, A., Thomann, E., & Weaver, K. (2021). Behavioural Governance in the Policy Process: Introduction to the Special Issue. *Journal of European Public Policy, 28*(5), 633–657. https://doi.org/10.1080/13501763.2021.1912153

Hallsworth, M., Egan, M., Rutter, J., & McCrae, J. (2018). *Behavioural Government. Using Behavioural Science to Improve How Governments Make Decisions*. London: The Behavioural Insights Team.

Henry, G. T., & Mark, M. M. (2003). Beyond Use: Understanding Evaluation's Influence on Attitudes and Actions. *American Journal of Evaluation, 24*(3), 293–314. https://doi.org/10.1177/109821400302400302

Howlett, M. (Ed.). (2023). *The Routledge Handbook of Policy Tools*. London and New York, NY: Routledge.

Leeuw, F. L., Rist, R. C., & Sonnichsen, R. C. (1994). *Can Governments Learn?: Comparative Perspectives on Evaluation & Organizational Learning*. New Brunswick, NJ: Transaction Publishers.

Motta, M., Callaghan, T., & Sylvester, S. (2018). Knowing Less But Presuming More: Dunning-Kruger Effects and the Endorsement of Anti-Vaccine Policy Attitudes. *Social Science & Medicine, 211*, 274–281. https://doi.org/10.1016/j.socscimed.2018.06.032

Ostrom, E. (2005). *Understanding Institutional Diversity*. Princeton, NJ and Woodstock: Princeton University Press.

Palenberg, M., & Paulson, A. (Eds.). (2020). *The Realpolitik of Evaluation: Why Demand and Supply Rarely Intersect*. New York, NY: Routledge.

Rieper, O., Leeuw, F. L., & Ling, T. (Eds.). (2012). *The Evidence Book. Concepts, Generation, and Use of Evidence*. New Brunswick, NJ: Transaction Publishers.

Smith, P. (1995). On the Unintended Consequences of Publishing Performance Data in the Public Sector. *International Journal of Public Administration, 18*(2&3), 277–310.

Straßheim, H. (2020). The Rise and Spread of Behavioral Public Policy: An Opportunity for Critical Research and Self-Reflection. *International Review of Public Policy, 2*(1), 115–128. https://doi.org/10.4000/irpp.897

Index

Page numbers in *italics* indicate figures, while page numbers in **bold** mark tables.

academic journals 178
Access to Public Information Act 67
accountability 6, 117, 167
addressees, mental models of 109
administrative activities, and decision-
making 76
age/crime curve 41
age of enlightenment 10, 25n3
Agricultural Sustainability and Advisory
Programme (ASSAP) (Ireland) 48–49, 52
Alford, J. 37
Alkin 165, 167
Alkin, M. C. 150
alternative facts 29, 57, 72n1
ambiguity 16, 21–22, 51
see also uncertainty
Amelina, M. 153
American Evaluation Association 139
*Annals of the American Academy of
Political and Social Science, The Role
of Evaluation in Building Evidence-
Based Policy* 3–4
argument-building strategies 111, *112*
attention-getting 104–6
Augustine 58
Australia 66, 79, 117–18
and evidence-informed policymaking
120, *121–25*, 126
authority, Weber on 14
auto manufacturers 31
availability heuristic 22, 80, **81**, 82, 86,
90, 195–96

"backfire effect" 11
Baiocchi, G. 159–60
Bartocci, L. 154, 159
Battaglio, R. P. 79–80

behavioral economics 78
behavioral governance discipline (BG) 77
behavioral public administration (BPA)
76–77
behavioral public policy (BPP) 76, 80
behavioral sciences 24, 76, 79, 87–88
Behavioural Insights Team 80
Belgium 117, **120**, *121–25*, 126
benevolence 103
Bentham, Jeremy 62–63
Berlusconi, Silvio 59
Bernstein, Carl 68–69
Bertsou, E. 116
Beuermann, D. W. 153
biases 77–78, 194, 197–98
education biases 119, 121, *122–23*
and truths 11
see also cognitive biases
Biden administration 139–40, 142
Biden, Joe 57
Binnema, H. 119
boosting 87–89
bounded rationality 21, 78–79, 97, 162
Boyle, Richard 6–7, 37–54, 193–94, 198
Brazil 153–55
Brexit 1, 11, 30, 32–33, 83, 156, 165
see also United Kingdom
Bundi, Pirmin 116–29, 193, 196
Burns, D. 34
Burr, E. M. 185
Bush, George W. administration 135

Cabannes, Y. 153
Cairney, P. 21–22, 188
Cambridge Analytica/Facebook scandal 61
campaign pledge evaluation tools
(CPETs) 69–70

202 *Index*

Campbell Collaboration, the Coalition for Evidence-Based Policy 135
Canada 117, 160
  Elections Act (2018) 68
  and evidence-informed policymaking **120**, *121–25*, 126
Caputo, D. 118
Caramani, D. 116
Cato Institute 177
characters 100
China *see* pre-imperial China
"choice architecture" 79
Christie, C. A. 180
citizens:
  and evidence 119–20, 128–29
  and evidence informed policymaking 117–19, **120**, *121–25*, 126–29, 159
  and participatory budgeting 154–56, 164
clearinghouses 135, 141–43, 176–78
climate change denialism 84
Clinton, Hillary 29, 36*n*1
codes of conduct 67–68
cognitive biases 21, 24, 79, **81**
  anchoring bias 80, **81**, 82–83, 90
  availability bias 22, 79–80, **81**, 82, 86, 89–90
  bandwagon effect 80, **81**, 84, 90, 197
  confirmation bias 78, 80, **81**, 84–86, 90, 196
  countering 87–91
  loss aversion 80, **81**, 85, 90
  myopia 80, **81**, 85–86, 89–90, 196
  optimism bias 22, 80, **81**, 86
  overconfidence 80, **81**, 86, 90
  salience effect 71, 80, **81**, 86–87, 195
cognitive dissonance 22, 25*n*4
  and fact-checking 70
  triggering 110
cognitive errors 91
cognitive heuristics 79
cognitive shortcuts 21–22, 89–90
cognitive systems 89
cognitive traps 77
Cohen, D. 30
collaboration:
  and evaluation 16
  lack of 141
collaborative governance 17, 23, 166
  see also participatory budgeting (PB)
Commission for Evidence-based Policymaking 7

communication 16
complexity 150
  and wicked problems **40**
  youth crime/justice 40
complex policy environments, and evaluative information 37
comprehensive rationality 21
concealment 61, **65**
Confucian virtues 103
Conklin, J. 48
consensus building 48
consequentialist theories 63
Conservatism, and populism 15
"Context-Mechanism-Outcome" (CMO) relationships 168
co-production 16–17, 23–24
  of evidence 50–51
cost-benefit analyses 34–35
COVID-19 82, 84, 116–18, 157
  and evidence-informed policymaking **120**, *121–25*, 126
CRAP test 72*n*2
critical narrative analysis 100–101
cultural traditions, and problem-solving 98
Czercky, H. 2, 5

data 19, 177
data collection 43, 186–87
Davies, William 10
Dawkins, Richard 25*n*3
The Death of Expertise (Nichols) 10
deception 60–61, **65**, 193
decision-making 176, 194
  and administrative activities 76
  and behavioral science 77
  disregarding evidence xii, 1, 3
  and evaluators 98, 193
  and evidence 143
  and expertise 4–5
  long-term implications of 111
  and participatory budgeting 163–64
  and policy evaluation 4–5
  political 19
  in the post-truth era 97
  process 3, 78–79
  taxonomy 80
democracy 66, 117, 198
  see also participatory budgeting (PB)
Demosthenes 66
Dennett, Daniel 25*n*3
deontology 64–65

Index   203

deplorables 29, 36*n*1
devil's advocate role 90
Dewey, J. 20
Dewulf, A. 51, 53
Dialectical Behavioral Therapy (DBT) 110
dictatorships 1
Diemand-Yauman, C. 90
digital data, availability of 12
digital transformation 23
divergence of opinion **40**, 41
Drieschova, A. 117
Dudley, S. E. 80
Duke, Richard 199*n*1

economic/social anxieties 14–16
"electoral" lies 57
electoral promises, keeping 69–70
elites:
   and alternative facts 29
   denunciations of 12
   distrust of 117, 159
   Gallston on 14
energy efficiency 85–86, 91
episteme 17
Epstein, B. 34
evaluation xi–xii, 12, 18–19, 23, 72, 97,
   179, 181, 189, 197–98
   audiences 109
   behavioral perspectives on 24
   bottom-up approaches to 194
   citizen involvement with 118–20,
      127–29, 180
   commissioners of 180, 184
   communicating 128–29
   data analysis **183–84**, 185
   data collection **186**
   executive summaries of 187
   and free trade 34
   impacted by polarization 2–3, 23
   as multilog 193, 199*n*1
   and participatory budgeting 164–67, 170
   and policymaking 12–13
   professionalization of 179
   realist framework 168–69
   research into 118, 126–29, 167
   roles for 11
   as social practice 5
   structuring/planning 182, **184**
   as *techné* 17–18
   tools for **183–84**, 186
   use of 180, 187–89

evaluation capacity 143–44
evaluation literature 110
evaluation models 127
evaluation-politics relation xi–xii
evaluation skills:
   forming 19–20
   needed 24, 182, 189–90
evaluation theory, and policymakers 20
Evaluation Tree framework 150, 165, 168
evaluation use 97, 138–40, 179, 188–89
evaluative information, and complex
   policy environments 37
evaluative knowledge 13, 23
evaluative research 13, 179
evaluators 181–82, 186
   and decision-making 98, 194
   and information quality 72
   judgement/reporting **183**, 186–87
   needed skills 23, 181, 188
   and participatory budgeting 166–69
   and professionalism 7–8
   professionalization of 180–81
   and psychological processes 77
   and public policy 194–98
   and research access 179
   and stakeholders 127–28, 179, 182,
      185–88, 190
   tools of **183–84**
evidence 127–28, 136
   and agency cultures 143–44
   challenges of 140–43
   disagreements about 141
   and government performance
      assessments 134–37
   living evidence 142
   and politicians 177
   users of 143
evidence-based policymaking (EBPM) 3,
   7, 116, 136–37, 145, 176, 188
   see also policymaking
   United States
evidence-based uprisings 3
evidence-informed policy 134
evidence-informed policy assessments 13,
   116, 141–42
evidence informed policymaking 116, 194
   attitudes towards **120**, *121–25*, 126
   and the Biden administration 139–42
   and citizens 117–20, 126–28
experiential learning 23
"experimentalist governance" 19

204   *Index*

expertise:
  and accountability 117
  and decision-making 4–5, 188
  distrust of 117
  and evaluation 13
  and political decision-making 116
  and wicked problems 50

fact-checking 58, 61, 69–71
facts:
  and lived reality 18
  see also alternative facts
fake news 61, **65**, 71, 83, 89, 168, 170
"Family 500+" child allowance 83
farmers, and trust 48–49, 52
far-right political parties, growth of 11
Feng Ji 106
"focusing events" 82
font studies 90
Foucault, M. 2–3, 14
frame reflection 53
framing effects 22, 80, 110, 196
France 67, 117, **120**, *121–25*, 126, 160
free trade 30–35
  see also welfare theory
Free-Trade Agreements 30
fuel surcharges 91
Fukushima disaster 82
funeral narrative 107
Fung, A. 119

Gaber, I. 60
Gallston, W. A. 14–15
games 111
"gangs" 41–42
Ganuza, E. 160
Gayer, T. 86
Germany 82
Gertler, M. 48
Gil de Zúñiga, H. 71
Gonçalves, S. 152
governmentality, and knowledge/power 2
government performance assessments 134–35
government service delivery 134
Greene, J. C. 180
Greentown 42–45, 50, 52, 54n4
Grillo, Beppe 25n7
groupthink 22
Guerrero O, R. Pablo 6–7, 29–36, 193, 195–96

Hallsworth, M. 197
Han Feizi 100
Harris, Sam 25n3
Hart, Nicholas 7, 134–45, 194–95
Head, B. W. 37, **40**, 41, 45
Heller, R. H. 30–31
Hernandez, I. 90
Heuristics & Biases School 88
Hirschman, A. 16
Hitler, Adolf 59
Hui Ang 102–3
Huizi 107
Hummel, D. 88
hydromorphology 46

illusion of similarity 197–98
illusions of control 22
immigrants, perceptions of 11
incrementalism 38
Indonesia 160
inequality, growth of 14
informational surveillance systems, and the SDGs 5
information bubbles 82, 160, 169–70
information cascades 82
information processing 77
infotainment 59
Inishowen River Trust 50
inoculation theory 88–89
institutional trust 159–60
intellectual authority, distrust of 14
interest group politics, and participatory budgeting 163
Iraq war 57, 69
Ireland 7, 41
  water governance in 7, 38, 40, 46–49, 52–53
  youth crime study 42–45, 50, 52, 54n4

Jacob, Steve 7, 57–72, 193
Jacoby, Marcin 7, 97–113, 195, 197
job losses, from free trade 31
Johnson, Boris 83
Joint Research Council of the European Commission 2, 25n2

Kahneman, D. 5, 11, 77–78, 82–86, 89
Kant, I. 58, 64
Kim, M.-S. 119
knowledge:
  abstract 19

Index 205

co-production of 17, 24
craft knowledge 46, 48–49, 53
evaluative 18, 181
experiential 48–49, 53
local 119
vs. politics 178
practical 19, 23
scientific 51
situational knowledge 20
tacit 19–20
techné 17
knowledge users 109, 144–45
Kota Kita 160
Krawiec, Jakub 7, 76–91, 193
Kuhn, T. 37
Kwiatkowski, R. 21–22

La politique mensonge [Lying Politics]
  (Schwartzenberg) 62
leadership, sword metaphor 102
legitimation 14
Lemire, Sebastian 7–8, 150, 165, 168,
  176–89, 193
Lichtenstein, S. 81
Li Dui 104
lies 11, 57, 59, 61, 64–65, 71, 193
literature myopia 111
living evidence 142
local governance, and participatory
  budgeting 153
long-term implications 111
Lubell, M. 48
Lüshi Chunqiu (LSCQ) 100, 102–3, 107

Machiavelli, N. 58, 62
Maedche, A. 88
Mair, D. 2
Malaysia 160
manipulation 109
Mark, M. M. 180
Marra, Mita 1–8, 10–24, 193–99
Marshall, H. 117
McGuire, W. J. 88
measure fixation 198
mechanisms (realist evaluation
  framework) 169–70
Medellin, Colombia 160
media:
  and fact-checking 70
  growing distrust of 10–11, 117
  and post-truth politics 117, 160

and the War on Terror 69
media discourse 5
medical professionals 84
mental models, of addressees 109
metis 17–18
Mexico 33
Michels, A. 119
Milkman, K. L. 90
Milot-Poulin, Jeanne 7, 57–72, 194
misinformation 61, **65**, 70, 89
Mo Di 103
moral actions 64
Moran, D. 29
Morra Imas, L. G. 186
motivated reasoning 22
Moy River Trust 49
Murray, Patty 136, 138

NAFTA *see* North American Free Trade
  Agreement (NAFTA)
National Technical Implementation Group
  (NTIG) (Ireland) 47, 53
need for coherence," 22
neoliberalism 15
Newcomer, Kathryn 7, 134–45, 193–95
"the New Optimists" 25*n*3
New Zealand Commission 67
Nichols, T. M. 2, 11
  The Death of Expertise 10
Nielsen, Steffen Bohni 7–8, 176–9, 180
Nixon, Richard 68
Norberg, Johan 25*n*3
Norgrove, David 83
Norris, P. 124–25
North American Free Trade Agreement
  (NAFTA) 30–33
nuclear power 82
Nudge:
  Improving Decisions about Health,
    Wealth, and Happiness (Thaler and
    Sunstein) 78–79
nudging 78–79, 87–88

Obama administration 135–36, 142
Obameter 69
Olejniczak, Karol 1–8, 97–113, 192–99
Oliver, K. 188
optimism bias 22, 80, **81**, 86
Organisation for Economic Co-operation
  and Development (OECD) 165
output legitimacy 116–17

206 *Index*

Papageorgis, D. 88
paradigms 37
Park, Yaerin 151–70, 193
participatory budgeting (PB) 7, 150
  and bounded rationality 162
  and citizens 153–56, 164, 170
  and decision-making 163–64
  defined *152*, 155
  and evaluation 165–69, 171
  explanatory accounts 169
  impacts of 152–53
  "Mini Atlas" 160
  in NYC 153, 156, 160, *161*
  as policy tool 159–60
  and the post-truth world 155–56, 159, 169–70
  and social justice 167–68
  and social media 157–58, 164
Patton, M. Q. 166
Pattyn, Valérie 116–29, 193–94, 196
Paul, J. R. 32
Paulson, Arne 1–8, 192–99
Pawson, R. 44, 168
peer-review practices 24
performance, measuring 18
persuasion strategies 7
persuasive narratives 100
Pinker, Steven 25n3
plot 101
Poland 83
polarization 1–2, 11, 156
polarized politics 2–3, 23, 118, 177
policy awareness 195
policy development, politicization of 1–3
policy evaluation 4–5, 198
policymakers 3, 20–21, 111, 116
  and anchoring bias 83
  and availability heuristics 82
  and the bandwagon effect 84
  vs. citizens 78
  and confirmation bias 85
  and evidence-based solutions 188
  lack of stakeholder involvement with 6
  myopia 85–86
  and optimism bia 86
  perceptions of 15, 17
policymaking 20–21, 150, 194
  and behavioral sciences 76, 79
  and evaluation 11–13
  long-term implications of 111

and "post-factual" society challenges 83, 169
  see also evidence-based policymaking (EBPM)
policy problems 4, 195–96
policy solutions 196–98
policy studies 21
political advertising 59
political bundling 90–91
political decisions 19, 116
political ideology, and evidence-informed policymaking *124–25*, 126
political legitimation, and evaluation xi
political lying 58, 60, 62–64, 66, 71, 156, 193
politicians 60, 68, 177
politics 18–19, 58, 60, 62, 177
politics-administration dichotomy 162–63
populism 12, 34
  and Conservatism 15
  and discontent 32, 34
  and distrust 66
  growth of 10, 13, 57, 71
  and policymakers 20
  and the post-truth world 1
  and reality 29–30
  in response to globalization 15
  and technocratic public policies 5, 16
Porto Alegre, Brazil 7, 151, 155, 163
  see also Brazil
Portugal 160
"post-factual" society challenges 83
postmodern philosophies, and knowledge/power 2
post-truth 29, 91, 97, 192–93, 198
  framings in 53
  and participatory budgeting 155–56, 159, 169
  and polarization 11
  public policy framing 12
post-truth evidence use 176
post-truth mechanisms 1, 11, 77
post truth opinions, and wicked problems 50
"post-truth politics" 10, 117–18, *124–25*
post-truth world 13, 159, 166, 169–70, 179, 188, 198
pragmatic reasoning strategy 106–8
pre-imperial China 99, 101–8, 110, 112–13
  see also specific texts
  Warring States Period

Preston, J. L. 90
privacy concerns 87
program evaluation 17, 167–68
*The Promise of Evidence-Based
Policymaking* (2017) 137
propaganda 58–59
prospect theory 22, 85, 90
public policy 34, 57, 110
PytlikZillig, L. M. 158–59

Radaelli, C. M. 116
Ramsey, F. P. 29
rationality 10, 24
realist evaluation framework 168–69
Redmond, Sean 6–7, 37–54, 192–93, 196
red-teaming 90–91
Rein, M. 53
"repair-shop principle" 196
representativeness heuristic 22
research:
    access to 177–78
    and politics 177
research literacy 187
Results for America 139
retraining programs 33–34
rhetoric 16, 104, 110
rhetoric narratology 100, 104
rhetoric strategies 110
Ricoeur, Paul 178
righteousness 103
Rist, R. C. 186
Rittel, Horst 38–40, 42, 51
Rivers Trusts 49, 51
Roderik, D. 32
*The Role of Evaluation in Building
    Evidence-Based Policy (Annals of the
    American Academy of Political and
    Social Science)* 3–4
Roosevelt, Franklin 63
Roozenbeek, J. 88
Russia 153
Russia-Ukraine war (2022-) 1
Ryan, Paul 136, 138

Sabel, C. 19, 46
Scharpf, F. W. 117
Scheer, Andrew 68
Schenk, D. H. 87, 91
Schmieg, G. 1, 5–6
Schön, D. A. 53
Schorr, L. B. 49

Schwandt, T. 8, 129, 179
Schwartzenberg, Roger-Gérard, *La
    politique mensonge [Lying Politics]* 62
science 2–3, 5, 10, 17, 23
scientific evidence, perceptions of 127–28
scientific method, modern advances in 21
scientific truths 37
Scott, J., *Seeing Like a State* 17–19
Scott, R. E. 32
Seeing Like a State (Scott) 17–19
Seinsge-bundenheit 3
Sen, A. 34
service design 109
setting 100
Shaw, I. F. 180
Sherif, M. 82
Simon, H. A. 162
Simon, Herbert 76
simplification 7
situational responsiveness 13
Skolits, G. J. 185
Sliwowski, Pawel 7, 76–91, 193
Slovic, P. 81
social cost-benefit analysis, and free trade
    34–35
social injustice 119
    evidence-informed priorities for
        142–43
social media 156–60, 164, 169, 176
social network analysis 51
social norms 88
    see also nudging
Sparrow, M. K. 52
Speaking Truth to Power (Wildavsky) 2
spinning 60–61, **65**
stakeholders:
    advisory/steering groups 184–85
    analysis of 184
    and evaluators 127–28, 178, 181,
        184–87, 189
    and evidence informed policymaking
        118–20
    lack of involvement in policymaking 6
    and research 178
    varied priorities of 45
    views on evidence 127–28
    wider involvement of 45
status quo bias 22
storytelling 101–10
suicides *vs.* homicides 81–82
Suiter, J. 117

208 Index

sunk costs fallacy 22
Sunstein, Cass 78–79
Sunzi's Art of War (Sunzi Bingfa) 99, 113
Su Qin 100, 104–5
Sustainable Development Goals (SDGs), assessing 5–6
Switzerland 117, **120**, *121–25*, 126
systemic errors 79

tame problems 39–40
tariffs 30
taxes 87–88
techné 17–18
terms of reference 180, 184–85
Thaler, Richard 78–79
themes 101
theories of change 110
Theory of Disproportionate Information-Processing 194
Tiefenbeck, V. 91
Tilley, N. 168
Timiraos, N. 33
Tocqueville, Alexis de 14
Touchton, M. 152–53
Toulmin, S. E. 111
Trade Adjustment Assistance (TAA) program 33
trade theory 30
Tramontano, K. A. 34
transparency regulations 67–68, 158–59
tribalism 159
Trump administration 66, 139, 156
Trump, Donald 1, 36*n*1, 66
trust:
    declining 66, 126–27, 156–59, 167, 169–70, 177
    and expertise 117, 177
    and fact-checking 70–71
    and farmers 49, 52
    and transparency regulations 67
truth 29, 37, 53, 57–58, **65**, 66
Truth Decay report (2018) 1
truths, and biases 11
truth-telling 60, 63
Tversky, Amos 11, 82–86
"Twinsight" 43

uncertainty 22, **40**
    and data 19
    and overconfidence 86

and wicked problems **40**, 50–51
youth crime/justice 40
see also ambiguity
United Kingdom 66, 83
see also Brexit
United States 117, 134, 160
    in the 1970's 39
    clearinghouses 135, 141–43
    Commission on Evidence-Based Policymaking 136–41
    common evidence framework 136
    Evidence Act (Foundations for Evidence-Based Policymaking Act, 2019) 136–38, 144–45, 176
    evidence challenges in 140–43
    and evidence-informed policymaking **120**, *121–25*, 126
    Freedom of Information Act (FOIA) 67
    My Brother's Keeper 142
    New York City 1, 151, 160, *161*
    Office of Management and Budget (OMB) 135–36
    and post-truth politics 118, 125
    Save More Tomorrow 88
    social media use 156–58
    suicides *vs.* homicides 81–82
    trust in 66
    see also North American Free Trade Agreement (NAFTA)
Universal Declaration of Human Rights and the International Covenant on Civil and Political Rights 67
US Agency for International Development (USAID) 134
user experiences, and collaborative governance 17
USS *Greer* 63
utilitarianism 62–64
utilization 97

Van der Linden, S. 88
Vedung, Evert 178, 187
Vietnam war 57
virtue ethics 63–64
Viscusi, W. K. 86

Waldo, D. 162–63
Wampler, B. 152–53
warnings 88
    see also nudging
War on Terror, and the media 69

Warring States Period 99, 103, 106
  see also pre-imperial China
  specific texts
wars, false information justifying 57, 69
watchdogging 58, 68–69
Water Forum (Ireland) 47–48, 53
Watergate scandal 68–69
water governance/quality 7, 38, 40,
  45–49, 52–53
Webber, Melvin 38–40, 42, 51
Weber, Max 14
Weeks, B. 71
Wei Chou 107
Weiss, Carol xi–xii, 97, 178
welfare theory 30–34
"wicked" policy problems 37–39, **40**, 51–52
  and evaluative information 37–38
  and expertise 53
  post-truth opinions about 50
  sizing 52
  solution tendencies 44
  and uncertainty **40**, 51
  see also water governance/quality
  youth crime
  youth justice

Wildavsky, A. B., *Speaking Truth to
  Power* 2
Wolfe, D. 48
Woodward, Bob 68–69
World Bank 134
World War I 58
World War II 63
written language 178

Xie, Z. 80

Yong Rui 107
youth crime 7
  age/crime curve 41, 50
  data 41–44
  and Greentown 42–45, 50,
    52, 54n4
youth justice 38, 40–41, 50

Zeitlin, J. 19, 46
Zhanguoce (ZGC) 100,
  103–6, 113
Zhang Yi 100
Zhuang Zhou 100, 102
Zhuangzi (ZZ) 100, 102

9781032719313